Empire of Timber

Labor Unions and the Pacific Northwest Forests

The battles to protect ancient forests and spotted owls in the Northwest regularly splashed across the evening news in the 1980s and early 1990s. *Empire of Timber* re-examines this history to demonstrate that workers used their unions to fight for a healthy workplace environment and sustainable logging practices that would allow themselves and future generations the chance to both work and play in the forests. Examining labor organizations from the Industrial Workers of the World in the 1910s to unions in the 1980s, this study shows that conventional narratives of workers opposing environmental protection are far too simplistic and often ignore the long histories of natural resource industry workers attempting to protect their health and their futures from the impact of industrial logging. Today, when workers fear that environmental restrictions threaten their jobs, learning the history of alliances between unions and environmentalists can build those conversations in the present.

Erik Loomis is Assistant Professor of History at the University of Rhode Island. He previously taught as a visiting assistant professor at Southwestern University and the College of Wooster. He is the author of *Out of Sight: The Long and Disturbing Story of Corporations Outsourcing Catastrophe*, published in 2015. He writes on labor, environmental, and political issues at the blog *Lawyers, Guns, and Money*. His series at LGM, "This Day in Labor History," won a Cliopatria Award from the History News Network in 2011. His writing has appeared in *Alternet*, *Truthout*, *Salon*, *In These Times*, *Counterpunch*, and many other publications. He lives in Providence, Rhode Island.

Studies in Environment and History

Editors

J.R. McNeill, Georgetown University
Edmund P. Russell, University of Kansas

Editors Emeritus

Alfred W. Crosby, University of Texas at Austin
Donald Worster, University of Kansas

Other Books in the Series

David A. Bello *Across Forest, Steppe, and Mountain: Environment, Identity, and Empire in Qing China's Borderlands*

Peter Thorsheim *Waste into Weapons: Recycling in Britain during the Second World War*

Kieko Matteson *Forests in Revolutionary France: Conservation, Community, and Conflict, 1669–1848*

George Colpitts *Pemmican Empire: Food, Trade, and the Last Bison Hunts in the North American Plains, 1780–1882*

Micah Muscolino *The Ecology of War in China: Henan Province, the Yellow River, and Beyond, 1938–1950*

John Brooke *Climate Change and the Course of Global History: A Rough Journey*

Emmanuel Kreike *Environmental Infrastructure in African History: Examining the Myth of Natural Resource Management*

Paul Josephson, Nicolai Dronin, Ruben Mnatsakanian, Aleh Cherp, Dmitry Efremenko, Vladislav Larin *An Environmental History of Russia*

Gregory T. Cushman *Guano and the Opening of the Pacific World: A Global Ecological History*

Sam White *Climate of Rebellion in the Early Modern Ottoman Empire*

Alan Mikhail *Nature and Empire in Ottoman Egypt: An Environmental History*

Edmund Russell *Evolutionary History: Uniting History and Biology to Understand Life on Earth*

Richard W. Judd *The Untilled Garden: Natural History and the Spirit of Conservation in America, 1740–1840*

James L.A. Webb, Jr. *Humanity's Burden: A Global History of Malaria*

Frank Uekoetter *The Green and the Brown: A History of Conservation in Nazi Germany*

Myrna I. Santiago *The Ecology of Oil: Environment, Labor, and the Mexican Revolution, 1900–1938*

Matthew D. Evenden *Fish versus Power: An Environmental History of the Fraser River*

Nancy J. Jacobs *Environment, Power, and Injustice: A South African History*

Adam Rome *The Bulldozer in the Countryside: Suburban Sprawl and the Rise of American Environmentalism*

Judith Shapiro *Mao's War against Nature: Politics and the Environment in Revolutionary China*

Edmund Russell *War and Nature: Fighting Humans and Insects with Chemicals from World War I to Silent Spring*

Andrew Isenberg *The Destruction of the Bison: An Environmental History* Thomas Dunlap *Nature and the English Diaspora*

Robert B. Marks *Tigers, Rice, Silk, and Silt: Environment and Economy in Late Imperial South China*

Mark Elvin and Tsui'jung Liu *Sediments of Time: Environment and Society in Chinese History*

Richard H. Grove *Green Imperialism: Colonial Expansion, Tropical Island Edens and the Origins of Environmentalism, 1600–1860*

Elinor G.K. Melville *A Plague of Sheep: Environmental Consequences of the Conquest of Mexico*

J.R. McNeill *The Mountains of the Mediterranean World: An Environmental History*

Theodore Steinberg *Nature Incorporated: Industrialization and the Waters of New England*

Timothy Silver *A New Face on the Countryside: Indians, Colonists, and Slaves in the South Atlantic Forests, 1500–1800*

Michael Williams *Americans and Their Forests: A Historical Geography*

Donald Worster *The Ends of the Earth: Perspectives on Modern Environmental History*

Samuel P. Hays Beauty *Health, and Permanence: Environmental Politics in the United States, 1955–1985*

Warren Dean *Brazil and the Struggle for Rubber: A Study in Environmental History*

Robert Harms *Games against Nature: An Eco-Cultural History of the Nunu of Equatorial Africa*

Arthur F. McEvoy *The Fisherman's Problem: Ecology and Law in the California Fisheries, 1850–1980*

Alfred W. Crosby *Ecological Imperialism: The Biological Expansion of Europe, 900–1900, Second Edition*

Kenneth F. Kiple *The Caribbean Slave: A Biological History*

Donald Worster *Nature's Economy: A History of Ecological Ideas, Second Edition*

Empire of Timber

Labor Unions and the Pacific Northwest Forests

ERIK LOOMIS

University of Rhode Island

CAMBRIDGE
UNIVERSITY PRESS

University Printing House, Cambridge CB2 8BS, United Kingdom

One Liberty Plaza, 20th Floor, New York, NY 10006, USA

477 Williamstown Road, Port Melbourne, VIC 3207, Australia

314-321, 3rd Floor, Plot 3, Splendor Forum, Jasola District Centre, New Delhi - 110025, India

103 Penang Road, #05-06/07, Visioncrest Commercial, Singapore 238467

Cambridge University Press is part of the University of Cambridge.

It furthers the University's mission by disseminating knowledge in the pursuit of education, learning and research at the highest international levels of excellence.

www.cambridge.org
Information on this title: www.cambridge.org/9781107125490

First published 2016

A catalogue record for this publication is available from the British Library

ISBN 978-1-107-12549-0 Hardback

To my father, for instilling in me a love of the forests even as he worked himself to the bone in the plywood mills to keep our family fed and clothed.

And to my mother, for giving her undying love and support in all the decisions I've ever made.

Contents

Acknowledgments

As anyone who has ever written an academic book knows, the process is both solitary and collaborative at the same time. One relies on friends, family, and colleagues to discuss ideas, work through problems, and stay grounded in real life. Or at least that was the case with me. I have been lucky to have supportive colleagues at all three institutions where I have taught. I've had outstanding colleagues who mentored me as a scholar, writer, and teacher. These acknowledgments can barely begin to pay back the debts I owe all these people.

My current colleagues at the University of Rhode Island are outstanding. Many, many thanks to Tim George, Rob Widell, Rosie Pegueros, Rae Ferguson, Miriam Reumann, Joelle Rollo-Koster, Alan Verskin, Mike Honhart, Eve Sterne, James Ward, Marie Schwartz, Rod Mather, Bridget Buxton, and Cathy DeCesare. Thanks a ton also to my department administrator, Nancy Woyak, for sorting through the various messes of my professional life.

I also had very generous funding from the University of Rhode Island to complete this book, specifically from the Center for the Humanities and the Council for Research. I was also a Grey Towers Scholar in Residence at Grey Towers National Historic Site, the home of Gifford Pinchot. The U.S. Forest Service funds this fellowship. Thanks to all who agreed to fund my research.

At Southwestern University, I want to heartily thank Thom McClendon, Elizabeth Green Musselman, Shana Bernstein, Steve Davidson, Daniel Castro, Melissa Byrnes, Rachel Nunez, Laura Hobgood-Oster, Melissa Johnson, Carina Evans, Julia Johnson, Eric Selbin, and Elizabeth Stockton.

At the College of Wooster, my deepest thanks go to Greg Shaya, Shannon King, Madonna Hettinger, Ibra Sene, Jeff Roche, Katie Holt, Ryan Edgington, Hayden Schilling, Joan Friedman, Peter Pozefsky, Marc Goulding, Jennifer Graber, Travis Foster, Phil Mellizo, and Charles Peterson.

This process started in graduate school and I was lucky enough to have an amazing cohort of graduate students to work with. Through good times and bad, we were a friendly and supportive group. Thanks to Bill Convery, Scott Meredith, Erin Cole, Meg Frisbee, Lincoln Bramwell, Sarah Payne, Laurie Hinck, Blair Woodard, Sonia Dickey, Kim Klimek, Amy Scott, James Martin, Courtney Collie, Sarah Grossman, Elaine Nelson, Kent Blansett, Colin Snider, Joe Lenti, Chad Black, Alden Big Man, Mark Duimstra, Brandon Morgan, and Brad Shreve.

I owe an immense amount to Virginia Scharff, who directed my dissertation and who took it upon herself to reshape my writing style during that process. That process was hard at the time, but it created the historian I have become and which I hope shows through in this book. My ability to write for different audiences, political, general, and academic, is a reflection of her own career. She decides what she wants to write, whom she wants to write it for, and then writes it. That's the model I have followed.

My other mentors at the University of New Mexico also have earned my lifelong appreciation. Thanks to my dissertation committee that included Sam Truett, Andrew Sandoval-Strausz, and Alex Lubin for approving a very early version of what became this book. Thanks as well to Linda Hall, Elizabeth Hutchison, Judy Bieber, Melvyn Yazawa, Cathleen Cahill, Beth Bailey, Enrique Sanabria, and David Farber for their mentorship.

Probably the second most important person in the shaping of this project is Jeff Sanders. No one read more bad chapter drafts all the way through the book stage. Yet he continued to agree to keep reading. This was interspersed with walks across the cities of the American West when we met for conferences or happened to be in the same place at the same time. Let us continue this through our next book projects.

Special thanks also go to other historians who suffered through drafts of some of these chapters, especially Ryan Edgington, Jacob Remes, and Paul Adler. Your comments were hugely helpful.

In the years since I started this dissertation, I have lost too many mentors: Tim Moy, Ferenc Szasz, Richard Maxwell Brown, and especially Susan Becker. Each of you guided me as a scholar and teacher in profound ways and I greatly miss my conversations with all of you.

I also want to thank the staff of Cambridge University Press, especially Deborah Gershenowitz, for their extraordinary support of this project. Many thanks to Ed Russell, John McNeill, and the anonymous readers of this manuscript for doing so much to make this book a reality.

This book became much easier to write when my political writing began to gain more attention, leading to me writing two books in one year; it turns out that this is possible. Thanks to Jed Bickman, Sarah Jaffe, and Lindsay Beyerstein, and the staff of The New Press for believing in my book *Out of Sight*, about the problems with outsourcing and globalized capitalism. Their belief in that project gave me the confidence to finish this one.

My colleagues at *Lawyers, Guns, and Money* have allowed me to work out many of the ideas of this book in their modern context on their site. Thanks to Scott Lemieux, David Watkins, David Brockington, Bethany Spencer, Steven Attewell, Scott Eric Kaufman, David Noon, Paul Campos, and Katie Surrence. Particular thanks also goes to Robert Farley for not only putting up with my political writing on his site but for hosting me in his home as I was doing dissertation research so many years ago.

Archivists are always priceless resources and the staff of the special collections at the University of Oregon, the Oregon Historical Society, the Washington Historical Society, the University of Washington, Humboldt State University, the University of Montana, the National Archives repository in Seattle, and the Montana Historical Society were all extremely helpful with everything I needed during this process. Special thanks to Edith Butler at Humboldt State University and Linda Long at the University of Oregon, both of whom suggested archival collections that significantly improved this project.

Jeff and Jen Sanders deserve a special line for getting me out of the archives during my research trips and into the forests and breweries of Oregon.

Scott Greacen found me interesting people to talk to about forest issues in northern California, which enriched the project significantly. Jerry Lembcke opened his home to me to talk about unions and forests in the 1970s. And I cannot thank Denny Scott enough. A key player in this book, Denny and I had long conversations about forestry, unions, environmentalists, and the complexities of fighting for working people in times of change. Denny is a great unionist and I have the utmost respect for him. Getting to know him was one of the real highlights of this project.

Last but most certainly not least is my family. My family doesn't exactly have a lot, or any, PhDs, so it wasn't always easy explaining just what I actually was doing with my time. But they have always been extraordinarily supportive of everything I do. My brother, Daryl Loomis, and my sister, Kris DiOrio, and her family Carlie DiOrio, Aaron Voigt, and Grace DiOrio, are always wonderful.

My in-laws and their sizable family accepted me from the very beginning and I thank Bill and Cassie McIntyre; Siobhan, Mike, Pat, Anne, Maggie, Luke, and Nora Bubel; Bill McIntyre; Kevin, Clare, Ryan, Griffin, Declan, and Maeve McIntyre; Sean, Megan, Ciara, and Aine McIntyre; Maura Ryan; and Siobhan and Sean Murphy.

Of course, my parents, to whom this book is dedicated, get their own paragraph. This book is my reckoning with growing up in the middle of the spotted owl crisis in Oregon in the 1980s and my father always made sure that I understood that the forests were a resource that not only put food on our table but also brought joy to our lives. My mother is the most supportive person on the face of this planet. Neither of them graduated from college but they were determined that I would. Not only did I achieve that, but I used that education to contextualize the history of the industry that defined so much of their own lives. I hope this book is useful to them and is a slight repayment for all they have done for me throughout the years.

Finally, there is my wife, Kathleen McIntyre, who has shown constant pride in me and has supported my work in innumerable ways that cannot be listed here because I do not have the words to describe it. Being married to an academic has its share of hardships in a world where jobs at the same school are tough to come by, but together we have seen much of the Americas through our jobs and our families and our research and our travels. I cherish you and the life that we have built. I love you.

Introduction

I was born into an Oregon logging family in 1974 and grew up in the middle of one of the biggest battles between environmentalists and natural resource industries in American history: the spotted owl crisis of the 1980s. This book is my attempt to reckon with the dominant event of my childhood: loving the forests while relying on my father harvesting them so we could eat. *Empire of Timber* is the story of timber workers and the environment created by industrial forestry in the twentieth century. It argues that workers long used their labor organizations to fight for their own environmental needs, be that a healthy and safe working environment, a forest managed for their interests rather than that of their employers, or work for the unemployed.

My family had long toiled in the hard, tiring, and poisonous work of turning the raw materials of the Pacific Northwest into industrial products. Ranching and logging were common jobs on my father's side, working for the Hanford nuclear site on my mother's. My father came home every morning from his graveyard shift at a plywood mill covered with industrial glue, his shirts stained purple. Scars crisscross his arms from a lifetime of wood splinters cutting his skin. He worked forty to sixty hours a week in an intense, fast-paced repetitive motion job that eventually necessitated carpal tunnel and rotator cuff surgeries. He worked very hard and when his body finally would not let him go on any longer, in his early sixties, he settled into a deserved retirement.

As relief from the daily toil of his job, when my brother and I were growing up, despite his exhaustion, he took us to the Cascade Mountains whenever he could. We might go fishing for the day at Leaburg Lake or take a drive to Crater Lake National Park or hike in the Three Sisters

Wilderness Area. We passed innumerable clearcuts on these drives and he would point to timber company signs saying "Next Harvest, 2010" or "Planted 1972" and tell us how the trees were a renewable resource that would come back and keep the next generation working while providing the beauty Oregon was known for. Today, although I live in faraway Rhode Island, I never feel more at home than on a trail in the Cascades or driving across Oregon's scenic McKenzie Pass. My father instilled that love of the Pacific Northwest forests in me.

But when I first flew in 1994, at the age of twenty, my life changed forever. I was shocked at the horrible damage to the forests I could see from the air. Everything I thought I knew about clearcuts was a lie. They were scars upon the landscape. Maybe the trees would grow back someday but the environmental impact of the timber industry became clear to me for the first time. Moreover, by 1994 the forests no longer even supported families like mine as the short-sighted timber industry prioritized short-term profits over long-term community stability and had laid off thousands of people they no longer needed to process their industrial forests. A transforming timber industry threatened my father's livelihood as well, through technological automation, overcutting the forests, the export of unprocessed logs to Japan, and an increasingly globalized timber resource.

Despite the complexity of the industry's changing economics, like thousands of other loggers and mill workers and their families in the 1980s, my father and the rest of my family pointed their fingers for job losses at the Northwest's growing community of environmentalists. "Save a Logger, Eat an Owl," "Earth First, We'll Log the Other Planets Later," and "Are You an Environmentalist or Do You Work for a Living?" became popular bumper stickers in my hometown when I was a teenager.[1] In the 1980s, environmentalists, organizing to hold the timber industry accountable to federal environmental laws enacted in the 1960s and 1970s, identified the northern spotted owl as a species that needed old-growth timber to survive. Its plummeting numbers became evidence that the timber industry not only had plundered the forest, but had also violated federal law in doing so. In particular, the National Forest Management Act of 1976, which required the U.S. Forest Service to maintain "viable populations" of native species, gave greens a new tool

[1] Richard White, "Are You an Environmentalist or Do You Work for a Living?," in William Cronon, ed., *Uncommon Ground: Rethinking the Human Place in Nature*," (New York: Norton, 1995), 171–85.

to change how the government operated the forests. Environmentalists sued to make it do so. The timber industry then blamed greens for all the job losses, using them as a convenient excuse to avoid responsibility for its culpability in unemployment. Despite industry attempts to paint them as outsiders, in fact local environmental groups made up of Northwestern residents, recent arrivals, or Oregonians for generations, powered much of the opposition to timber industry practices. Environmentalism was as native-born to Oregon as the timber workers.

Rhetoric ran high on both sides of the debate, with environmentalists accusing the timber industry of destroying the forests and loggers like my father pointing to the indifference of many environmentalists regarding the human costs of environmental protection. While some environmentalists certainly did show indifference toward workers' future, mostly this charge was unfair, although easy for desperate workers to believe. Still, some environmentalists did use harsh rhetoric against the timber industry and its workers. Too typical was Roy Keene's 1990 *High Country News* article entitled, "Raping the Private Forests." Keene's criticism of multinational corporations that abandoned small Oregon towns through unsustainable logging, the environmental impact of clearcutting, and log exports was valid. These issues had potential for building bridges with workers. Yet while the word "rape" may have caught readers' attention and galvanized people to action, it certainly did not generate understanding with the timber workers struggling to hold onto their jobs.[2] Rhetoric that the timber industry was "raping" the forest was overly harsh and unnecessarily sexualized, tapping into long-held gendered relationships with nature, but the long-term effects of clearcutting on forests, mountainsides, streambeds, and wildlife did engender an urgency among greens. The last old-growth forests were disappearing fast. Simplifying the timber industry into a monolith without differentiating between workers and owners might have made rhetorical sense, but did not accurately describe how many loggers felt about the forests. People such as my father and the many other timber industry employees I grew up with had complex relationships with the forest, loving the outdoors as much as greens but also having no way to make a living without permanently altering that forest.

[2] Roy Keene, "Raping the Private Forests," *High Country News*, November 19, 1990, 13–14. Of course, many publications provide article titles for pieces accepted so I do not know whether it was Keene or *High Country News* staff who suggested this term.

Growing up torn between environmentalism and work, between the conservative logging town of Springfield and the counterculture environmentalism of nearby Eugene, between the extractive and ecotopian Northwest, shaped who I am and stoked my desire to tell a more complete story about the history of the Northwest forests. As a historian who came to graduate school with a strong environmental ethic and with a background in the labor movement, I found myself drawn back to this foundational story of my youth and of Pacific Northwest history. As an environmentalist, I came to understand that the environmental critique of the timber industry was spot on and as a unionist, I felt deeply for the men and women and children like myself and my family who found their lives torn asunder by a timber industry mismanaging the forests.

The history of the forest is one of trees and owls, of timber executives and government foresters. But it is also a history full of human stories, lives crafted cutting down old-growth timber, laboring in remote timber camps, and dying in timber mills' saws. It is a history of workers acting collectively to demand that industry respect the integrity of their bodies and the long-term health of the forest. Logging transformed the forest into an industrial environment that loggers and mill workers had to negotiate every day to stay alive and employed. They worried about a future without timber. They went hunting and camping and hiking in their free time. They produced forest products and consumed forest leisure. Throughout the twentieth century, they acted collectively to press their interests on all of these issues.

This story places the actions of timber workers and their labor organizations at the center of twentieth-century forest history. The Northwest timber industry began in the mid-nineteenth century and scholars have explored its development in depth, centering around the tensions between the growing industry and the rise of conservationists trying to develop the forests rationally. Compared to the twentieth century, little labor agitation or worker critique of timber industry practices, either in its logging methods or working conditions, marked the period.[3] This changed with the rapid expansion of the timber industry after 1890. By the 1900s,

[3] Among the most important literature on the early history of logging in the Northwest is Robert Ficken, *The Forested Land: A History of Lumbering in Western Washington* (Seattle: University of Washington Press, 1987); Norman H. Clark, *Mill Town: A Social History of Everett, Washington, from Its Earliest Beginnings on the Shores of Puget Sound to the Tragic and Infamous Event Known as the Everett Massacre* (Seattle: University of Washington Press, 1970); Thomas R. Cox, *Mills and Markets: A History of the Pacific Coast Lumber Industry to 1900* (Seattle: University of Washington Press, 1974); Robert

Northwestern workers began organizing around the increasingly brutal conditions of their work, leading to the rise of the Industrial Workers of the World in the forests beginning in 1907. The labor history of the timber industry has detailed how loggers in the 1910s became radicalized and engaged in widespread strikes. These historians have expressed more interest in the radicalism of workers and the violence used against them by employers than placing them within the larger context of the larger twentieth-century timber industry.[4] The smaller labor history of the New Deal-era timber-worker unions either sees them as a minor part of a larger

Bunting, *The Pacific Raincoast: Environment and Culture in an American Eden, 1778–1900* (Lawrence: University of Kansas Press, 1997); Richard White, *Land Use, Environment, and Social Change: The Shaping of Island County, Washington* (Seattle: University of Washington Press, 1980); William G. Robbins, *Hard Times in Paradise: Coos Bay, Oregon, 1850–1986* (Seattle: University of Washington Press, 1988); Michael Williams, *Americans and Their Forests: A Historical Geography* (New York: Cambridge University Press, 1989), 289–330; Greg Gordon, *When Money Grew on Trees: A.B. Hammond and the Age of the Timber Baron* (Norman: University of Oklahoma Press, 2014). On the development of conservation and the forests, see Samuel P. Hays, *Conservation and the Gospel of Efficiency: The Progressive Conservation Movement* (Cambridge: Harvard University Press, 1959); Samuel P. Hays, *Wars in the Woods: The Rise of Ecological Forestry in America* (Pittsburgh: University of Pittsburgh Press, 2007); David Clary, *Timber and the Forest Service* (Lawrence: University Press of Kansas, 1986); Henry Clepper, *Professional Forestry in the United States* (Baltimore: Johns Hopkins University Press, 1971); William B. Greeley *Forests and Men* (Garden City: Doubleday and Company, 1951); Harold T. Pinkett, *Gifford Pinchot: Private and Public Forester* (Chicago: University of Chicago Press, 1970); William G. Robbins, *American Forestry: A History of National, State, and Private Cooperation* (Lincoln: University of Nebraska Press, 1985); William G. Robbins, *Lumberjacks and Legislators: Political Economy of the U.S. Lumber Industry, 1890–1941* (College Station: Texas A&M University Press, 1982); Harold K. Steen, *The U.S. Forest Service: A History* (Seattle: University of Washington Press, 1976); Stephen Fox, *The American Conservation Movement: John Muir and His Legacy* (Madison: University of Wisconsin Press, 1986); Char Miller, *Gifford Pinchot and the Making of Modern Environmentalism* (Washington, D.C.: Island Press, 2001); Thomas R. Cox, *The Lumbermen's Frontier: Three Centuries of Land Use, Society, and Change in American Forests* (Corvallis: Oregon State University Press, 2010).

4 Carlos Schwantes, *Hard Traveling: A Portrait of Work Life in the Pacific Northwest* (Lincoln: University of Nebraska Press, 1994); Andrew Mason Prouty, *More Deadly Than War: Pacific Coast Logging, 1927–1981* (New York: Garland Publishing, 1985); Philip Dreyfus, "Nature, Militancy, and the Western Worker: Socialist Shingles, Syndicalist Spruce," *Labor* 1, no. 3 (2004): 71–96; Robert L. Tyler, *Rebels of the Woods: The I.W.W. in the Pacific Northwest* (Eugene: University of Oregon Press, 1967); John McClelland, Jr. *Wobbly War: The Centralia Story* (Tacoma: Washington State Historical Society, 1978); *Soldiers and Spruce: Origins of the Loyal Legion of Loggers and Lumbermen* (Los Angeles: Institute of Industrial Relations, University of California, Los Angeles, 1963); Tom Copeland, *The Centralia Tragedy of 1919: Elmer Smith and the Wobblies* (Seattle: University of Washington Press, 1993); Vernon Jensen, *Lumber and Labor* (New York: Farrar and Rinehart, 1945).

organization, in the case of those affiliated with the United Brotherhood of Carpenters (UBC), or focuses on internal radical politics in the case of the International Woodworkers of America (IWA). This has led to large gaps in our understanding of the role timber-worker unions have played in shaping the timber industry through the twentieth century.[5]

If the history of workplace activism remains largely unconnected to the Northwest's larger environmental debates, the sizable literature on forest policy and environmental debates in the postwar period has mostly relegated workers and their unions to passing references and footnotes. The postwar housing crisis and political pressure to increase the cut led to a vast overharvesting of the national forests after World War II. In the 1950s, wilderness advocates began putting pressure on the government to preserve not only high mountain areas but also valuable stands of old-growth timber from the saw. The Forest Service sought to exclude these forests from preservation and the cut largely continued unabated. By the 1970s, the growing environmental movement began using the courts to enforce environmental legislation such as the Endangered Species Act and National Forest Management Act. This included suing to protect the northern spotted owl, whose habitat requires preserving the last old-growth forests in the region. The growing ecological crisis in the forest, embodied in the spotted owl controversy, began to make national headlines as environmentalists clamored for locking up the remaining old growth and the timber industry proclaimed the doom that would result.[6]

[5] Jerry Lembcke & William M. Tattam, *One Union in Wood: A Political History of the International Woodworkers of America* (New York: International Publishers, 1984); Andrew Neufeld and Andrew Parnaby, *The IWA in Canada: The Life and Times of an Industrial Union* (Vancouver: IWA Canada/New Star Books, 2000); Walter Galenson, *The United Brotherhood of Carpenters: The First Hundred Years* (Cambridge: Harvard University Press, 1983).

[6] On logging and forestry after World War II, see Paul Hirt, *A Conspiracy of Optimism: Management of the National Forests since World War Two* (Lincoln: University of Nebraska Press, 1996); Nancy Langston, *Forest Dreams, Forest Nightmares: The Paradox of Old Growth in the Inland West* (Seattle: University of Washington Press, 1995); Susan R. Schrepfer, *The Fight to Save the Redwoods: A History of Environmental Reform, 1917–1978* (Madison: University of Wisconsin Press, 1983); James Morton Turner, *The Promise of Wilderness* (Seattle: University of Washington Press, 2012); Richard Rajala, *Clearcutting the Pacific Rain Forest: Production, Science, and Regulation* (Vancouver: University of British Columbia Press, 1998); David Clary, *Timber and the Forest Service* (Lawrence: University of Kansas Press, 1986); Carsten Lien, *Olympic Battleground: The Power Politics of Timber Preservation* (San Francisco: Sierra Club Books, 1991); Ben W. Twight, *Organizational Values and Political Power: The Forest Service versus the Olympic National Park* (State College: The Pennsylvania State University Press, 1983); Gerald W. Williams, *The U.S.*

With few exceptions however, the literature on forest history largely leaves everyday workers out of the discussion. If workers play a role in these histories, they only participate in protests against spotted owl protection without exploring these actions in the context of workers' historical relationships with the forest and their employers.[7] In contrast, *Empire of Timber* places labor organizations squarely at the center of the environmental history of the Pacific Northwest forests through the twentieth century. Individual loggers had very little power to transform their day-to-day interactions with the forests; employed as an independent contractor or as an employee of a large corporation, the logger's or millworker's day meant the production of timber in order to keep his (and increasingly by the 1970s, her) job. However, like laborers throughout the nation, timber workers created or joined labor organizations, whether labor unions or cooperatives, to advance their personal and political goals. They sought an equitable environment that prioritized both shepherding of the timber resource and workplace protection from the dangers of industrial logging. Different union cultures created different reactions to the rise of environmentalism and environmental organizations found common ground with some unions for the mutual benefit of both.

Forest Service in the Pacific Northwest: A History (Corvallis: Oregon State University Press, 2009); Mark Harvey, *Wilderness Forever: Howard Zahniser and the Path to the Wilderness Act* (Seattle: University of Washington Press, 2005); Kevin Marsh, *Lines in the Forest: Creating Wilderness Areas in the Pacific Northwest* (Seattle: University of Washington Press, 2009); Darren Speece, "From Corporatism to Citizen Oversight: The Legal Fight over California Redwoods, 1970–1996," *Environmental History* 14, no. 4 (October 2009): 705–36; Speece, "Defending Giants: The Battle over Headwaters Forest and the Transformation of American Environmental Politics, 1850–1999," Ph.D. Dissertation, University of Maryland, 2010; Douglas Bevington, *The Rebirth of Environmentalism: Grassroots Activism from the Spotted Owl to the Polar Bear* (Washington, D.C.: Island Press, 2009; Christopher McGrory Klyza and David J. Sousa, *American Environmental Policy, 1990–2006: Beyond Gridlock* (Cambridge: The MIT Press, 2007); Christopher Klyza, *Who Controls Public Lands?: Mining, Forestry, and Grazing Policies, 1870–1990* (Chapel Hill: University of North Carolina Press, 1996); Thomas R. Wellock, "The Dickey Bird Scientists Take Charge: Science, Policy, and the Spotted Owl," *Environmental History* 15, no. 3 (July 2010): 381–414; Hans Brendan Swedlow, "Scientists, Judges, and Spotted Owls: Policymakers in the Pacific Northwest," Ph.D. Dissertation, University of California, 2002; William Robbins, *Nature's Northwest: The North Pacific Slope in the Twentieth Century* (Tucson: University of Arizona Press, 2011); William Robbins, *Landscapes of Conflict: The Oregon Story, 1940–2000* (Seattle: University of Washington Press, 2004).

7 The most prominent exception is Robbins, *Hard Times in Paradise*. By non-historians, see Brinda Sarathy, *Pineros: Latino Labour and the Changing Face of Forestry in the Pacific Northwest* (Vancouver: University of British Columbia Press, 2012); Beverly A. Brown, *In Timber Country: Working People's Stories of Environmental Conflict and Urban Flight* (Philadelphia: Temple University Press, 1995).

In examining these issues, this book builds upon the growing literature on work and nature to center the role played by labor unions in shaping workers' responses to a natural world transformed by industrialization.[8] Labor unions are the most established method of workers channeling discontent toward employers and displaying power on the job. Understanding how labor unions shaped the responses to people knowing nature through labor must be central to the environmental history of work. Examining how unions conceptualized nature to appeal to members or how unions articulated a specific environmental program that shaped resource usage are understudied questions in the environmental history of work. Labor historians have begun exploring these questions, particularly how unions began influencing environmental policy based upon members' desire for leisure. However, there remains a great deal of room for expanding our understanding of the roles working people have played in environmental debates.[9]

This book focuses on five labor organizations to tell the story of timber workers' activism over the industrial forests created by the timber

[8] Thomas G. Andrews, *Killing for Coal: America's Deadliest Labor War* (Cambridge: Harvard University Press, 2008); Scott Dewey, "Working for the Environment: Organized Labor and the Origins of Environmentalism in the United States, 1948–1970," *Environmental History* 3, no. 1 (January 1998): 45–63; Myrna Santiago, *The Ecology of Oil: Environment, Labor, and the Mexican Revolution* (New York: Cambridge University Press, 2006); Gunther Peck, *Reinventing Free Labor: Padrones and Immigrant Workers in the American West, 1880–1930* (New York: Cambridge University Press, 2000); Gunther Peck, "The Nature of Labor: Fault Lines and Common Ground in Environmental and Labor History," *Environmental History* 11, no. 2 (April 2006): 212–38; Don Mitchell, *The Lie of the Land: Migrant Workers and the California Landscape* (Minneapolis: University of Minnesota Press, 1996); Mitchell, *They Saved the Crops: Labor, Landscape and the Struggle over Industrial Farming in Bracero-Era California* (Athens: University of Georgia Press, 2012); Chad Montrie, *Making a Living: Work and Environment in the United States* (Chapel Hill: University of North Carolina, 2008); Stefania Barca, "Laboring the Earth: Transnational Reflections on the Environmental History of Work, *Environmental History* 19, no. 1 (January 2014): 3–27; Gregory Rosenthal, "Life and Labor in a Seabird Colony: Hawaiian Guano Workers, 1857–1870," *Environmental History* 17, no. 4 (October 2012): 744–82; Kathryn Morse, *The Nature of Gold: An Environmental History of the Klondike Gold Rush* (Seattle: University of Washington Press, 2003).

[9] Lawrence Lipin, *Workers and the Wild: Conservation, Consumerism, and Labor in Oregon, 1910–1930* (Urbana: University of Illinois Press, 2007); Lisa M. Fine, "Workers and the Land in US History: Pointe Mouillée and the Downriver Detroit Working Class in the Twentieth Century," *Labor History* 53, no. 3 (August 2012): 409–34; Scott Dewey, "Working for the Environment: Organized Labor and the Origins of Environmentalism in the United States, 1948–1970," *Environmental History* 3, no. 1 (1998): 45–63.

industry. First, it examines the Industrial Workers of the World (IWW). The IWW organized Northwest loggers between 1907 and World War I, focusing primarily on the brutal conditions industrial capitalism forced upon timber workers: flea-ridden bedding, adulterated food, unsanitary toilets, untreated disease, death and dismemberment from logging machines. Second, it considers the Loyal Legion of Loggers and Lumbermen (Four-L), an industry-wide company union created by the U.S. Army in 1918 in order to organize loggers to cut trees for military airplane production. Crafted as a response to the IWW and continued on a voluntary basis until 1937, the Four-L solved most of the sanitation problems that led Wobbly loggers to strike, demonstrating the power of workers to force responses to environmental problems, even outside of unionization. Third, the book explores the International Woodworkers of America in significant detail. Organized in 1937, the Congress of Industrial Organizations-affiliated IWA was the first union to challenge timber-industry forestry policy, going so far as to hire a professional forester to lobby for its agenda of federal regulation over private forestry. The IWA built connections with environmental organizations from the 1930s to the 1980s, supported wilderness areas, and argued for forest protection based upon protecting members' right to recreate after collectively bargained higher wages and shorter hours gave them the ability to play in the forests. In the 1970s, the IWA used environmental language to reinvigorate its workplace health program, pushing companies and the federal government for a reshaping of the timber workplace environment. However, the IWA was not the only labor union representing timber workers. Fourth, the book examines the United Brotherhood of Carpenters. The UBC opposed the IWA forestry agenda from the 1930s through the 1980s, arguing that real worker representation meant opening more forests to logging. Particularly in the response to Redwood National Park expansion in the 1970s, the Carpenters channeled worker activism in opposing greens as anti-worker outsiders. Finally, the book takes countercultural reforestation workers in the 1970s and 1980s seriously. It details how their experiences with herbicide poisoning shaped their life within the forest, built class consciousness among people who thought of themselves as independent operators in the forest, and created the potential for a new alliance between traditional labor unions and these new forest workers. The IWA, UBC, and reforestation cooperatives all created and adjusted to a radically transforming Pacific Northwest forest economy, one that laid off thousands of workers to increase corporate profits while the region's changing demographics meant that many forests had more economic value remaining standing than being logged.

Examining these five organizations helps elucidate three major themes in the historical relationship between work, unions, and the Northwest forests. First, life in the forest placed timber workers on the front line of environmental transformations and they acted to protect themselves from the worst effects of the new timber ecology. Limiting a discussion of loggers' environmental activism to forest policy would sell short the loggers' own understanding of the environmental impact of logging, which they also connected to the physical impact upon their bodies. It would also reinforce popular notions of environmentalism as "out there," not in the workplace, home, and body. Rather, timber workers responded to the "workscape" created by the timber industry by organizing to moderate its impact upon their bodies.[10] Environmental historians have developed a vigorous literature on health and the body in recent years that demonstrates the centrality of understanding landscape and protecting oneself from the impact of industrial hazards for environmental history, a literature to which this book contributes.[11]

In their daily lives in the logging camps, timber workers faced a "slow violence" to their bodies, "a violence that occurs gradually and out of sight . . . an attritional violence that is typically not viewed as violence at

[10] Thomas Andrews defines the "workscape" as "a place shaped by the interplay of human labor and natural processes," a concept "that treats people as laboring beings who have changed and been changed by a natural world that remains always under construction." Andrews, *Killing for Coal*, 125.

[11] Linda Nash, *Inescapable Ecologies: A History of Environment, Disease, and Knowledge* (Berkeley: University of California Press, 2006); Conevery Bolton Valencius, *The Health of the Country: How American Settlers Understood Themselves and Their Land* (New York: Basic Books, 2002); Nancy Langston, *Toxic Bodies: Hormone Disruptors and the Legacy of DES* (New Haven: Yale University Press, 2010); Gregg Mitman, "In Search of Health: Landscape and Disease in American Environmental History," *Environmental History* 10, no. 2 (April 2005): 184–210; Gregg Mitman, *Breathing Space: How Allergies Shape Our Lives and Landscapes* (New Haven: Yale University Press, 2009); Neil M. Maher, *Nature's New Deal: The Civilian Conservation Corps and the Roots of the American Environmental Movement* (New York: Oxford University Press, 2008); On the environment of the workplace, see Brett Walker, *Toxic Archipelago: A History of Industrial Disease in Japan* (Seattle: University of Washington Press, 2010); Christopher Sellers, *Hazards of the Job: From Industrial Hygiene to Environmental Health Science* (Chapel Hill: University of North Carolina Press, 1998); David Rosner and Gerald Markowitz, *Dying for Work: Workers' Safety and Health in Twentieth-Century America* (Bloomington: Indiana University Press, 1986); Arthur McEvoy, "Working Environments: An Ecological Approach to Industrial Health and Safety," *Technology and Culture* 36 (April 1995): S145–73.

all," to borrow from literary scholar Rob Nixon.[12] Focusing on the material conditions of loggers' lives, I detail the impact of the timber industry on workers' bodies, the meeting point of labor and nature. The IWW focused on those same conditions in convincing workers indifferent to larger theoretical questions but desperate to improve their own lives to join the organization. The sights, sounds, smells, and tastes of the logging camps constructed as cheap and temporary housing by timber operators, disgusted workers. This environment included flea-infested bedding, venereal disease spreading through bunkhouses, rancid butter, workers drowning in log ponds and rivers, and workers' inability to clean themselves. Loggers responded to this environmental injustice through joining the IWW. Strikes convinced some timber operators to implement reforms they hoped would buy off worker discontent through better food, clean sheets, and sanitary toilets. This history reflects larger transformations of the American workplace during this era, when radical unionism and everyday workers forced reformers to make important health and safety improvements to stave off unionism. By 1915, however, most workers' lives remained untouched by these minimal changes and the IWW continued organizing in the forests.

Wobbly loggers striking in 1917 to end the slow violence to their lives forced federal intervention to implement the sanitary changes they demanded when the nation entered World War I and the military needed timber for airplanes. The military created the Spruce Production Division, a division of soldiers who would serve as loggers. The military wanted to integrate soldiers among the camps to avoid the appearance of strikebreaking. However, the sanitation of the camps was below military standards. Colonel Brice Disque convinced employers to join what he called the Loyal Legion of Loggers and Lumbermen (4-L). This government-sponsored company union required workers to renounce the IWW but also forced the companies to improve sanitation, bunkhouses, and food in order to receive soldier-loggers. The largest timber companies continued the company union on a voluntary basis after the war, institutionalizing the sanitary reforms and setting a baseline of acceptable working conditions. The Great Depression ravaged the timber industry and the 4-L shrunk drastically as companies withdrew to save money. Loggers finally organized into their own unions in the mid-1930s, but while the work was still dangerous, issues of sanitation and environmental justice were almost

[12] Rob Nixon, *Slow Violence and the Environmentalism of the Poor* (Cambridge: Harvard University Press, 2011).

completely off the table, as nearly twenty years of sanitation made a return to the old days unthinkable.

While protecting the body from indignities did not play a major role in the 1930s strikes that allowed timber workers to organize on a mass scale for the first time, the continued dangers of the industry made health and safety a priority for both workers and union leaders. Between the 1940s and 1960s, unions attempted to negotiate slow and steady improvements in workplace safety through union contracts and worker-management safety committees, but by the 1970s the timber industry remained one of the nation's most dangerous sectors. Nationally, the 1970s witnessed both environmentalism's rise and blue-collar discontent. The IWA tapped into both of these trends through revitalizing its workplace safety program. Invigorated by new leadership taking power in 1972, the IWA used the Occupational Safety and Health Administration (OSHA) to empower workers to protect their bodies from chemicals and industrial disease on the job. Environmentalism provided the IWA with new language to discuss health and safety. Calling health and safety "the total work environment," it tried using OSHA regulations to challenge corporate control over worker health. It became a national leader among labor unions on OSHA enforcement, conducting research on the unlabeled chemicals, building connections with American, European, and Japanese health researchers to run tests on loggers to gain necessary scientific knowledge, and encouraging members to refuse work if they thought the job unsafe. Conceptualizing these problems as environmental issues allowed the IWA to tap into the growing concerns during the 1970s that Americans had about the effects of unregulated corporate pollution on their lives. However, attacks on OSHA from the Reagan administration in the 1980s and declining timber employment undermined the health and safety program. The IWA allied with environmentalists to bolster both movements against Reagan's budget cuts. This alliance fought for chemical right-to-know legislation in the Oregon legislature and the failure to pass the bill shows both the potential and tenuous nature of these blue-green alliances. Despite these decades of struggle, today the timber industry still has one of the nation's highest fatality rates.

Workers most consistently felt the impact of industrializing the forests in their bodies. However, by the 1930s forest policy also played a major role in timber unions' environmental agenda, both in silvicultural practices and recreational opportunities. The book's second major theme is that labor unions represented their members' interests in natural resource policy. Moreover, this representation was not monolithic but rather represented different union cultures that could channel worker activism into different sides of a forestry debate. Beginning in 1938, the IWA lambasted the timber industry for destructive forestry practices. It pointed to the timber industry's long history of deforestation, using its own members' memories of the despoiling of Wisconsin, Michigan, and Minnesota as evidence. The union claimed the same thing was happening in the Pacific Northwest and called for federal regulation of private forestry in order to make the forests work for the people rather than the capitalists, creating community stability instead of profit. The United Brotherhood of Carpenters, one of the most powerful and politically conservative unions in the country and the IWA's bitter rival for the allegiance of timber workers, denounced this critique as anti-employer and communistic. The two timber unions battled over the creation of Olympic National Park in 1938 with the IWA providing key labor support for the bill.

After World War II, the IWA made a congressional forestry bill mandating federal regulation over private forestry its top legislative priority. It became the nation's first union to hire a professional forester to shape this program that included the end of clearcutting, federal agents choosing which trees private companies could harvest, and a federal road program to open the national forests to small foresters that could compete with private monopolies through federal assistance. Although this attempt to wrest control over the nation's forests from corporations failed in the postwar conservative backlash, the union not only crafted alliances with the growing conservation movement but also became a regional force for working-class environmentalism. Throughout the 1950s and 1960s, the union provided support for wilderness protection in the Northwest, even when it would take timberlands out of production. IWA leadership justified these positions by talking of the need to protect the forest for workers' recreation. Good union contracts with higher wages and shorter hours turned workers into consumers of forest recreation as well as producers of timber products and the IWA tried to balance the need for jobs with life amenities for its members. Overall, the IWA provided the timber industry with the most serious grassroots challenge to its control over the Northwest forests until the environmental movement of the 1970s.

The Carpenters continued opposing these conservation measures, offering a vision of work in the forest consisting of good wages and no environmental protections that would reduce harvests or jobs. The 1968 creation of Redwood National Park caused some controversy, but when plans for park expansion rose in the 1970s, the UBC led the opposition to taking timber land out of production, the first wide-scale working-class protest against environmentalism in the Pacific Northwest. Workers' rallies in Eureka, Sacramento, and Washington, D.C., portended two decades of angry loggers denouncing environmental protections. Despite this acrimony, the American Federation of Labor and Congress of Industrial Organizations (AFL–CIO) and Sierra Club allied to create a landmark compensation package for workers unemployed by environmental protections. The Redwood Employee Protection Program provided long-term benefits for those laid off because of environmental protections. Importantly, while the Carpenters led the opposition to the park, it was the IWA that took the lead in administering REPP and generating community support for the controversial and generous compensation program. This potentially important precedent for workers could have created a new welfare program committing the government to stabilizing communities when natural resource production ended. However, it was sabotaged in the conservative counterrevolution beginning to transform the nation in the 1980s. REPP died in 1982, considered a failure by workers.

The Redwood National Park controversy spoke to the rapid changes transforming the Pacific Northwest after 1965, both within the timber industry and society as a whole. Understanding how workers negotiated and contested these changes is the book's third major theme. New corporate policies promoting the export of unprocessed logs to Japan, the automation of thousands of jobs in new, more efficient timber mills, the rapid harvesting of the last high-profit old-growth trees, and capital mobility away from the Northwest to the American South, Canada, New Zealand, and tropical forests all threatened the future of the timber industry as the Northwest's dominant industry. The number of people employed in the timber industry plummeted. New residents changed the Northwest as well. The region's natural beauty began attracting amenity migrants, tourists, people looking to live alternative lifestyles, and new industries such as computing. For these residents, the forests had far greater value standing than harvested and processed into plywood or exported to Japan. In 1960, the timber industry had almost undisputed precedence in forest management. By 1975, that dominance was challenged on many fronts.

These new residents to the Northwest also brought new forms of work to the forest. In the 1970s, countercultural cooperatives began winning reforestation contracts from federal agencies. Hoping to regenerate the forests through their work outside of mainstream society, hundreds of young people brought a new sense of purpose to some of the most exploitative work in the industry. Founded in 1970 by returned Peace Corps volunteers in Eugene, Hoedads, the largest cooperative, became an important force in the forest by the late 1970s. Its members envisioned physical labor rejuvenating themselves and the forest, living in relative freedom as their own bosses, and presenting a cooperative economic and ecologically friendly work culture to the counterculture. But their vision of a life in the forest was challenged after exposure to the chemical herbicides used to eliminate competition to valuable seedlings. Anger over toxic exposure created political activists out of this new class of workers. Laborers and environmentalists both, Hoedads and other cooperatives had the potential to build bridges between labor and environmental movements. Cooperative members created the Northwest Forest Workers Alliance to lobby state legislatures and federal land management agencies for changes in spraying regulations. When meaningful change proved frustrating, some explored affiliating with the International Woodworkers of America in 1979. The IWA was excited about the idea but Hoedads, who saw unions as bureaucratic and corrupt institutions, shot the plan down. The tentative alliance died and soon after so did Hoedads, as changes in the reforestation contracting process placed power back in the hands of contractors employing undocumented labor. Yet Hoedads also show how changing populations with new ideas of working in the forest could build bridges with organized labor.

While countercultural reforestation workers brought new ideas of work to the forest, for many Northwest residents, all work that damaged rather than enhanced forest ecosystems was unacceptable by the 1970s. Timber workers had to negotiate their job losses and rapidly changing values of the timber country at the same time, as the Northwest transformed from a timber economy to an urban, high-tech economy where the forests' economic value resided in their preservation, not their harvest. The IWA attempted to balance its long history of environmentalist support and the need for workers to have jobs. It supported continued environmental legislation but wanted the end of lawsuits holding up most logging on national forest lands by the late 1970s. Final decisions on what could be logged would allow the union to plan for the future. But as during the Redwood Park expansion campaign, the Carpenters continued whipping up worker discontent toward environmentalists, despite the larger corporate strategies costing far more workers their jobs than environmental protection. Rank-and-file pressure from nervous workers led to the first grassroots challenge to the IWA environmental agenda and in 1987, new leadership turned the union away from its moderate past. This caused chagrin among greens used to the IWA providing labor cover for their agenda. Ultimately, however, a declining union in the face of rampant unemployment could no longer shape a broader moderate worker response to the ancient forest campaigns. Fifty years of IWA environmentalism came to an end in the face of immense challenges that doomed the union's existence, and in 1994 it merged with the International Association of Machinists. The IWA's long history of attempting to craft a working-class environmentalism suggests lost opportunities to create a more constructive response to the problems of sustainable labor and sustainable forestry.

It also suggests a way forward into the future. The history of timber worker unions has lessons for leaders of green and labor organizations today as they attempt to craft contemporary alliances. Historicizing the relationship between workers and nature, especially in an area with a heated recent past of conflict between labor and greens, both challenges the narrative that workers did not care about the forests and provides a usable past for activists. This project is rooted in one corner of the United States but has far broader implications because of the tenuous nature of both labor rights and ecological integrity in the early twenty-first-century system of global capitalism. This system in recent decades has undermined labor and environmental protections at home while shipping jobs, pollution, and poisonous work overseas. The decline of steady work and growth of economic instability have combined with a resurgent conservative movement and organized corporate lobby to depress both the labor and environmental movements' ability to influence national policy to the lowest point in decades. Unions are struggling for sheer survival. Economic instability has also meant that since the recession of the 1970s, environmentalists and labor have often found themselves at loggerheads, particularly over natural resource and pollution policy. Today, the United Mine Workers of America joins with the coal industry to fight the Democratic Party and environmentalists over regulations on coal-burning power plants. Environmentalists are trying to convince President Obama to reject the Keystone XL Pipeline while organized labor finds itself split on the issue. The AFL-CIO has announced partnerships with the Sierra Club while Laborers International Union of North America president Terry O'Sullivan decries environmentalists for opposing the pipeline and bullies other unions who dare speak out against it. The need for so-called blue-green alliances between the two movements in the present is enormous. The history of timber workers and the environment can help us understand how natural resource workers might balance work and the natural world in ways that could help those alliances form.[13]

[13] On blue-green alliances, see William Brucher, "From the Picket Line to the Playground: Labor, Environmental Activism, and the International Paper Strike in Jay, Maine," *Labor History* 52 no. 1 (January 2011): 95–116; Robert Gordon, "'Shell No!' OCAW and the Labor-Environmental Alliance," *Environmental History* 3, no. 4 (October 1998): 460–87; Richard Kazis and Richard L. Grossman, *Fear at Work: Job Blackmail, Labor, and the Environment* (New York: The Pilgrim Press, 1982); Andrew Szasz, *EcoPopulism: Toxic Waste and the Movement for Environmental Justice* (Minneapolis: University of Minnesota Press, 1994); Fred Rose, *Coalitions across the Class Divide: Lessons from the Labor, Peace, and Environmental Movements* (Ithaca: Cornell University Press, 2000); Brian K. Obach, *Labor and the Environmental Movement: The Quest for Common Ground* (Cambridge: The MIT Press, 2004); Les Leopold, *The Man Who Hated Work and Loved Labor: The Life and Times of Tony Mazzocchi* (White River Junction, VT: Chelsea Green Publishing, 2007).

1

Industrial Nature, Working Bodies

In 1917, a new logger came into an Oregon timber camp. His boss assigned him to a typical bunkhouse, crowded with eighty other workers in bunks. Those eighty men shared one sink and one towel. Unfortunately for his bunkmates, this new man had untreated gonorrhea. He used the towel to wipe his infected body. In the wet mountains the towel never dried and the gonorrhea culture stayed alive. Not knowing of their coworker's disease, the men continued to use the towel. Soon, an outbreak of gonorrhea set in the workers' eyes.[1]

American industry's rapid growth after the Civil War came at great expense to both the natural world and human bodies. The transformation of animals, plants, and minerals into industrial and consumer products occurred in workplaces that offered few safety precautions. Coal miners suffered from mine collapses and black lung disease, textile workers inhaled fibers that narrowed their airways, and meatpackers labored in frigid factories with dangerous animal carcasses and knives flying in seemingly every direction.[2] Thomas Andrews has written that "the reek

[1] W.N. Lipscomb, "Red Cross Man Urges Exercise of Great Care in Locating Camp Building," *West Coast Lumberman*, November 1917, 38–39.

[2] On coal mining, see Thomas G. Andrews, *Killing for Coal: America's Deadliest Labor War* (Cambridge: Harvard University Press, 2008); Alan Derickson, *Black Lung: Anatomy of a Public Health Disaster* (Ithaca: Cornell University Press, 1998); William Graebner, *Coal-Mining Safety in the Progressive Period: The Political Economy of Reform* (Lexington: The University Press of Kentucky, 1976). On textile workers, see Charles Levenstein and Gregory F. DeLaurier with Mary Dunn, *The Cotton Dust Papers: Science, Politics, and Power in the Discovery of Byssinosis in the U.S.* (Baywood, 2001); Susan I. Hautaniemi, Alan C. Swedlund, and Douglas L. Anderson, "Mill Town Mortality: Consequences of Industrial

of the industrializing West is lost to us."[3] Most of us living today in the developed world have lost the entire sensory overload of the industrializing landscape, whether the Gilded Age Chicago meatpacking district, the mines of West Virginia, or the maquiladoras and steel mills of the twenty-first-century developing world.

The sensory experiences of early twentieth-century timber workers have also disappeared from our eyes, ears, and noses. The timber industry's rapid expansion after 1900 created massive environmental change in the forests.[4] Loggers smelled, saw, heard, and tasted the products of industrializing nature created to maximize profit off both nature and workers. Industrial logging created a filthy and dangerous landscape in early twentieth-century Northwestern timber camps. Transforming the sun's energy into homes,

Growth in Two Nineteenth-Century New England Towns," *Social Science History* 23, no. 1 (Spring 1999): 1–39. On meatpacking, see Dominic A. Pacyga, *Polish Immigrants and Industrial Chicago: Workers on the South Side, 1880–1922* (Chicago: University of Chicago Press, 1991); Roger Horowitz, "'That Was a Dirty Job!' Technology and Workplace Hazards in Meatpacking over the Long Twentieth Century," *Labor: Studies in Working Class History of the Americas* 5, no. 2 (Summer 2008): 13–25. On broader health and safety issues in workplace, see David Rosner and Gerald Markowitz, "The Early Movement for Occupational Safety and Health, 1900–1917," in Judith Walzer Leavitt and Ronald L. Numbers, eds., *Sickness and Health in America: Readings in the History of Medicine and Public Health*, 2nd edn., Rev. (Madison: University of Wisconsin Press, 1985), 507–21; Rosner and Markowitz, *Deadly Dust: Silicosis and the Politics of Occupational Disease in Twentieth-Century America* (Princeton: Princeton University Press, 1991); Alan Derickson, *Workers' Health Workers' Democracy: The Western Miners' Struggle, 1891–1925* (Ithaca: Cornell University Press, 1988).

[3] Andrews, *Killing for Coal*, 50.

[4] On early logging in the Northwest, see Robert Ficken, *The Forested Land: A History of Lumbering in Western Washington* (Seattle: University of Washington Press, 1987); Norman H. Clark, *Mill Town: A Social History of Everett, Washington, from Its Earliest Beginnings on the Shores of Puget Sound to the Tragic and Infamous Event Known as the Everett Massacre* (Seattle: University of Washington Press, 1970); Thomas R. Cox, *Mills and Markets: A History of the Pacific Coast Lumber Industry to 1900* (Seattle: University of Washington Press, 1974); Robert Bunting, *The Pacific Raincoast: Environment and Culture in an American Eden, 1778–1900* (Lawrence: University of Kansas Press, 1997); Greg Gordon, *When Money Grew on Trees: A.B. Hammond and the Age of the Timber Baron* (Norman: University of Oklahoma Press, 2014). On the environmental changes of logging, see Richard White, *Land Use, Environment, and Social Change: The Shaping of Island County, Washington* (Seattle: University of Washington Press, 1980); Nancy Langston, *Forest Dreams, Forest Nightmares: The Paradox of Old Growth in the Inland West* (Seattle: University of Washington Press, 1995); William G. Robbins, *American Forestry: A History of National, State, and Private Cooperation* (Lincoln: University of Nebraska Press, 1985); William G. Robbins, *Hard Times in Paradise: Coos Bay, Oregon, 1850–1986* (Seattle: University of Washington Press, 1988); Michael Williams, *Americans and Their Forests: A Historical Geography* (New York: Cambridge University Press, 1989), 289–330.

mine timbers, railroad ties, and fuel did not require creating a landscape of illness and death, but timber operators indifferent to workplace safety or sanitation produced a deadly environment. Loggers suffered from a slow violence of disease, filth, insect bites, bodies ground down through hard work, drafty housing, and soaked clothing. Laborers, unmarried and transient, rode the railroads from job to job. Carrying their waterlogged and flea-infested bedrolls on their backs, loggers suffered through respiratory illnesses, filth, and miserable discomfort. Operators constructed drafty housing with hay for a mattress, refused to install modern sanitary facilities, and provided adulterated food that made workers sick. New technologies lacking safety precautions killed and maimed workers daily. From the venereal disease racking their bodies to the tree limbs crushing their heads, loggers may have known nature through working in a beautiful forest but they suffered the consequences of an industrialized, polluted landscape.

The sensory experiences of loggers, moving in and out of the all-too permeable borders between the nature inside and outside the body, eventually led them to challenge the timber industry in the 1910s for control over the industrialized nature created by the intensive logging that characterized the region. Like many other contemporary workers, loggers saw labor unions as a tool to protect their interests. Beginning in 1907, loggers joined the Industrial Workers of the World to fight for sanitation, cleanliness, and dignity, as well as higher wages and shorter hours. Over the next decade, the working and living environment became ever more central to IWW organizing. Although IWW organizers wanted workers to become revolutionaries, they learned that cleanliness and healthy food motivated workers. Thus the union grounded its efforts in the daily relationships between timber workers and the industrialized nature of the logging camp. It wrapped its radical rhetoric in a package of safe food, clean water, and healthy bodies. Wobbly literature contrasted the beautiful healthy forests with loggers' unhealthy lives, urging them to create a masculine proletarian identity based upon dignified work in healthy nature. The IWW demonstrated how organizing around the indignities in their lives could build collective power. In doing so, it gave a voice to workers desperate to keep themselves safe, clean, and healthy.

Loggers demanded what today we would call environmental justice, defined broadly as the equitable distribution of environmental burdens, as they struggled for dignity and safety in the places they worked and lived. Working-class people have long fought for safe food and water, sturdy housing, and protection from the illnesses created by the industrial landscape of manufacturing. Struggling against the slow violence of the environmental injustice they faced daily, invisible to the world outside the timber camps, loggers generated a labor movement in the 1910s that roiled the timber industry and began a nearly century-long tradition of timber workers using their unions to challenge employers' control over the nature in which they lived and worked.[5]

THE TIMBER CAMP ENVIRONMENT

Millennia of sun, rain, life, and death created the vast forests of the north Pacific Coast that seemed inexhaustible to the first Europeans to arrive there. The late eighteenth-century British explorer David Thompson gushed about the size of the trees and the fecundity of the forests, writing that he "measured a very tall Pine forty two feet girth: the Raspberry stalk measured eighteen to twenty one feet in height, and the size of a man's arm."[6] Regional timber operations began with a Hudson's Bay Company mill at Willamette Falls in 1828. Small mills harvested local timber, mostly supplying markets in California and a growing Pacific economy, including Hawaii, Australia, and China. New technologies transformed the industry, ecosystem, and workers' lives in the late nineteenth century. In 1882, California lumberman

[5] Among the most important of the voluminous literature on environmental racism and environmental justice are Luke W. Cole and Sheila R. Foster, *From the Ground Up: Environmental Racism and the Rise of the Environmental Justice Movement* (New York: New York University Press, 2001); Robert D. Bullard, *Dumping in Dixie: Race, Class, and Environmental Quality* (Boulder: Westview Press, 1990); Andrew Hurley, *Environmental Inequalities: Class, Race, and Industrial Pollution in Gary, Indiana, 1945–1980* (Chapel Hill: University of North Carolina Press, 1995); Ted Steinberg, *Acts of God: The Unnatural History of Natural Disaster in America*, 2nd ed. (New York: Oxford University Press, 2006); Steve Lerner, *Diamond: A Struggle for Environmental Justice in Louisiana's Chemical Corridor* (Cambridge: MIT Press, 2006); Steve Lerner, *Sacrifice Zones: The Front Lines of Toxic Chemical Exposure in the United States* (Cambridge: MIT Press, 2010); Sylvia Hood Washington, *Packing Them In: An Archaeology of Environmental Racism in Chicago, 1865–1954* (Lanham, MD: Lexington Books, 2004); Jill Lindsey Harrison, *Pesticide Drift and the Pursuit of Environmental Justice* (Cambridge: MIT Press, 2011); Pete Daniel, *Toxic Drift: Pesticides and Health in the Post-World War II South* (Baton Rouge: Louisiana State University Press, 2007); Daniel Faber, *Capitalizing on Environmental Justice: The Polluter-Industrial Complex in the Age of Globalization* (Rowman & Littlefield, 2008); JoAnn Carmin and Julian Agyeman, eds., *Environmental Inequalities beyond Borders: Local Perspectives on Global Injustices* (Cambridge: The MIT Press, 2011); Rob Nixon, *Slow Violence and the Environmentalism of the Poor* (Cambridge: Harvard University Press, 2010), esp. 1–44. My conception of the ecological body is drawn from Linda Nash, *Inescapable Ecologies: A History of Environment, Disease, and Knowledge* (Berkeley: University of California Press, 2006), esp. 1–15.

[6] David Thompson, *David Thompson's Narrative of His Exploration in Western America, 1784–1812* (Toronto: The Champlain Society, 1916), 504–05.

John Dolbeer patented what he called a "Steam Logging Machine." Soon known as a donkey engine, this was a large engine attached by cables to felled logs that dragged them to a central location. The donkey engine freed operators from expensive animal and skilled human labor previously used to move logs to market. High-lead logging further transformed the forest. First used in the Northwest in 1906, cables were connected from logged trees to a spar tree that remained in the ground, using a donkey engine to swing those fallen trees through the air to a rail line or water deposit, thus avoiding the difficult terrain of the forest floor entirely and allowing for more rapid logging. The donkey engine and high-lead logging not only allowed the exploitation of ever more remote forests, but also contributed to the proletarianization of the timber workforce by undermining worker control over production, a process workers experienced throughout the nation in the early twentieth century. Operating a lever in a logging operation required less skill than driving oxen and workers earned lower wages than nineteenth-century loggers.[7] The completion of the Northern Pacific Railway in 1883 and Great Northern Railway in 1893 brought the Northwest's giant trees to the eastern market. Rapidly advancing logging technologies, the railroad's arrival, and the nation's insatiable need for timber meant the Northwest soon replaced the logged-out Great Lakes and South as the center of American timber production. In 1899, only 5 percent of the nation's lumber came from Douglas fir, the region's dominant commercial species. By 1911, this rose to 14 percent and continued to expand.[8]

The arrival of industrial logging quickly challenged the belief that the forests would last forever. Timber companies had felled over three million acres of timber in western Oregon and western Washington by 1910. Western Washington's nineteen counties alone lost 365,000 acres (570 square miles) of timber per year.[9] As early as 1881, the New Tacoma newspaper *North Pacific Coast* warned readers that the timber could disappear very quickly without protection. Overcutting had already led to difficulty finding "timber within a marketable distance of the water courses." Therefore, "the territorial government should, by the wisest legislation possible, preserve every stick of timber not in the way of

[7] Richard Rajala, *Clearcutting the Pacific Rain Forest: Production, Science, and Regulation* (Vancouver: University of British Columbia Press, 1998), 7–30.

[8] On the technological changes, Rajala, *Clearcutting the Pacific Rain Forest*, 14–30. See also Greg Gordon, *When Money Grew on Trees*, 290–92.

[9] Byron Hunter and Harry Thompson, "The Utilization of Logged-Off Land for Pasture in Western Oregon and Western Washington, United States Department of Agriculture," *Farmers' Bulletin* 462 (Washington, D.C.: Government Printing Office, 1911), 5.

populating the country."[10] The *Jacksonville* (OR) *Sentinel* expressed similar worries, noting that fire and overcutting threatened the regional climate and stating, "the farmers and the town people should be equally interested with the timbermen in the preservation of the forests of this section for tree-clad hills would mean less floods in the winter and more water in the summer in the streams and the climate would be more equitable and not so dry and hot in the summer."[11] The nascent conservation movement called for timber companies to invest in reforestation in order to create a long-term timber industry in the Northwest. While the creation of the U.S. Forest Service in 1905 was an important new step in federal resource management, the forest reserves consisted of higher-elevation and largely unlogged land. The vast forests of the Pacific lowlands and coastal ranges remained under private control.[12]

The timber industry's rapid expansion also brought the problems of Gilded Age workplaces and cities to the forests. Like workers throughout the country, loggers would deal with substandard housing, adulterated and rotting food, communicable diseases, exposure to heat and cold, and a general lack of sanitation, ironically while laboring far from cities. Rapid capital mobility defined the industry, with operations moving from forest to forest. Nineteenth-century loggers usually worked near homes and farms, but the requirements of early twentieth-century capital created a transient workforce, and the lack of workplace standards allowed companies to provide only the most minimal necessities of life to labor. Labor reformer

[10] "Destruction of Timber in the Territory," *North Pacific Coast*, June 15, 1881.

[11] *Jacksonville Sentinel*, August 21, 1903.

[12] Samuel P. Hays, *Conservation and the Gospel of Efficiency: The Progressive Conservation Movement* (Cambridge: Harvard University Press, 1959); Samuel P. Hays, *Wars in the Woods: The Rise of Ecological Forestry in America* (Pittsburgh: University of Pittsburgh Press, 2007); David Clary, *Timber and the Forest Service* (Lawrence: University Press of Kansas, 1986); Henry Clepper, *Professional Forestry in the United States* (Baltimore: Johns Hopkins University Press, 1971); William B. Greeley *Forests and Men* (Garden City: Doubleday and Company, 1951); Harold T. Pinkett, *Gifford Pinchot: Private and Public Forester* (Chicago: University of Chicago Press, 1970); William G. Robbins, *American Forestry: A History of National, State, and Private Cooperation* (Lincoln: University of Nebraska Press, 1985); William G. Robbins, *Lumberjacks and Legislators: Political Economy of the U.S. Lumber Industry, 1890–1941* (College Station: Texas A&M University Press, 1982); Harold K. Steen, *The U.S. Forest Service: A History* (Seattle: University of Washington Press, 1976); Stephen Fox, *The American Conservation Movement: John Muir and His Legacy* (Madison: University of Wisconsin Press, 1986); Char Miller, *Gifford Pinchot and the Making of Modern Environmentalism* (Washington, D.C.: Island Press, 2001); Thomas R. Cox, *The Lumbermen's Frontier: Three Centuries of Land Use, Society, and Change in American Forests* (Corvallis: Oregon State University Press, 2010).

Carleton Parker estimated in 1914 that loggers in the California lumber camps only stayed on the job between fifteen and thirty days before hopping a train and moving on. Temporary worksites allowed timber operators to construct logging camps that lacked even basic sanitation. Loggers' bodies became as degraded as the deforested landscape.[13]

Logging was seasonal, with frequent layoffs during slow economic periods and bad weather. Washington Labor Commissioner Edward Olson estimated in 1912 that industry needed 50 percent fewer laborers during the winter, when masses of unemployed loggers descended upon the cities, and a 1914 study of the unemployed in Portland estimated that loggers were unemployed 130 days a year.[14] When loggers found a job, companies provided room and board, deducting the cost from wages. The new employee usually saw a wooden barrack with double bunks on three sides, a single window on one end, and a stove in the middle.[15] Operators squeezed as many workers as possible into the bunkhouses. One Brooks-Scanlon company camp provided a floor space of merely 3,586 square feet for 108 men to live and sleep on.[16] Logger H.J. Cox described the bunkhouses as "an architectural abortion," saying, "Floor cracks reduced sweeping to a minimum. Shake roof, one door on leather strap hinges, one window with sliding window pane."[17]

Loggers carried their own blankets on their back from job to job. Most companies did not provide mattresses for the bunks. Instead, loggers

[13] Carleton H. Parker, "Preliminary Report on Tentative Findings and Conclusion in the Investigations of Seasonal, Migratory, and Unskilled Labor in California," Report to U.S. Commission on Industrial Relations, 1914, 10; Arthur Evans Wood, *A Study of the Unemployed in Portland, Oregon* (Reed College: Social Service Bulletin, 1914). Mark Wyman, *Hoboes: Bindlestiffs, Fruit Tramps, and the Harvesting of the West* (New York; Hill and Wang, 2010); Carlos Schwantes, *Hard Traveling: A Portrait of Work Life in the Pacific Northwest* (Lincoln: University of Nebraska Press, 1994), 25–45; Greg Hall, *Harvest Wobblies: The Industrial Workers of the World and Agricultural Laborers in the American West, 1910–1930* (Corvallis: Oregon State University Press, 2001); Frank Tobias Higbie, *Indispensable Outcasts: Hobo Workers and Community in the American Midwest, 1880–1930* (Urbana: University of Illinois Press, 2003); Peter Boag, *Same-Sex Affairs: Constructing and Controlling Homosexuality in the Pacific Northwest* (Berkeley: University of California Press, 2003), 15–44. For a worker's perspective, see G.R. "Tramping the Northwest," *Industrial Pioneer* September 1921, 45.

[14] U.S. Commission on Industrial Relations, *Industrial Relations: Final Report and Testimony, Vol.* V (Washington: Government Printing Office, 1916), 4121, see also 4108; Wood, *A Study of the Unemployed in Portland, Oregon*, 14.

[15] See USCIR, *Final Report and Testimony*, 4211 for a typical description of the bunkhouses.

[16] Brice Disque Papers, University of Washington Special Collections, Box 3, Folder V0257a.

[17] H.J. Cox, *Random Lengths: Forty Years with "Timber Beasts" and "Sawdust Savages"* (Eugene, OR: publisher unknown, 1949), 8.

collected hay for makeshift padding. The hay, unwashed bedding, and moisture from rain-soaked bedrolls combined to create a perfect environment for flea infestations. Torger Birkeland remembered his first night in a logging camp, at the age of eleven. He looked around for leftover hay to create his bed. He described his sleep as "not too good. The fleas, having found their way out, were having a grand time, jumping around and feeding on brand-new, tender skin. Sleep came after my little friends had all been fed and had crawled back under the bottom blanket again."[18] George Davidson's underwear became so full of vermin he had to throw them out and sleep outside, exposed to the elements.[19] The bunkhouses also stank. Each night, loggers hung their drenched socks near the bunkhouse's single heater to dry before the next day's work. The smell of dozens of pairs of drying socks nearly sickened many loggers. As H.J. Cox recalled, "the steaming aroma ... permeated the same feeling of life as from the windward whiff of a country backhouse."[20]

Timber companies argued that they could not provide better housing because of low profit margins and mobile operations. Frank Hobi's father expressed a typical attitude about camp quarters in his operation near Aberdeen, Washington, around 1910. The camp had no road leading into it and everything came in and out of camp by horse and river. Hobi used the camp's remoteness to justify why his father "furnished double bunks with split cedar boards and straw in place of mattresses."[21] Companies were as reluctant to build sanitary latrines as sturdy bunkhouses. Many camps located toilet facilities near water supplies or the kitchen, allowing for an increased risk of cross-contamination and gastrointestinal diseases. Seattle minister Oscar McGill talked of one camp where the owners placed the toilets between the bunkhouses, leading to a smell so foul that the workers slept on the ground in the forest rather than in their bunks.[22]

Anyone walking into the mess hall at a logging camp saw an enormous spread of food.[23] Even the stingiest operators understood loggers' sheer caloric needs. Logging millennia of the sun's energy required a

[18] Torger Birkeland, *Echoes of Puget Sound: Fifty Years of Logging and Steamboating* (Caldwell, ID: The Claxton Printers Ltd., 1960), 19–21.

[19] "Poor, Often Rotten," *Industrial Worker*, June 23, 1917.

[20] Cox, *Random Lengths*, 8–9.

[21] Frank Hobi Reminiscence, University of Washington Special Collections, 9.

[22] USCIR, *Final Report and Testimony*, 4385.

[23] On food in logging camps, see Joseph R. Conlin, "Old Boy, Did You Get Enough of Pie? A Social History of Food in Logging Camps," *Journal of Forest History* 23, no. 4 (October 1979): 164–85.

tremendous amount of energy from workers. A 1915 study of Maine loggers used as a model by Northwestern operators estimated that loggers ate 6,783 calories a day, of which 3,434 came from meat.[24] Birkeland remembered the breakfast table "loaded with meat, spuds, oatmeal, hot cakes, and other food" where loggers could eat enough to get through the morning's hard work.[25] However, commonly for the period, operations often sacrificed food quality for higher profit. Kitchen facilities were as shoddily built as bunkhouses. Companies stored meat in the open air, allowing flies unlimited access. A lack of garbage disposal meant mounds of trash that attracted even more flies.[26] A logger writing in 1910 described the butter served in camps as "white as wax, and as rotten as a putrid carcass, if smell goes for anything."[27] A man sitting next to Egbert Oliver in one camp opened three successive eggs, each inedible. In the third was a half-formed chick. The logger ran outside and vomited.[28]

This poor food made gastrointestinal diseases common. Edward Gilbert told U.S. Commission on Industrial Relations investigators that he worked at a Maplewood, Oregon, camp for only a few days when he contracted a stomach illness and had to quit work for two weeks.[29] These were hardly the only health hazards in the timber camp ecology. As Ern Hanson remembered, "Bunkhouses were jammed with double decker bunks with two men in each bunk and if one man got the flu or pneumonia, it spread like fire. You no sooner boiled out your clothes and blankets and got rid of the lice and bedbugs when some new worker bedded with you and you were freshly colonized."[30] Bunkhouse stoves got so hot in the

[24] M.E. Jaffa, "The Uses and Values of Foods," *The Timberman, November* 1915, 60–61.

[25] Birkeland, *Echoes of Puget Sound*, 21.

[26] USCIR, *Final Report and Testimony*, 4211–12. On food in the Gilded Age, see Roger Horowitz, *Putting Meat on the American Table: Taste, Technology, Transformation* (Baltimore: Johns Hopkins University Press, 2006), 59. On food quality in the Gilded Age, see also Uwe Spiekermann, "Redefining Food," *History & Technology* 27, no. 1 (March 2011): 11–36; Gabriella M. Petrick, "An Ambivalent Diet: The Industrialization of Canning," *OAH Magazine of History* 24, no. 3 (July 2010): 35–38; Jason Pickavance, "Gastronomic Realism: Upton Sinclair's The Jungle, The Fight for Pure Food, and the Magic of Mastication," *History and Culture of Human Nourishment* 11, no. 2–3 (April 2003): 87–112; Ronald F. Wright and Paul Huck, "Counting Cases about Milk, Our 'Most Nearly Perfect Food,' 1860–1940," *Law and Society Review* 36, no. 1 (March 2002): 51–111."

[27] A Logger, "Who Says a Logger Lives?" *Industrial Worker*, July 2, 1910.

[28] Egbert S. Oliver, "Sawmilling on Grays Harbor in the Twenties," IWA Box 275, Folder 6.

[29] Unpublished notes on the interviews with Mr. John L. Spicer and Mr. Edward Gilbert," United States Commission on Industrial Relations, Microfilm Reel 6.

[30] Bert Russell, ed., *Hardships and Happy Times in Idaho's St. Joe Wilderness* (Caldwell, ID: Lacon Publishers, 1978), 103–04.

winter that loggers would leave the doors open so they could sleep, which they blamed for colds, rheumatism, and other diseases.[31] Untreated venereal disease spread through the camps, through sex between loggers and through the general lack of sanitation, such as the gonorrhea epidemic described at the opening of this chapter.[32] Cooks often had untreated respiratory or venereal disease that disgusted workers. Logger Edward Gilbert told the USCIR he knew of at least two cases of cooks with active venereal disease.[33]

After a day's work in the forests, mud, dust, tree needles, and other logging residue covered workers' bodies. The filth caked onto loggers' bodies often proved difficult to wash off because few camps provided decent bathing facilities. Ern Hanson remembered that loggers improvised a shower by punching holes in a five-gallon oil can, attaching it to a stand, and then pouring warm water through it.[34] Clean water could attract loggers to a particular camp. For instance, Torger Birkeland enjoyed working near Washington's Hood Canal because it gave him a way to clean himself. He called the canal "a godsend for the grimy logger after a day of toil."[35]

Timber mill workers lived in cities and towns, with generally permanent housing and access to recreation and amenities, avoiding loggers' itinerancy and isolation. But workers in company towns suffered much of the same discomfort as loggers. The Grays Harbor Commercial Company provided a stipend to workers if they wanted to live on their own, but that stipend covered only half the going rate for boarding. This forced 575 of its 650 workers into profit-generating company housing. Most lived in cheaply built wooden cabins, each partitioned into two units. In one area, the mill built fifteen cabins. The thirty men shared only one toilet and a small pipe for water, creating an atmosphere described as "extremely filthy."[36]

[31] USCIR, *Final Report and Testimony*, 4211.

[32] On same-sex relationships between migrant loggers, see Boag, *Same-Sex Affairs*, 15–44. On sexuality within the migrant labor community more broadly, Todd DePastino, *Citizen Hobo: How a Century of Homelessness Shaped America* (Chicago: University of Chicago Press, 2003), 81–91.

[33] Unpublished notes on the interviews with Mr. John L. Spicer and Mr. Edward Gilbert," United States Commission on Industrial Relations, Microfilm Reel 6.

[34] On company towns in the Northwest, see Linda Carlson, *Company Towns of the Pacific Northwest* (Seattle: University of Washington Press, 2003); Russell, *Hardships and Happy Times in Idaho's St. Joe Wilderness*, 104.

[35] Birkeland, *Echoes of Puget Sound*, 23.

[36] USCIR, *Final Report and Testimony*, 4551–52.

Both camp and mill workers felt the pain and shock of severe injury in a dangerous and highly mechanized working environment and saw workers die horrible deaths. These technologies made logging a more dangerous and deadly job. Cables and machines broke, becoming deadly whipsaws. The flying logs of high-lead logging crushed workers' heads. The state of Washington began collecting data on workplace injuries in 1912. Between that date and 1929, between 124 and 261 loggers died every year in the timber industry.[37] In 1914, 63,350 people worked in the timber industry, 35 percent of the state's workforce. In the first five months of that year, there were 4,928 reported accidents that injured or killed timber workers.[38]

Working in the region's watery environment contributed to this death toll. The Northwest's cold rain and snow made workers sick while the workers toiling on floating logs in log ponds or river drives risked their lives. At least nine loggers drowned on the job in 1906, including J.W. Roth of Springfield, Oregon, and Ralph Leedy of Hoquiam, Washington, who died in separate incidents on log ponds, as well as J.K. Lynn, who fell into a river near Hoquiam while rafting logs. Alfred Aasen fell into a cold river while working in the spring of 1916. He did not drown, but he caught pneumonia while riding on a rail car the ten miles back to camp in soaking clothes and soon died.[39]

Machines killed far more workers than water and cold. On August 28, 1905, Clise Houston reached to clear an obstruction from his saw. He fell into it and died. Finnish immigrant John Koski found a job with the Simpson Logging Company in a camp near Matlock, Washington. On June 18, 1904, nearby tree fallers shouted "Timber!" He did not move and the tree landed directly on top of him, crushing him beyond recognition. Koski had no family in America and his coworkers had no way to inform his relations in Finland of his demise. The company paid for the burial. Karl Carlson worked in the Anderson & Middleton mill in Aberdeen, Washington. In 1905, a belt fell off its course and Carlson tried to guide it back on to the pulley with a shovel. The shovel became

[37] Andrew Prouty, *More Deadly Than War: Pacific Coast Logging, 1927–1981* (New York: Garland Publishing, 1985), 186–87.

[38] *Eleventh Annual Report of the American Red Cross for the Year 1915* (Washington: Government Printing Office, 1916), 34.

[39] "Fatal Accidents" *West Coast and Puget Sound Lumberman*, January 1906, 230; "Fatal Accidents" *West Coast and Puget Sound Lumberman*, April 1906, 528; Lionel Youst, *She's Tricky Like Coyote: Annie Miner Peterson, an Oregon Coast Indian Woman* (Norman: University of Oklahoma Press, 1997), 144.

entangled with the belt and he lost control of it. The machine tore the shovel from his hands and plunged it, handle first, through his body. Carlson lingered for a day before dying, leaving behind a wife and child.[40]

The lucky workers were merely maimed. Morris Campbell worked in J.E. Nichols' sawmill in La Conner, Washington. In the last days of 1899, he caught his arm in a mill saw. It was amputated at the shoulder. In 1900, Frank Lang lost most of his left hand running a band saw in the Centralia Shingle Mill in Centralia, Washington. In 1901, Martin Boyer's foot got caught in machinery in a Centralia mill. Doctors amputated. In a nation without a social safety net, injured workers often fell through the cracks into a lifetime of poverty. Workers such as Campbell, Lang, and Boyer faced grim futures as disabled persons, as did many people disabled on the job before the passage of the Civilian Vocational Rehabilitation Act in 1920, which provided occupational training and job placement for those injured at the workplace. Many workers chose self-medication. Joseph Gillis of Seattle lost a leg while working at the McDougal and Jackson logging camp near Buckley, Washington. He sued for $10,000 but overdosed on the laudanum he used for pain the day before he lost his suit.[41]

Like with food and sanitation, companies used medicine to profit off their workers' bodies. They frequently signed medical contracts with hospitals that took advantage of workers' transience. The Northwestern Hospital Association in Portland advertised its services to timber companies, offering a medical plan for $1 a month per worker, including limited burial expenses, hospital transportation, and some drugs in the camps.[42] That dollar fee became standard in the industry, often paid in twenty-cent increments the first five days of the month worked. If a logger took a job and was fired or quit six days later, he already had

[40] "Fatal Accidents," *West Coast Lumberman*, September 1905, 777; "Fatal Accidents" *West Coast and Puget Sound Lumberman*, July 1904, 669; "Fatal Accidents" *West Coast and Puget Sound Lumberman*, May 1905, 508.

[41] "Fatal Accidents" *West Coast and Puget Sound Lumberman*, January 1900, 134; "Fatal Accidents" *West Coast and Puget Sound Lumberman*, April 1900, 28; "Fatal Accidents" *West Coast and Puget Sound Lumberman*, January 1901, 150; "Fatal Accidents," *West Coast and Puget Sound Lumberman* October 1903, 158. On disability during the early twentieth century, Beth Linker, *War's Waste: Rehabilitation in World War I America* (Chicago: University of Chicago Press, 2011), 148–49; See also Katherine Ott, David Serlin, and Stephen Mihm, eds., *Artificial Parts, Practical Lives: Modern History of Prosthetics* (New York: New York University Press, 2002); Paul Longmore and Lauri Umansky, eds., *The New Disability History: American Perspectives* (New York: New York University Press, 2001); Susan M. Schweik, *The Ugly Laws; Disability in Public* (New York: New York University Press, 2010).

[42] *The Timberman* September 1911, 57.

paid a full month's hospital bill and would have to pay again starting the first day of his next job.[43]

A camp cook named Doc Wilson wrote to the *Pacific Monthly* in 1908 to complain about the lives of loggers. In a verse he titled "The Bunk House," Wilson expressed the depressing reality:

O! Bunks and bunks
Valises and trunks
Blankets and swags by the score;
Smoky oil cans,
Old spittoon pans,
Scattered all over the floor!

Old gunny sacks
Filled from the stacks
Of hay in the field nearby;
Under your nose
Pillow your clothes
And sleep with many a sigh.

Old broken door
Drags on the floor,
Overhead the nightbats hide;
The roof's too thin
And rain drips in
The bunk where Anderson died.

Old shirts and coats
Where Spider gloats
On the flies and moths in his lair.
Rusty old stove,
Socks by the grove,
Polluting the room's warm air.

Off to the junks!
Bunkhouses and bunks!
For the toiler requires rest.
A clean, warm bed,
Or home, instead
And then his labors are blest.[44]

Around these issues, loggers began a long road to demanding dignity and environmental justice.

[43] USCIR, *Final Report and Testimony*, 4187.

[44] Quoted in A.B. Wastell, "Illustration of Housing and Feeding Logging Camp Outfit on Wheels," *The Timberman*, August 1910, 50–51.

THE INDUSTRIAL WORKERS OF THE WORLD

Increasingly desperate to protect themselves from the ravages of timber camp life, loggers began organizing with the Industrial Workers of the World in 1907. Over the next decade, the IWW built a core membership of committed radicals to recruit disaffected loggers. Although it hoped for a revolution to replace capitalism, the IWW gained followers in the timber camps because it focused on environmental inequities of workers' lives. Wobbly organizers and literature spoke to the daily concerns of loggers, empowering them with hope for a dignified and sanitary future. The historiography on the IWW has explored the union from any number of vantage points. This includes a focus on the working conditions of itinerant labor in the western natural resources industries. However, the effects of environmental injustice as the motivating factor behind the Wobblies' success in the region is largely understudied; as this section shows, the IWW tried a variety of methods for organizing the loggers in its first years in the woods before settling upon issues such as sanitation, food, and health.[45]

Except for shingle weavers, the timber industry remained almost wholly unorganized into the twentieth century's first decade. Shaping pieces of wood into roofing shingles using unprotected saws, shingle weavers suffered dearly from severed fingers. They went through several unions beginning in 1890, but they struggled to remain viable and had little influence in the rest of the timber industry. The American Federation of Labor (AFL)-chartered International Brotherhood of Woodsmen and Sawmill Workers only had 8,000 members in 1912, and the national AFL was little concerned with itinerant, unskilled loggers. The timber industry

[45] Among the most important books in the gigantic historiography on the IWW are Melvyn Dubofsky, *We Shall Be All: A History of the Industrial Workers of the World* (Chicago: Quadrangle Press, 1969); Howard Kimeldorf, *Battling for American Labor: Wobblies, Craft Workers, and the Making of the Union Movement* (Berkeley: University of California Press, 1999); Salvatore Salerno, *Red November, Black November: Culture and Community in the Industrial Workers of the World* (Albany: State University of New York Press, 1989); Joseph R. Conlin, *Bread and Roses Too: Studies of the Wobblies* (Westport, CT: Greenwood Press, 1969); Joseph R. Conlin, ed., *At the Point of Production: The Local History of the I.W.W.* (Westport, CT: Greenwood Press, 1981). For the IWW in the West outside of logging, see Hall, *Harvest Wobblies*; Wyman, *Hoboes*; Nigel Anthony Sellars, *Oil, Wheat, and Wobblies: The Industrial Workers of the World in Oklahoma, 1905–1930* (Norman: University of Oklahoma Press, 1998); Clemens P. Work, *Darkest before Dawn: Sedition and Free Speech in the American West* (Albuquerque: University of New Mexico Press, 2005).

did not consider it a serious threat.[46] The IWW first appeared in the timber industry in 1907 when workers demanding shorter hours and a minimum of $2.50 a day went on strike. Within two weeks the Wobblies claimed a membership of over 1,500 men in Portland. The strike collapsed in April after mill owners hired strikebreakers with the approval of the AFL.[47]

By late 1907, Wobbly organizers worked in the Grays Harbor area of southwestern Washington, Bellingham, western Montana, the redwood forests of California, and Vancouver, British Columbia.[48] Wobblies targeted the region for its free speech fights, when law enforcement officials would arrest IWW members for public speaking, leading to radicals arriving from around the nation to reinforce them, filling the jails, and embarrassing public officials. In 1909, Wobblies began a free speech fight in Spokane, Washington, after they publicly spoke out against the employment agencies that itinerant loggers used to find work. These agencies sometimes made bargains with employers who would fire workers upon their arrival. Loggers then returned to the agency to pay for another, possibly fraudulent, job. Spokane's leaders passed ordinances banning public gatherings after Wobbly speakers began making speeches on town streets opposing these practices. Hundreds of radicals were arrested, though fearing lawsuits and bad publicity the city dropped all charges, repealed the offending ordinance, and closed employment agencies in March 1910.[49]

[46] Vernon Jensen, *Lumber and Labor* (New York: Farrar and Rinehart, 1945), 117–19; Philip Dreyfus, "Nature, Militancy, and the Western Worker: Socialist Shingles, Syndicalist Spruce," *Labor* 1, no.3 (Summer 2004): 80–84; USCIR, *Final Report and Testimony*, 4207.

[47] "Strikers Gain in Mill Fight," *The Oregonian*, March 6, 1907; "Portland Men Mill Strike," *Industrial Union Bulletin*, March 16, 1907; "'Stand Pat' at Portland," *Industrial Union Bulletin*, April 6, 1907; "Four Big Lumber Mills Shut Down," *The Oregonian*, March 8, 1907; "Still Gaining at Portland," *Industrial Union Bulletin*, March 30, 1907. "The Millworkers' Strike," *The Oregonian*, March 8, 1907. "Portland Strike Off," *Industrial Union Bulletin*, April 20, 1907.

[48] "Local Executive Board" *Industrial Union Bulletin*, May 11, 1907; "Untitled Editorial" *Industrial Union Bulletin*, May 25, 1907; "Lumber Jacks Taken In" *Industrial Union Bulletin*, November 2, 1907; "Kalispell Lumbermen Get It Right" *Industrial Union Bulletin*, December 7, 1907; "Somers Lumbermen Back in Line," *Industrial Union Bulletin*, December 14, 1907; "Untitled Editorial" *Industrial Union Bulletin*, December 21, 1907; "Substantial Progress at Bellingham, Wash." *Industrial Union Bulletin*, December 21, 1907; "Resolutions: In Support of the Striking Lumber Men in Missoula, Mont." *Industrial Union Bulletin*, August 8, 1908; E.J. Foote, "The Strike of the Montana Lumber Workers" *Industrial Union Bulletin*, August 22, 1908, "Hell Popping in Montana," *Industrial Union Bulletin*, November 7, 1908.

[49] USCIR, *Final Report and Testimony*, 4208. On the free speech struggles, Robert L. Tyler, *Rebels of the Woods: The I.W.W. in the Pacific Northwest* (Eugene: University of Oregon

In 1912, the IWW targeted the Grays Harbor region of southwestern Washington for organizing. In Aberdeen, organizers intended to organize loggers, but that goal quickly took a backseat to the free speech struggle. "Stumpy" wrote in *Industrial Worker* that with the arrival of street speakers "the woods and mills and vessels and city streets on Grays Harbor will soon ring with the cry of victory for the workers!"[50] However, Stumpy or the many other Wobbly writers on the struggle never articulated why average workers would support these free speech struggles. Instead the language surrounding these fights revolved around the evils of capitalism, the hypocrisy of politicians, and the brutality of the police, with very little connecting the struggles to the lived experiences of loggers. Frank Schleis told *Industrial Worker* readers about the tough lives of hoboes during the Aberdeen free speech struggle, but this was simply to note how proud these men were of being called Wobblies and that they would rush from around the Northwest to support the struggle because "they have nothing to lose."[51] Even when the IWW won the free speech fights, it never led to refocusing attention on the daily lives of timber workers. Local repression crushed organizing in Aberdeen while providing a slight increase in wages. This defeat decimated active IWW membership, but the union continued to organize in the woods.[52]

Early IWW campaigns to organize loggers show a wide variety of strategies. The 1907 Portland strike revolved around wages. In February 1911, attempting to convince mill workers in Bellingham to walk off the job, one Wobbly writer challenged workers to leave their fourteen-hour-a-day jobs, saying that such men "were better dead and resting in the grave."[53] The IWW also organized around technological change and the decline of skilled labor. Charles Bernat wrote that high-lead logging means "you can go and seek a job elsewhere while the boss doubles his profits."[54] In 1912, the *Industrial Worker* pushed for loggers to strike

Press, 1967), 33–39; David M. Rabban, *Free Speech in Its Forgotten Years* (New York: Cambridge University Press, 1997), 77–127; Margaret Kohn, *The Privatization of Public Space* (New York: Routledge, 2004), 18–35; Dubofsky, *We Shall Be All*, 173–97.

50 "Preparing the Ground in Aberdeen," *Industrial Worker*, January 11, 1912.

51 "To the Mayor and Officials of Aberdeen," *Industrial Worker*, December 7, 1911.

52 Joyce Kornbluh, ed., *Rebel Voices: An I.W.W. Anthology* (Ann Arbor: The University of Michigan Press, 1964), 252.

53 "A Modern Hell-Hole," *Industrial Worker*, February 16, 1911.

54 "To Loggers and Lumberjacks on the Coast," *Industrial Worker*, June 11, 1910. See also, "The Evolution in Logging," *Industrial Worker*, November 23, 1911.

over wages, presenting suggested wage scales for each position within the timber industry.[55]

However, fighting for sanitary logging camps soon became the leading argument made by Wobbly organizers. The connection between sanitation and class became a common rhetorical strategy for Wobbly organizers. Emil Herman noted that it was illegal to spit on the sidewalk because rich people might catch disease. But the rich had no problem providing loggers with bunkhouses so filthy that they might as well spit on the floor. The difference was "Because while both are liable to spread disease, only the former is liable to spread until it reaches some parasite and thus hurries him on to the home beyond the grave which his agents in the pulpit picture as being a beautiful, glorious, and all-ideal place."[56] So the IWW subsumed its ideology behind environmental inequality, attempting to convince loggers that capitalism itself was to blame for the filth, odors, and illness they faced.[57]

Loggers' traveling from camp to camp on trains gave organizers space away from bosses to talk to workers.[58] This mobility also meant coordinating action was much harder than a shop floor or a mill town. Thus, IWW newspapers played a vital role in organizing. Conversations about organizing and political strategy had to take place in the newspapers because there was no other effective way to disseminate information. Organizers presented ideas that clearly show strategies in development. J.H. Reynolds of Grays Harbor urged the IWW to focus on getting camp delegates to larger central meetings at least once a year in order to focus on "methods and means of organizing." John Pancner, organizing in Coos Bay, created an organizing plan on his own. Delineating it in the pages of *Industrial Worker*, although never declaring the reasons workers would

55 "Wage Scale for Logging Camps," *Industrial Worker*, April 25, 1912.

56 "Lumberjacks: What Are They Up Against," *Industrial Worker*, October 1, 1910.

57 Industrial Workers of the World, *The Lumber Industry and Its Workers*, 52; Elizabeth Attridge, "My Findings on the Centralia Case," University of Washington Archives, 1; "Fifty Thousand Lumberjacks," IWW Songbook, University of Washington Archives, 43.

58 Among the most important works on the history of mobile labor in American history are Higbie, *Indispensable Outcasts*; Sarah Deutsch, *No Separate Refuge: Culture, Class, and Gender on an Anglo-Hispanic Frontier in the American Southwest, 1880–1940* (New York: Oxford University Press, 1989); Cindy Hahamovitch, *The Fruits of Their Labor: Atlantic Coast Farmworkers and the Making of Migrant Poverty, 1870–1945* (Chapel Hill: University of North Carolina Press, 1997); and Gunther Peck, *Reinventing Free Labor: Padrones and Immigrant Workers in the North American West, 1880–1930* (New York: Cambridge University Press, 2000).

strike, Pancner wanted to establish branch offices in the nearby towns of Coquille and Bandon, seek volunteers to organize each camp and mill, teach members Wobbly tactics and ideology, and strike across the region once they had achieved "a strong minority." This strategy if "used nationally would surely bring to terms the Lumber trust."[59]

More useful to everyday workers was how IWW newspapers became public information sheets, publicizing camp conditions. Earl Osborne warned loggers in 1913 to stay away from a Coos Bay operation with overcrowded bunkhouses, no way to dry their drenched work clothes, and a hospital fee of $1 a month for a "doctor" that was just a practicing medical student. H.H. told workers to avoid Stimson Timber Company operations near Union City, Washington. The food was good but not plentiful enough, forcing workers to fight for every last scrap. Worse was a pig pen just off the kitchen that created a smell wafting over the dining hall as well as "an open cesspool outside the door of the kitchen that would smell worse only the pigs keep a person's nose so busy." When workers entered a camp with better conditions, they wrote to inform each other about that as well. One 1916 article urged loggers to come to Bend, Oregon, where "men who work hard can make what is considered good wages under the general conditions of slavery."[60]

Organizers and writers soon picked up on the importance of sanitation and food, emphasizing the real possibilities of better conditions if workers stuck together and organized. In March 1910, "McKenzie" appealed to loggers in the pages of *Industrial Worker* by honing in on the environmental injustice they faced. McKenzie challenged loggers to stand up for themselves by organizing against the overcrowded bunkhouses and wet clothing, comparing owners ensuring their own horses stayed warm after a day in the cold while dooming loggers to the drafty bunkhouses. He spoke to the conversations loggers had with each other food in the camps, noting that when asked about why loggers quit, two-thirds answered that the food was "why I bunched the job."[61] Earl Osborne used similar language, telling loggers to ask themselves, "How would it be to have these bunkhouses well lighted, properly ventilated, rooms instead of

[59] "The Logger Will Organize," *Industrial Worker*, November 23, 1911; John Pancner, "To Coos Bay Lumber Workers," *Industrial Worker*, February 1, 1912.

[60] "Camp Conditions at Coos Bay," *Industrial Worker*, June 5, 1913; "Terrible Working Conditions," *Industrial Worker*, October 7, 1916; "Lumber Workers Needed in Bend, Oregon," *Industrial Worker*, October 28, 1916.

[61] "Logger Speaks to the Loggers," *Industrial Worker*, March 12, 1910.

bunks, with springs, mattresses and bedclothes furnished, wash rooms, drying rooms, bath rooms, reading and writing rooms?"[62]

These issues appealed to thousands of workers. A Swedish immigrant logger explained his reasons for IWW membership simply: "We did not need to live in misery."[63] Andrew Hanson was a typical IWW recruit. Thirty years old when a U.S. Commission on Industrial Relations investigator interviewed him in September 1914, Hanson emigrated from Sweden, moving to Iowa before coming to the Pacific Northwest in 1913. He moved from logging camp to logging camp, dealing with frequent unemployment, bad food, dirty bunkhouses, and polluted air. One company superintendent beat him and robbed him of all his possessions. Hanson did not admit to IWW membership, but he expressed sympathy with the union.[64]

Wobblies often found particular success organizing around food. As Donald Worster has said, "environmental history begins in the belly," a sentiment with which loggers, with their internal organs rumbling from adulterated and poor quality food might, well have agreed.[65] "A. Rebel" wrote of his experiences working in the Fordney Lumber Company camp cookhouse. Rebel described how the company focused on "efficiency" in the cookhouse, with the head cook paid $25 extra per month for saving money. This gave the cook incentive to buy low-quality food. He created tapioca cooked in a dirty pot with food coloring to give it an appealing look after "the dirt and flies were skimmed off." Wormy cabbage and rotten meat were common. He noted that if workers knew what they ate, "there would be a lot of vomiting."[66] Bad food gave Wobbly organizers the chance to show how collective power could work. IWW organizer and writer Ralph Winstead wrote of how rancid butter spurred one logging camp to organize. Winstead tried to convince his coworkers of the need

[62] "An Address to Loggers," *Industrial Worker*, July 9, 1910.

[63] John Pancner, "The Spokane Free-Speech Fight – 1909," in Philip S. Foner, ed., *Fellow Workers and Friends: I.W.W. Free-Speech Fights as Told by Participants* (Westport, CT: Greenwood Press, 1981), 71–75; "To Coos Bay Lumber Workers," *Industrial Worker* February 1, 1912. "Why I Am a Member of the I.W.W." *Four L Bulletin*, October 1922, 9, 34–36. See Cloice R. Howd, "What Kind of Man Are You?" *Four L Bulletin*, July 1922, 10–11 for a contemporary analysis of these migratory networks. For an excellent discussion of these regional Wobbly networks, see Higbie, *Indispensable Outcasts*.

[64] Unpublished Notes on interview with Andrew Hanson, United States Commission on Industrial Relations, Microfilm Collection, Reel 6.

[65] Worster quote from Nicolaas Mink, "It Begins in the Belly," *Environmental History* 14, no. 2 (April 2009): 312.

[66] "Stomach-Robbing the Lumberjacks," *Industrial Worker*, November 4, 1916.

for revolution to no avail. However, when the company ordered the bad butter, Winstead directed the workers' anger. He saw food as only a step toward revolution: "Now, anybody knows that fightin' for good butter ain't the social revolution, but anybody also knows that hittin' a punchin' bag ain't knockin' Dempsey out, neither. Both of these stunts is good practice for the event aimed at, and if enough pep is showed up in the practice, why, this practice is sure goin' to help in the big event." Winstead and two other men formed a committee, took the bad butter to the superintendent, and convinced him to send it back. The company fired Winstead three days later.[67] But as Winstead suggested, the potential for collective action over food was great. When the Stimson Lumber Company fired its cook at Bryant, Washington, to replace him with someone who would work for less, forty loggers walked off the job over the suddenly poorer food, demanding the return of the old cook at his standard wages.[68]

Wobblies also organized around workplace safety and the destruction of workers bodies through preventable accidents and bad medical care. Timber workers' broken bodies were a visceral symbol of how little loggers had to lose by joining the IWW. Timber faller Emil Herman wrote of seeing three men killed and two seriously injured in two months. He connected workplace safety with environmental inequality, writing in 1910, "When the lumberjack is not fighting fleas, bedbugs, and disease in the bunkhouse during the short time allotted him for rest, he is risking life and limb in the woods, producing wealth for his master."[69] Tom Scribner became a Wobbly in 1917 after nearly dying several times from logging accidents, including once when a log rolled over his chest, crushing several ribs and ripping open his sides to the point that "the doctor had to stuff my intestines back in like they were rope, curling them and shoving them back up inside of me." Scribner's respect for the IWW came from how it stood up for worker safety, noting its role in fighting against the unsafe machines.[70]

The IWW also organized around the environmental hazards of the mills. One writer invoked the tale of a young man who died after working in an Idaho mill, remarking, "You will remember, fellow workers, that

[67] Ralph Winstead, "Chin-Whiskers, Hay-Wire and Pitchforks," *One Big Union Monthly*, n.d., found in Luke May File, Box 1.2, Folder VO260, University of Washington Special Collections, 32–37.

[68] "What the Lumberjacks Are Doing," *Industrial Worker*, December 1, 1917.

[69] "Lumberjacks: What They Are Up Against," *Industrial Worker*, October 1, 1910.

[70] Stewart Bird, Dan Georgakas, and Deborah Shaffer, eds., *Solidarity Forever: An Oral History of the IWW* (Chicago: Lake View Press, 1985), 210.

this boy was suffering from tuberculosis, contracted during his confinement in Weyerhaeuser's 'black hole' in Moscow."[71] The IWW proclaimed solidarity with shingle weavers when they turned to the *Industrial Worker* to complain about their own AFL-affiliated union's unwillingness to press the companies for better safety standards. One shingle weaver wrote in March 1913, "We have not been able to get the owners to install blowers for taking up the poisonous cedar dust, that has sent many men to premature death, and shorten the life of every man that is compelled to inhale it." The shingle weaver urged his coworkers to reject "the Gompersonian reactionary cry" and become socialists.[72]

IWW songs show this attention to the details of loggers' living and working environment. Art played an important role in Wobbly organizing. Through well-illustrated newspapers, posters, poems, and songs, the Wobblies crafted a message comprehensible to the polyglot and often illiterate workers of early twentieth-century America. Sociologist and hobo participant-observer Nels Anderson wrote that the IWW songs created "the strongest form of group solidarity in the hobo world." Wobbly art constituted an interplay between the artists themselves, who were often committed believers in anarcho-syndicalism, and the workers who had flexible beliefs but concrete demands to improve their lives.[73]

The often anonymous authors of songs such as "Fifty Thousand Lumberjacks" urged loggers to sing about their struggles. The song talked of loggers sleeping in bunks "full of things that crawl," and striking because of the "fifty thousand dirty rolls of blankets on their backs." This song laid out clear demands for employers that would get them back on the job:

> Take a tip and start right in – plan some cozy rooms.
> Six or eight spring beds in each, with towels, sheets
> and brooms;
> Shower baths for men who work keeps them well and fit;
> A laundry, too, and drying room, would help a little bit.

[71] "Lumber Workers' Bulletin" *New Solidarity*, November 16, 1918.

[72] "Some Strong Words from a Shingle Weaver," *Industrial Worker*, March 13, 1913.

[73] Nels Anderson, *On Hoboes and Homelessness* (Chicago: University of Chicago Press, 1998), 209–10; Nels Anderson, *The Hobo – The Sociology of the Homeless Man* (Chicago: University of Chicago Press, reprint 1961), 214; Salvatore Salerno, *Red November, Black November: Culture and Community in the Industrial Workers of the World* (Albany: State University of New York Press, 1989), 120–40. On Anderson and other participant observations of poverty, see Mark Pittenger, *Class Unknown: Undercover Investigations of American Work and Poverty from the Progressive Era to the Present* (New York: New York University Press, 2012).

Singing brought participants together in mutual solidarity to fight for better conditions. The beds, the showers, and the bunkhouses: these were physical manifestations of loggers' suffering around which the IWW could organize. "Fifty Thousand Lumberjacks" said this about food:

> Get some dishes, white and clean; good pure food to eat;
> See that cook has help enough to keep the table neat.
> Tap the bell for eight hours; treat the boys like men,
> And fifty thousand lumberjacks may come to work again.[74]

Other versions of the same song talked of the "Fifty thousand lumberjacks/ Goin' in to eat/Fifty thousand plates of slum/Made from tainted meat."[75] Wobblies raised funds by selling cards and pamphlets with songs and poems to workers that promoted the union message. One had "The Lumber Jack's Prayer." This prayer revolved around the logger's dream for tasty food. He prays of fried potatoes, ham, and eggs, even quail on toast. He concludes by asking the Lord to take away the food he eats every day. "With Alum bread and Pressed-Beef butts/Dear Lord you damn near ruin'd my guts/Your white-wash milk and Oleorine/I wish to Christ I'd never seen." The Wobbly Christ is a distant deity, for "He believes in letting us fight it out along the lines of Industrial Unionism."[76]

After 1912, the IWW increasingly committed to environmental justice as its core organizing strategy in the woods. In June 1913, after 85 percent of voting members approved of a strike in the Puget Sound region, loggers' demands included not only the eight-hour day and minimum wages of $3 a day, but also towels and soap for bathing, "clean sanitary bunkhouses" with mattresses and blankets, and safety equipment around dangerous machinery in the mills. In publicizing the strike, the IWW asked, "Are you dissatisfied with living ... in miserable bunkhouses?" If so, "refuse to work under bad conditions, demand better camp conditions and pure food." Fifty camps shut down during this brief and unsuccessful strike, which fell apart in July. However, these actions slowly built IWW membership in the woods over the next two years; by the eve of America's entrance into World War I, the Wobblies had made themselves the single organization in the forests willing to stand up to provide ecological democracy in the camps.[77]

[74] Industrial Workers of the World Songbook, Industrial Workers of the World Collection, Box 7, 43, University of Washington Special Collections.

[75] Kornbluh, *Rebel Voices*, 267.

[76] "The Lumber Jack's Prayer," from Kornbluh, *Rebel Voices*, 268.

[77] "Strike Proclamation," *Industrial Worker*, June 5, 1913; "Responding to Strike Call," *Industrial Worker*, June 12, 1913; "Opening Reports Are Encouraging," *Industrial Worker*, June 12, 1913; "Lumber Strike Called Off," *Industrial Worker*, July 10, 1913.

While organizing for that ecological democracy, Wobbly propagandists attempted to create a working-class manhood based upon toiling with other men in the healthy forests. Most logging camps were all-male spaces and Northwestern demographics were skewered toward men, with Seattle, Portland, and Spokane among the top five American cities in percentage of men among the population in 1900.[78] The isolated locations and itinerant labor made it virtually impossible for workers to bring families into logging camps. The constant mobility and struggle for stable work had widespread regional implications of single men roaming between city and country, constituting an unmoored and potentially politically radicalized populace that made Northwestern elites concerned about crime and agitation. The IWW sought to build upon these men as a proletarian masculine vanguard of worker solidarity. Nationally, 54 percent of men over the age of fifteen were married in 1890, but only 41 percent in the Pacific Northwest.[79] Carleton Parker estimated in 1918 that only 10 percent of the "hobo lumberjacks" had ever married, and most of these had either divorced or abandoned their wives.[80] This did not mean men did not want to marry. However, when they did marry, they usually left the camps for jobs in the timber mills. When camp operators hired women, they often married loggers, as happened in 1903 when the S.A. Soule Logging Camp hired six women to work in its cookhouse and each one married a logger almost immediately and quit her job.[81] In one camp, the cook threatened to quit because he had to train new female assistants constantly. The camp manager quieted the cook's complaints by telling him, "We'll have men flunkies after this. The loggers and mill-workers won't be marrying them."[82] Such frequent incidents led most camps to hire only men for the kitchen.[83]

Drawing stark comparisons between the degrading conditions of work and the healthful forests around the camps, Wobbly organizers and writers urged loggers to use the forests as an organizing tool. They tied ideas of labor, manhood, and nature together to help workers reclaim their

78 See Carlos A. Schwantes, "The Concept of the Wageworkers' Frontier: A Framework for Future Research," *The Western Historical Quarterly* 18, no.1 (January 1987): 45.

79 Boag, *Same-Sex Affairs*, 18.

80 Carleton Parker, *The Casual Laborer and Other Essays* (New York: Harcourt, Brace, and Howe, 1920), 113–14.

81 "By the Way," *West Coast and Puget Sound Lumberman*, June 1903, 520.

82 "Lumber Town Folks," *Four L Bulletin*, October 1925, 10.

83 Ah Sam to John Campbell, March 2, 1898, Port Blakely Mill Company Papers, UW, Box 35, Folder 51; List of Wages, n.d., Port Blakely, Box 30, Folder 3; C.W. Buckner, "Sanitary Logging Camps," *The Timberman* September 1914, 58–59.

dignity as well as to explain to workers the regional labor situation. In doing so, they deployed stereotypes about women both to promote loggers as single men and to explain their own organizing failures with mill workers.[84] The IWW assigned Ralph Chaplin, writer of the lyrics to "Solidarity Forever" and editor of *Industrial Worker*, to cover the logging strikes. Chaplin described loggers as the "husky and unconquerable workers of the Northwest" who would not submit to capitalist authority. Loggers walked, lived, worked, and ate together. Through living with other men and in the forests, the logger "resents industrial slavery as an insult." Reflecting struggles to organize the timber mill workers, Chaplin contrasted the masculine resistance of the logger to the feminized and defeated mill worker. Loggers had the "physical strength, cleanliness, and mental alertness" that mill workers did not. Loggers worked hard, moving on when they no longer cared to work for a particular boss because they were the "perfect proletarian type – possessionless, homeless, rebellious."[85]

For Chaplin and other Wobbly writers, loggers faced challenges to proletarian manhood from not only capitalists, but from women too. They split women into two groups – wives and prostitutes – constructing a paradigm of imperiled masculinity around stereotypes of these women. When loggers were in the forests, they wanted nothing more than the company of a woman. This drove them to distraction and disease after they satisfied their urges by visiting prostitutes when they returned to town. These prostitutes were parasites who "fattens on the worker in industry" and destroyed workers' bodies through venereal disease.[86] But if a logger avoided prostitutes and married, his manhood was equally at peril. Wobblies knew that companies preferred married men to the single, itinerant logger, for the married worker was easier to control and "less apt

[84] On the masculinity during this period, see Gail Bederman, *Manliness and Civilization: A Cultural History of Gender and Race in the United States, 1880–1917* (Chicago: University of Chicago Press, 1995); Elliott J. Gorn, *The Manly Art: Bare-Knuckle Prize Fighting in America* (Ithaca: Cornell University Press, 1986); and Kristin L. Hoganson, *Fighting for American Manhood: How Gender Politics Provoked the Spanish-American and Philippine-American Wars* (New Haven: Yale University Press, 1998). For broader overviews of American masculinity, see Michael S. Kimmel, *Manhood in America: A Cultural History*, 2nd edn. (New York: Oxford University Press, 2006); and E. Anthony Rotundo, *American Manhood: Transformation in American Masculinity from the Revolution to the Modern Era* (New York: Basic Books, 1993).

[85] Ralph Chaplin, *The Centralia Conspiracy: The Truth About the Armistice Day Tragedy* (Chicago: IWW General Defense Committee, 1920) 35, 19, 17, 16.

[86] W.F. Dunn, *The Crime of Centralia*, IWW Archives, University of Washington Special Collections, 2; see also, Industrial Workers of the World, *The Lumber Industry and Its Workers*, 57.

to exhibit those admirable – but to the bosses undesirable – qualities of independence and rebellion than the unencumbered migratory worker."[87] Wobblies' reports frequently complained about married loggers refusing to go on strike because of the fear of not being able to take care of their families.[88] The manly single logger pitied his mill worker brethren, but once married, a logger entered an unanswerable paradox. If the mill worker "subordinates his manhood and sacrifices his independence to the will of the company, he is rewarded by a life of grinding poverty, hopeless drudgery, and a condition of economic dependence and insecurity." But if he stands up for himself, "he faces discharge and the blacklist, which, if he is a married man, means the breaking up of his home, and separation from wife and children.[89]

These ideas did not go unchallenged within the IWW. Fred Hegge used constructions of masculinity based upon men protecting their families to exhort loggers to organize, telling workers, "Let us all dig in and do our share to stop this damnable system of exploitation and robbery that takes away our lives and liberty, forces our sisters and daughters into the streets and deprives our little children of their natural rights – a happy childhood of play and development." Hegge's conception of masculinity provided a useful counter to the common rhetoric used by the IWW. Even though the logging camps were largely all-male spaces, the exclusionary aspect of Wobbly masculinity marginalized and demonized the wives of mill workers, who also struggled with the poverty of their families.[90]

Reverend Oscar H. McGill, Social Service Secretary for the Methodist Church in Seattle, traveled to many logging camps as part of his job. He stated that "the cause of the discontent very largely ... is because these workmen have been exploited in way that is indescribable."[91] Workers' responses to their lives of endless exploitation caught the attention of timber executives in the early 1910s. Some bosses wanted to ignore the IWW, others to crush it without remorse. Still others responded by providing just enough reform to the timber camp ecology to reduce the slow

[87] Chaplin, *The Centralia Conspiracy*, 14; James Rowan, *The I.W.W. in the Lumber Industry* (Seattle Lumber Workers Industrial Union No. 500, 1919), 7–8.

[88] See, for instance, "Call the Hand of Timber Trust," *The New Solidarity*, September 27, 1919.

[89] Rowan, *The I.W.W. in the Lumber Industry*, 9.

[90] Fred Hegge, "Lumber Workers' Bulletin," *The New Solidarity*, November 16, 1918. See also Alice Kessler-Harris, *Gendering Labor History* (Urbana: University of Illinois Press, 2007), 146.

[91] USCIR, *Final Report and Testimony*, 4382.

violence of workers lives or by exploring new systems of labor to turn workers into stakeholders without giving up any meaningful power over the industry.

Like their contemporary industrialists, most employers believed workers consented to conditions when they took the job. Thus owners had no tolerance for any unions, especially the IWW. Neil Cooney reassured Edwin G. Ames of the Pope & Talbot Lumber Company in 1911 that his workers were "too wise" to be convinced by the IWW.[92] A more chilling response came from Mark Reed of the Simpson Logging Company. Reed wrote to Ames of a worker killed on the job in 1911. While calling the death a "misfortune," Reed's real concern was that the worker had an IWW card in his personal effects. He called for "a concerted effort ... to thwart this organization."[93] Ames indeed made a concerted effort to keep the Wobblies out of his workforce. The manager of one Ames mill saw unknown visitors skulking about. He assumed they were Wobblies and "immediately organized a posse" to catch them, only to find upon questioning they were Ames' friends.[94]

A more constructive industry response came from supporting workers' compensation legislation. Nineteenth-century workers assumed risk to their bodies on the job, a doctrine backed up by judges in compensatory lawsuits since the 1830s.[95] However, beginning with the 1898 case *Holden* v. *Hardy*, when the Supreme Court upheld a law limiting smelter workers' hours due to the toxic nature of fumes, courts began slowly moving toward a doctrine of state regulation of workplace health and safety.[96] Timber executives breathed a sigh of relief in 1901 when a Lewis County, Washington, judge dismissed a case filed by a mill sawyer who sued for $6,000 over the loss of three fingers.[97] Similarly, in 1905, the Washington Supreme Court overturned a lower court's decision to award the family of George Stratton $20,000 after he was killed by a saw in a timber mill.[98] But courts increasingly did find for workers. In 1904, a Washington court granted a worker who lost both legs in a mill accident

[92] Neil Cooney to E.G. Ames, November 29, 1911, Ames Box 4, Folder 2.

[93] Mark Reed to E.G. Ames, December 1, 1911, Ames Box 4, Folder 2.

[94] Unknown author to E.G. Ames, March 30, 1912, Ames Box 4, Folder 10.

[95] Jonathan Levy, Freaks of Fortune: The Emerging World of Capitalism and Risk in America (Cambridge: Harvard University Press, 2012), 7–20.

[96] Christopher C. Sellers, *Hazards of the Job: From Industrial Disease to Environmental Health Science* (Chapel Hill: University of North Carolina Press, 1997), 47.

[97] *West Coast and Puget Sound Lumberman*, November 1901, 62.

[98] "Personal Injury Damage Case," *The Timberman*, August 1905, 18–19.

$50,000, leading George M. Cornwall, publisher of the industry journal *The Timberman*, to complain about these decisions "causing a flood of litigation of a very questionable character."[99]

Cornwall's concern over the impact of worker lawsuits against timber companies mattered because he was becoming a major force for reforming the timber camps as a way of achieving labor peace. A newspaper editor without a background in logging, Cornwall began what was originally known as *The Columbia River and Oregon Timberman* in 1899. Cornwall became a mainstay of the regional timber industry, promoting a modern, rationalized industry. A believer in the doctrine of efficiency that marked the Progressive Era, Cornwall promoted technological advancement, industry-wide organization, and humane labor relations, all in the name of steady profits.[100]

The changing legal climate led timber executives and allies such as Cornwall to support worker compensation laws. Such efforts received support from industrialists as a way to undermine class consciousness and "make the individual working man more of an individual," as Herbert Croly said.[101] Reformers around the nation, concerned about the unequal conditions of American society and the labor strife and violence that marked the Gilded Age, began supporting limited reforms in the early twentieth century to make the industrial workplace more humane. Child labor laws, fire safety laws for industrial buildings, and worker compensation laws all provided more equity to workers without seriously threatening the corporate dominance of the workplace.[102] Cornwall

99 "'Personal Injury Travesty,'" *The Columbia River and Oregon Timberman*, July 1904, 19.

100 For more on Cornwall, see Gage McKinney, "'A Man among You, Taking Notes': George M. Cornwall and The Timberman," *Journal of Forest History* 26, no. 2 (April 1982): 76–83. On the doctrine of efficiency, see Hays, *Conservation and the Doctrine of Efficiency*; Robert Wiebe, *The Search for Order, 1877–1920* (New York: Hill and Wang, 1967).

101 Quoted in David Montgomery, *The Fall of the House of Labor: The Workplace, the State, and American Labor Activism, 1865–1925* (New York: Cambridge University Press, 1987), 177.

102 Mark Aldrich, *Safety First: Technology, Labor, and Business in the Building of American Work Safety* (Baltimore: The Johns Hopkins University Press, 1997); Richard A. Greenwald, *The Triangle Fire, the Protocols of Peace, and Industrial Democracy in Progressive Era New York* (Philadelphia: Temple University Press, 2005); James D. Schmidt, *Industrial Violence and the Legal Origins of Child Labor* (New York: Cambridge University Press, 2010); Julian Go III, "Inventing Industrial Accidents and Their Insurance: Discourse and Workers' Compensation in the United States, 1880s-1910s," *Social Science History* 20, no. 3 (Autumn 1996): 401–38. See

announced his support to protect the industry from the growing number of lawsuits filed by "ambulance chaser lawyers" in 1909.[103] Washington and California passed worker compensation bills in 1911, while Oregon in 1913, Montana in 1915, and Idaho in 1917 did likewise.

Cornwall argued that workers' compensation would give workers a stake in timber capitalism, for they would know they were "not merely a particle of irresponsible drift floating on the industrial stream."[104] Each state's law required workers to trade their right to sue employers after accidents in return for state-determined compensation, leading to the AFL opposing these laws.[105] Although costs for employers briefly rose, successful attempts to keep compensation rates far lower than workers' lost wages limited employers' liability.[106] Washington's law only provided minimal compensation. One worker missed twenty-four days after an injury. He lost $108 in wages and his medical expenses came to $19.50. The state paid him $27.65. Another missed fifty-five days. He lost $192.50 in wages and had medical expenses of $55.50. He received $63.45 from the state.[107] Although better than no compensation, workers arguably had a better chance for a fair financial settlement through the courts than the state systems. Ultimately, worker compensation did little to tamper down worker dissent over the threats loggers faced to their bodies and lives. Washington banned employers from charging hospital fees if workers also paid into the state program. But many companies charged workers anyway, leading one IWW member to call the system "raw graft," made worse because doctors had little incentive to provide treatment to pre-paid patients and did not even provide basic first aid.[108]

The IWW's rise also convinced some operators to take workers' concerns about timber camp workscapes seriously and begin reforming the camps. As in much of American industry in the 1910s, some owners began

Randolph E. Bergstrom, *Courting Danger: Injury and Law in New York City, 1870–1910* (Ithaca: Cornell University Press, 1992) on the growing success of worker lawsuits against employers for workplace injuries that led to the compensation laws.

103 "Workmen's Liability Insurance," *The Timberman*, March 1909, 19.

104 "Compulsory Industrial Insurance," *The Timberman*, July 1909, 19. On the broader connections between workplace safety and anti-unionism, see David Noble, *Liberalism at Work: The Rise and Fall of OSHA* (Philadelphia: Temple University Press, 1986), 41.

105 Noble, *Liberalism at Work*, 54–55; Ruth O'Brien, *Workers' Paradox: The Republican Origins of New Deal Labor Policy, 1886–1935* (Chapel Hill: University of North Carolina Press, 1998), 8.

106 Aldrich, *Safety First*, 93–100.

107 USCIR, *Final Report and Testimony*, 4156, 4535.

108 "Hospital Fees – Raw Graft," *Industrial Worker* April 13, 1918.

seeking a welfare capitalism that would buy off workers' discontent without giving up control over the workplace and while possibly improving the bottom line. They tapped into an early twentieth-century discourse that connected the remaking of unruly landscapes to the disciplining of poorly behaved people. Whether in India, the Philippines, or the Central Valley of California, hygienists, doctors, and employers increasingly saw sanitation in the context of controlling unruly labor forces increasingly attracted to radical politics.[109] Carleton Parker argued that the IWW hall was the only home the logger had, a place where the logger can find "a light, a stove, companionship."[110] Timber companies did not want to provide stable homes for loggers, but the messages received at "home" in the IWW hall was the root of the labor problems faced by the companies. Remaking these landscapes could happen by creating something that looked like home for loggers, whether actual permanent homes or a camp built with the comforts of home. Ideally for operators, this would undermine Wobbly organizing and reduce labor strife.

Allowing workers to wash off the accumulated detritus of a day's work transforming the forest ecology was an easy way to achieve labor peace, according to Cornwall. He told employers at the first Pacific Logging Congress (PLC) meeting in 1909 that "men could entertain ideas on the substitution of a locomotive for an ox team, but to undertake the project of furnishing a bathtub and a clean towel to the men and charging for the service was a most momentous step that could not be taken without due deliberation."[111] By adapting household technologies to logging camps, Cornwall and his supporters hoped to create a docile labor force tied to the job. Industry reformers blamed workers for their own filth and disease, claiming their sloth helped create the unsanitary environment of the timber camp and their simplicity allowed them to be bamboozled by IWW class warriors. Washington State Commissioner of Health Eugene Kelley argued for voluntary camp reforms, but also said, "To be sure, some employes [sic] in camp certainly seem to like to have things as insanitary as they can."[112] Cornwall's opening address at the 1911 PLC referred to employers exercising a "generalship," needing to motivate the troops for proper work by providing sanitary conditions. Calling the bathtub "a

109 Nash, *Inescapable Ecologies*, 93–106.

110 Parker, *The Casual Laborer and Other Essays*, 115.

111 *The Timberman*, August 1909, 52.

112 "Industrial Hygiene Is an Important Factor," *The Timberman*, September 1914, 58.

civilizer," Cornwall stated, "supplying adequate facilities for bathing ... is the first step towards establishing permanency of occupation."[113]

Simple technological solutions were tools for effective workplace generalship, undermining unionism at a low price and without giving up control over the conditions of work. The Clear Lake Lumber Company provided workers with fresh water pumped to the camp, showers, and fresh bedding.[114] The Cherry Valley Timber Company constructed a new camp in 1915 that it could move on rail cars, an idea first implemented in the forests in 1910. Painting the rail cars yellow with white trimmings, the camp consisted of twelve cars. The cars were still quite crowded; the five cars used for bunkhouses held 150 men, with each car divided into three compartments. The company hoped smaller groups of men would coalesce into friends that would unite to keep the living quarters clean. The beds were made of steel and equipped with mattresses and springs. Two cars were used for dining, others for meat storage and cooking. The kitchen car had a water tank that supplied water to the camp. One car contained a shower and a drying room with steam heat for loggers to dry their drenched clothes that so offended noses throughout the region. Cherry Valley executive J.E. Gowen estimated a cost of $4,000–$6,000 to build this mobile camp, but believed it would pay off since the company no longer had to build temporary structures every time it cut down a new forest. He hoped the camp would "secure a higher and better class of employees by giving them thoroughly modern and sanitary quarters."[115] *The Timberman* described it as "how a model logging camp should be constructed."[116]

Cornwall used the PLC and his journal to promote reformist corporations like Cherry Valley and build connections between sanitary environments and labor peace. He argued for changes in "the physical conditions of camp life," for "no man is at his best when his body is dirty."[117] Many leading timbermen such as George Long of Weyerhaeuser and J.J. Donovan of Bloedel-Donovan supported Cornwall's cause and sought to bring efficient reforms into camps. But they had an uphill road against the inertia of

113 "Routine Work of the Congress," *The Timberman*, July 1911, 21.

114 "The Y.M.C.A. Welfare Dinner a Brilliant Feature of the Congress," *The Timberman*, September 1914, 82.

115 "Modern Camp Equipment," *The Timberman*, May 1915, 46–47. See also A.B. Wastell, "Illustration of Housing and Feeding Logging Camp Outfit on Wheels," *The Timberman*, August 1910, 50–51.

116 "Modern Camp Equipment," *The Timberman*, May 1915, 46–47.

117 "Saw Logs and School Teachers," *The Timberman*, March 1917, 1.

many camp owners. One called these ideas "too far advanced" for his camp, noting that all he wanted "is to get some good loggers."[118] Cornwall and his allies battled this attitude by framing sanitation in practical, efficient terms that would sell sanitary landscapes as an investment.[119] Dr. W.C. Belt spoke to the 1910 Pacific Logging Congress and sold sanitation to them in terms of profit. "Sanitation pays. It pays in cold-blooded dollars and cents, and it will return to you 25 per cent on the investment. It pays in the increased working efficiency of your men." Belt's suggestions included piped water, eliminating rotten food, sanitary outhouses, and regular inspections by outside doctors.[120]

As with so much in the camps, food played a central role in the camp environment debates. Reformers sought to bring a touch of home into the mess halls through providing better dishware and tablecloths. Operators investing in mobile camps on rail promoted their modern kitchens and dining rooms. Once again, reformers connected efficiency and food. Walter Belt urged corporations to pool their resources to buy good food at a low price to feed the hungry bodies of workers who would then cut more trees.[121] Frank Hobi did not mind losing money, as "so long as the cook served good meals, and the crew was satisfied, we directed our attention to other problems that affected our logging costs."[122] A 1917 survey showed some timbermen felt that running a deficit in the cookhouse was an acceptable loss if it made the men happy. Others insisted upon a profit. A.S. Kerry believed that without aiming for a profit, a loss would result. But profit incentivized serving low quality food and cutting corners on sanitation.[123]

Reformers also targeted disease as a major emphasis of camp reform. The early twentieth century saw a significant growth in the study of occupational disease but in timber relatively few camp owners took it

118 "Comments on 'Saw Logs and School Teachers'," *The Timberman*, May 1917, 1, 30–31.

119 Sanford Jacoby, Employing Bureaucracy: Managers, Unions, and the Transformation of Work in American Industry, 1900–1945 (New York: Columbia University Press, 1985), 123 on this argument in the broader context of American industrial reform.

120 W.C. Belt, "Camp's Maintenance of Sanitary Conditions Essential to Success," *The Timberman*, August 1909, 26; Belt, "Importance of Conservation of Human Energies in the Logging Camp," *The Timberman*, August 1910, 44–45.

121 Walter C. Belt, "Increased Efficiency Through Proper Diet and Sanitary Surroundings," The Timberman, July 1911, 32.

122 Frank Hobi Reminiscence, University of Washington Special Collections, 95.

123 J.J. Donovan, "Should the Cook House Make a Profit," *The Timberman*, November 1917, 59–61.

seriously before 1915.[124] Dr. E.A. Pierce told executives that a salubrious camp that provided well-ventilated sleeping quarters, pure water, and protection of food from flies would protect workers from tuberculosis.[125] *The Timberman* also promoted a tour of the camps made by Dr. W.N. Lipscomb, a staff doctor for the Red Cross. During the 1910s, the Red Cross began creating job safety and first-aid training for employers that meant to shift responsibility for safety from employers to workers.[126] In 1913, Lipscomb met Robert Allen, editor of the timber journal *West Coast Lumberman*. Their conversation got him interested in conditions in logging.[127] The Red Cross assigned him to the timber camps, where he made repeated tours stressing the need for sanitation. However, the Red Cross found timber operators had little interest in sanitation, noting with some disgust, "Finding it was practically impossible to obtain their financial cooperation, it was decided to inaugurate the instruction ourselves, hoping that a demonstration of its usefulness would convince those who employ lumbermen of the practical and economic value of such work, and appeal to them through their pockets, if not on purely humanitarian ground."[128]

Lipscomb expressed deep displeasure with what he saw, commenting, "I was rather amazed on going to Western Washington in 1915 and finding camp sanitary conditions as they were." Lipscomb told one story of a camp in eastern Oregon whose owner located it in a marsh when he could have built on higher ground 200 yards away. He described its camp toilets as "a disgrace; it is too close to the bunkhouses, too much open to flies and the location of same resulting in contamination of streams." Lipscomb worried that polluted water supplies would lead to a typhoid outbreak and complained that cooks did not keep their water barrels sanitary and shared drinking cups that could lead to syphilis and tuberculosis outbreaks.[129]

Timber operators also enlisted the Young Men's Christian Association to create sanitary homes in the woods. A central purpose of the YMCA

124 Sellers, *Hazards of the Job*, 111; Derickson, *Black Lung*, 60–86.

125 Dr. E.A. Pierce, "Preventive Measures for Combatting the White Plague in Lumber Camps," *The Timberman*, August 1910, 64K.

126 Marian Moser Jones, *The American Red Cross from Clara Barton to the New Deal* (Baltimore: The Johns Hopkins University Press, 2013).

127 "Red Cross in the Lumber Industry," *Lumber World Review*, November 10, 1915, 72.

128 Eleventh Annual Report of the American Red Cross for the Year 1915 (Washington: Government Printing Office, 1916), 33–34.

129 W.N. Lipscomb, "Red Cross Man Urges Exercise of Great Care in Locating Camp Building," *West Coast Lumberman*, November 1917, 38.

was fighting radicalism through "proper leisure activities within a moral environment," a program which took it from railroad camps to urban centers in the early twentieth century.[130] The YMCA set up several programs in camps beginning in 1911 with the Doty Lumber and Shingle Company in Doty, Washington.[131] Creating a home meant providing a place to play in workers' off hours that would distract them from drinking and radical politics. The Booth-Kelly Lumber Company had a mobile YMCA rail car where workers could visit for "physical, educational, and moral work," which included everything from a circulating library to a pool table, and outdoor games including boxing, fencing, and log rolling.[132] The YMCA worked with the Women's Christian Temperance Union to cleanse the camps of alcohol. Many timber operators supported temperance as a way to undermine violence in their camps and looked forward to Oregon's and Washington's temperance laws that went into effect in 1916.[133] But they were surprised that drinking did not explain their workers' radicalism, leading L.T. Hays to express indignation that "the strike seems to exist whether or not we have the liquor question."[134] Although the IWW often spoke out against alcohol as a substance that distracted workers from political solutions, some Wobblies justified loggers drinking to forget their unsanitary lives. A 1910 Wobbly newspaper article told loggers to reject prohibition because moderate drinking was an acceptable response to their miserable living environments. Only when "loggers don't have to sleep in dirty, lousy bunk houses, work hard and long hours like a black slave, and eat rotten grub like a hog in a garbage plant" would temperance make sense.[135]

The YMCA openly sided with employers in the period's labor battles, with its representatives actively working to keep labor in place. A YMCA general secretary named Sellwood overheard workers talking about

[130] Thomas Winter, *Making Men, Making Class: The YMCA and Workingmen, 1877–1920* (Chicago: The University of Chicago Press, 2002), 4; Jacoby, *Employing Bureaucracy*, 56–59. See also Richard White, *Railroaded: The Transcontinentals and the Making of Modern America* (New York: W.W. Norton, 2011), 279. On the connection between creating living spaces and docile labor, see Andrews, *Killing for Coal*, 201–04.

[131] "The Rose Lake Y.M.C.A.," *The Timberman*, September 1916, 37–38.

[132] Oregon Y.M.C.A. Car, *The Timberman*, May 1916, 34.

[133] A.H. Powers, "Accident Prevention in the Woods," *The Timberman*, September 1914, 42; J.P. Van Orsdell, "Labor Problems and the Logging Industry," *The Timberman*, December 1915, 31.

[134] J.J. Donovan, "Should the Cook House Make a Profit," *The Timberman*, November 1917, 59–61.

[135] "To the Loggers of Coos Bay," *Industrial Worker*, January 4, 1912.

moving onto another camp. He acted quickly. Three days later was July 4. He arranged with the camp cook to ship in a special order of ice and fresh fruit to make lemonade and cake and host a big dinner. He convinced the local train line to not stop at the camp on its next run. After the party, not a single worker hopped the train. The YMCA presented Sellwood's story to timber operators as a prime example of how a general secretary on the ground, listening to the complaints of workers, could hold them in place by providing minor amenities, building loyalty and increasing profits.[136]

However, many operators wanted an immediate payoff to the YMCA production of loyal labor. R.R. Lewis stated to his fellow timbermen that he had two camps with the YMCA and one without it. He could not see any discernible difference. Lewis thought the organization's benefits were good for his workers, but declaring himself "unable to look at it from the sentimental standpoint," he "wanted to see that it gets in logs cheaper" in order to keep it.[137] Other companies had greater expectations. One mill owner refused to continue paying for a YMCA secretary for his camps after that secretary refused to serve as a spy. He sent a letter excoriating the organization after the YMCA representative did not warn him of an upcoming strike, writing "If the secretary had had the company's interests at heart and been onto his job he would have been close enough to the men to have prevented this walkout, or notified us of the existence of I.W.W. organizers."[138] The IWW saw the YMCA in essentially the same terms. It warned loggers in 1912 that the companies brought in the YMCA "to chloroform the workers," noting that "whenever the bosses organize their slaves into the Y.M.C.A . . . it is for the purpose of keeping peace in the interest of the boss and against the interest of the workers."[139]

For many loggers, a settled family life was as much a dream as an indoor shower or clean sheets. By 1917, when the United States entered World War I and timber supplies became a national security issue, little had changed for most loggers, who still labored in temporary camps in unsanitary conditions. Despite industry reformers such as Cornwall and doctors such as Lipscomb, many timber operators were intransigent when it came to sanitary camps. For many, the sheer conception of a comfortable and safe

136 "Y.M.C.A. Welfare Dinner a Brilliant Feature and Inspiring Gathering," *The Timberman* October 1913, 88–91.

137 Ibid.

138 USCIR, *Final Report and Testimony*, 4383, 4532–33.

139 "Workers in Forest and Mill," *Industrial Worker*, September 26, 1912.

workspace seemed foreign. Perhaps this attitude was best summed up in a 1910 speech at the Pacific Logging Congress. Speaking to operators about the need for greater sanitation, Dr. E.A. Pierce made fun of anything more than the most basic sanitation, noting that a camp with electric lights might as well have "a French pastry cook or the latest brand of cigarettes, cocktails or mint juleps."[140] Even reformers could not visualize the modern conveniences of home in the forests.

Moreover, outside observers expressed skepticism of whether these reforms really created a landscape that provided workers with dignified lives. Sanitary housing and amenities cost money and with timber operators desperate to keep costs low in an industry subject to boom and bust cycles, many looked for cosmetic reforms and additional ways to generate profit from their workers. Oscar McGill testified to the USCIR about a company near Bellingham that claimed to have a beautiful recreation space for workers, replete with billiard and card tables. In fact, the company had just put a cheaply made second floor over the mess hall and then charged concessionaries high rates to provide those services, who then charged the workers.[141] Industrialists' discussions of reforms often turned into self-congratulatory promotions for very small changes that did little for workers' health. George Long gave a speech at the 1910 Pacific Logging Congress where he stated, "An age of big things calls for big men." The big men of the timber industry cared enough about his men to talk about tuberculosis in the camps and look upon his employees as a father giving advice. Long urged them to "study their wants, and correct as far as you can" and encourage them "in the friendly relations which in times past have been characteristic between the 'boss' and his men in logging camps." Long emphasized that the big man knew how to manage his men, not that actual improvement to fight tuberculosis needed to happen.[142]

For the IWW, any sanitary reforms were evidence of how radical solidarity could transform their lives. A 1916 *Industrial Worker* article talked of an Idaho operator bragging about his new camp, with each logger having his own room, quality food, and even movie screenings at night. The IWW writer noted that the real story was that operators

[140] Dr. E.A. Pierce, "Preventive Measures for Combatting the White Plague in Lumber Camps," *The Timberman*, August 1910, 64k.

[141] USCIR, *Final Report and Testimony*, 4384.

[142] George Long, "The Logger of the Pacific Northwest: His Opportunities and Duties," *The Timberman*, August 1910, 41–42.

granted concessions because they "feared further agitation." He asked, "if a little agitation by a few members can produce these results, what would not a vast propaganda achieve?"[143] In 1917, thousands of striking loggers would seek the answer of what would happen if they stood up against the slow violence of the timber camp environment.

[143] "I.W.W. Agitation Betters Conditions," *Industrial Worker*, August 12, 1916.

2

The Battle for the Body

In the summer of 1917, Industrial Workers of the World–affiliated loggers walked off the job in eastern Washington and northern Idaho in protest against the filth, disease, and long hours that dominated their lives. This strike soon spread to western Washington and into Oregon, making it the largest strike to that date in the Northwestern forests. In April 1917, the United States entered World War I and the military needed to harvest Northwestern trees to build airplanes for the war. The violence to loggers' bodies finally attracted government attention. In response, the army created the Spruce Production Division (SPD), a division of soldier-loggers interspersed in civilian logging camps, and the Loyal Legion of Loggers and Lumbermen (Four-L), an industry-wide company union dedicated to organizing workers for wartime production. This decimated the IWW as it banished active Wobbly members from work. Yet the government also initiated a sanitary revolution in the timber camps, granting most of the loggers' basic demands around sanitation and working hours to bring labor peace and get the wood cut. It established the eight-hour day, forced timber operators to clean up their camps in order to receive SPD troops, and sent inspectors into recalcitrant camp operations to enforce regulations.

The combination of worker agitation and government action transformed timber workscapes and loggers' bodies. Between 1918 and 1937, the filth and disease that motivated loggers to join the IWW nearly disappeared. After the war, the Four-L transitioned into a voluntary company union that allowed large timber operators to set standards of wages and working conditions in return for control over the labor force and steady work. It suppressed worker activism but also institutionalized sanitary landscapes. The Four-L attempted to instill loyalty and docility into the once rowdy and mobile workforce through applying simple technologies that made their life more comfortable, and producing stable workers through encouraging them to settle down with families that would theoretically undermine their radicalism.

However, this process of reform remained highly contested, with both the IWW and employers taking credit for sanitary reforms and bitterly denouncing the other. Repression of the Wobblies grew and on November 11, 1919, Wobblies shot four American Legion members during a raid on their hall in Centralia, Washington. In the aftermath, IWW organizer Wesley Everest was lynched and eight Wobblies sentenced to long prison terms. To defend its members and attack its opponents, the IWW and its opponents used constructions of loyalty, manhood, and work in the forests. The IWW declined in Centralia's aftermath but timber workers continued pressing their own agenda around the workplace environment. The Four-L may have institutionalized sanitary landscapes but it did not give workers power to shape their own lives. Some workers sought to make the Four-L serve as an organization to speak for them, but employers had no intention of it operating as a real union. When the Great Depression decimated the industry and the Four-L no longer could set wages and working conditions, timber workers rejected the company union and created their own organizations to represent themselves.

THE LOGGER REVOLT

The IWW's presence in the forests grew rapidly in 1916, as did the escalation of violence against them. In Everett, Washington, forty miles north of Seattle, timber operators organized to eliminate the Wobblies. On October 30, forty Wobblies took a boat to Everett from Seattle. They were met at the dock, rounded up, stripped naked, and forced to run the gauntlet while the vigilantes beat them. In response, the IWW sent 250 additional radicals on a boat from Seattle on November 5. When they arrived, a firefight broke out between the unionists and the police that led to four Wobblies dying from gunshot wounds, several more drowning, and the death of two deputies. The state charged the surviving Wobblies with murder, but the prosecutions galvanized attention on the violence, and after the first trial resulted in acquittal, the state dropped all charges.[1]

[1] Melvyn Dubofsky, *We Shall Be All: A History of the Industrial Workers of the World* (Chicago: Quadrangle Books, 1969), 338–43; Robert L. Tyler, *Rebels of the Woods: The*

The IWW organized from the Everett Massacre. Wobbly speaker Elizabeth Gurley Flynn visited Idaho logging towns in February 1917, whipping loggers' discontent into action.[2] On March 4, Wobblies established Lumber Workers Industrial Union No. 500 in Spokane to coordinate the upcoming IWW actions. In April, loggers near St. Maries, Idaho, walked off the job when their bosses refused demands for improved bunkhouses and better food, higher wages, and the eight-hour day. By June, some camps near St. Maries had forced employers to grant an eight-hour day.[3] Workers in the pine forests near Sandpoint, Idaho, then struck in protest of the camp conditions and the strike rapidly spread through eastern Washington, Idaho, and western Montana. Building upon the actions of the Idaho loggers, the IWW called for a strike in the pine country on June 20 and then an industry-wide strike effective through the Northwest on July 17. When workers at the Humbird Lumber Company demanded "clean bunk houses, decent food and the eight hour day," the company refused and the loggers joined the growing strike. The IWW expanded out of its eastern Washington and Idaho base, opening an office in Klamath Falls, Oregon, and leading western Washington loggers out of the forests in July.[4]

With loggers directing their own actions, timber camps had slightly different demands that often shifted by the week, but they fell into two general categories. First, loggers wanted to work fewer hours for more money. Their core demand was the eight-hour day, the fundamental goal of the American working class for decades. Wobblies walked out of a Big Lake, Washington, operation in order to make the camp "safe for the eight-hour day."[5] That included travel to and from the camps to the logging site, which could take up to an hour each way. Overtime and

I.W.W. in the Pacific Northwest (Eugene: University of Oregon Press, 1967), 62–84; Norman Clark, *Mill Town: A Social History of Everett, Washington from Its Earliest Beginnings on the Shores of Puget Sound to the Tragic and Infamous Event Known as the Everett Massacre* (Seattle: University of Washington Press, 1970), 168–242. For contemporary coverage, see "Shall Our Fellow Workers Be Murdered," *The Industrial Worker*, October 21, 1916; "I.W.W. Must Answer the Terrorism of Everett," *The Industrial Worker*, November 4, 1916; "Open Shop Advocates Take Death Toll," *The Industrial Worker*, November 11, 1916. Also, Walker C. Smith, *The Everett Massacre: A History of the Class Struggle in the Lumber Industry* (Chicago: I.W.W. Publishing Bureau, 1918).

2 "Closed Shops to Hear Flynn," *The Industrial Worker*, February 17, 1917.

3 "I.W.W. Disturbances," *West Coast Lumberman*, May 1, 1917, 30; "Results Organization in the Lumber Industry," *The Industrial Worker*, June 16, 1917.

4 "Later," *The Industrial Worker*, June 23, 1917; "Organizing Oregon," *The Industrial Worker*, June 23, 1917; "Big Lumber Strike Is Spreading," *The Industrial Worker*, June 30, 1917; "Monster Lumber Workers Strike," *The Industrial Worker*, July 21, 1917.

5 "Lumberjacks Defend Their Job Delegates," *The Industrial Worker*, February 2, 1918.

holiday pay joined the demands as the strike proceeded. By July, Wobblies demanded a minimum wage of $60 a month for loggers and $3.50 a day for sawmill workers ($1127 and $62.97 in 2014 dollars).[6]

The second set of demands revolved around revolutionizing loggers' workscapes. *The Industrial Worker* described the strike as "the gigantic struggle for decent conditions" for a class of long-abused workers.[7] One Wobbly strike poster listed very specific requirements for housing, including "sanitary sleeping quarters with not more than 12 men in each bunkhouse" that would have good lighting and reading tables. It also demanded laundry rooms and bathrooms with showers. Finally, workers wanted "wholesome food on porcelain dishes with no overcrowding at dining tables," and cookhouses that were well staffed "to keep them sanitary." Mill workers sought not more than two men per room. Wobblies called for the end of the timber camp medical system exploiting them, fighting for the end to hospital fees and incompetent company doctors.[8] Good food prepared in sanitary conditions remained central to workers' demands in the strike. Camps near Cle Elum, Washington, struck because of food described as "nauseating."[9] Striking meant that loggers lost their food supply, nauseating as it might be. The Cle Elum loggers had to walk four miles for food, where local miners fed them.[10] That summer, the fecundity of the Northwest forests fed many striking loggers. As E. Phelps put it when reporting on his strike in Stillwater, Washington, "the weather is fine, plenty of berries are at hand, there are lots of fish, and no scabs are coming in."[11]

Wobblies had long relied on the constant mobility of timber workers to spread their doctrine, but fighting for change meant convincing workers to stay on the strike in one place rather than hop a train for another town or job. A.L. Vecellio, reporting on a camp at Clear Lake, Washington, expressed frustration that, despite several short walkouts, the workers seemed unable to realize the need to stay and organize. He urged, "do not run away from the job because conditions are rotten – stay and fight. Don't think that in joining the I.W.W. you are undertaking a hard fight. It

6 "General Strike in Woods and Mines," *The Industrial Worker*, July 7, 1917: "Lumberworkers Standing Firm," *The Industrial Worker*, July 14, 1917; "Eight-Hour Day," *The Industrial Worker*, July 28, 1917. For the inflation calculator, http://data.bls.gov/cgi-bin/cpicalc.pl?cost1=60&year1=1917&year2=2014. Accessed June 14, 2014.

7 "General Strike in Woods and Mines," *The Industrial Worker*, July 7, 1917.

8 "Lumberworkers Standing Firm," *The Industrial Worker*, July 14, 1917; "Inland Empire I.W.W. Demands," *West Coast Lumberman*, April 1, 1917, 42.

9 "Real Solidarity Being Displayed by Workers," *The Industrial Worker*, June 23, 1917.

10 "Going Four Miles to Eat," *The Industrial Worker*, July 7, 1917.

11 E. Phelps, "Fish and Berries, But No Scabs," *The Industrial Worker*, August 4, 1917.

is far easier to change conditions than to endure them."[12] As this message sank in and Wobblies struck instead of ran, they made employers feel their wrath. Loggers in Eureka, Montana, left twelve million board feet of cut timber to rot on riverbanks, where Wobblies hoped it "will make a banquet for worms owing to the bullheaded tactics of the boss."[13] Not working also kept workers alive; there were 1,856 fewer timber workplace accidents in July than June due to the work stoppage.[14]

Employers rejected all of the strikers' demands. The workers' ability to shut down production depended on time and place; as timber executive Edwin Ames put it, "we hope to keep the mills running, but cannot tell one day what is going to happen the next." Complaining that the IWW had doubled the cost of labor, Ames called for the repeal of the Chinese Exclusion Act in order to flood the Northwest with cheap, pliable workers. With that not forthcoming, Ames urged federal intervention to crush the strike, writing Col. D.E. Dentley to ask for a military guard for his Port Ludlow and Port Gamble mills in order to repress any IWW activity.[15] George Cornwall and progressive operators still worked toward the moderate reform of camp spaces, but they had no tolerance for the IWW. Cornwall referred to the strike as "the reign of terror" in a *Timberman* editorial and urged the government to send federal troops to crush it.[16] The C.A. Smith Lumber and Manufacturing Company in Marshfield, Oregon, declared that they would close the mills permanently before recognizing the IWW, while the *West Coast Lumberman* proudly boasted of how the timber industry stood together against labor.[17] One sarcastic editorialist commented in that journal in August, "when the Labor Unions have confiscated the Saw Mills, when a Woman is President, when universal Peace is firmly established and when the country has eliminated all vice and selfishness – then life won't be worth a te-total tinkers Damn!"[18]

That the strike came after the United States joined World War I on April 6, 1917, gave the timber operators a new weapon against workers:

[12] A.L. Vecellio, "Need Permanent Organization," *The Industrial Worker*, April 14, 1917.

[13] "Lumberworkers Standing Firm," *The Industrial Worker*, July 14, 1917.

[14] "Lumberjacks Surer than Ever of Victory," *The Industrial Worker*, August 8, 1917.

[15] Edwin Ames to Jay Thomas, April 20, 1917, Ames Papers, University of Washington Special Collections, Box 16, Folder 4; Ames to Albert Johnson, May 23, 1917, Box 16, Folder 11; Ames to Col. D.E. Dentley, July 16, 1917, Box 16, Folder 18; Ames to C.R. Cranmer, Box 16, Folder 20.

[16] George Cornwall, "Your Country and Mine," *The Timberman*, July 1917, 1.

[17] "Close Mill before Yielding to Union," *West Coast Lumberman*, July 1, 1917, 34; "The Strike Accomplished Much," *West Coast Lumberman*, September 15, 1917, 1.

[18] *West Coast Lumberman*, August 1, 1917, 1.

accusing them of treason and sabotage. Workplace resistance around the nation spiked in 1917, with nearly 3,000 strikes in the first six months after the United States entered the war. This caused a tremendous backlash from employers determined to maintain control over the open shop, especially in the American West. Frank Little's murder in Butte and the Bisbee Deportation are the most famous, but hardly isolated, violent acts against the IWW that year. The Espionage Act, passed in 1917, and the Sedition Act, passed in 1918, cracked down on internal dissent and led to the arrest of hundreds of radicals, the confiscation of radical literature and property, and the deportation of immigrant leftists, including thirty-six from the Pacific Northwest that left Seattle on February 7, 1919.[19]

Timber owners wanted to apply the Espionage and Sedition Acts to their unruly workers. J.J. Donovan complained of a worker who told others to quit after eight hours of work. Donovan griped, "Were it not for the bad blood such things stir up, I would make complaint against this man under the Espionage Act."[20] Both Oregon and Washington passed criminal syndicalism bills.[21] A *West Coast Lumberman* editorial said the IWW "should right now be forever crushed in the Pacific Northwest."[22] The near lynching of a Wobbly in Hood River, Oregon, and a public burning of IWW literature in Aberdeen, Washington, showed increasing violence against radicals in the timber country.

Employers attempted to taint the Wobblies with accusations of arson. Fires plagued mills and forests throughout the early twentieth century. The notorious 1910 fires in Washington, Idaho, and western Montana burned three million acres and killed eighty-seven people.[23] Lightning started many fires, but the methods of industrial logging vastly increased the problem. Donkey engines sent off sparks that frequently set a dry forest ablaze. The dead slash left behind by a logging operation served as

[19] Joseph A. McCartin, *Labor's Great War: The Struggle for Industrial Democracy and the Origins of Modern American Labor Relations, 1912–1921* (Chapel Hill: University of North Carolina Press, 1997), 39; Dubofsky, *We Shall Be All*, 308–13, 376–97; Clemens P. Work, *Darkest Before Dawn: Sedition and Free Speech in the American West* (Albuquerque: University of New Mexico Press, 2005); David M. Rabban, *Free Speech in Its Forgotten Years* (New York: Cambridge University Press, 1997).

[20] J.J. Donovan to Brice P. Disque, July 22, 1918. Brice P. Disque Collection, University of Oregon Special Collections, Box 2.

[21] John McClelland, Jr., *Wobbly War: The Centralia Story* (Tacoma: Washington State Historical Society, 1978), 37; "I.W.W. Aimed at in Senate Bill," *Seattle Union Record*, January 13, 1919.

[22] "I.W.W." *West Coast Lumberman*, July 15, 1917, 1.

[23] Steven Pyne, *Year of the Fires: The Story of the Great Fires of 1910* (New York: Viking, 2001).

ideal fuel for growing fires. Huge piles of sawdust in mills could spontaneously combust. Dealing with fire was a major theme of timber industry conferences. The 1913 meeting of the Western Forestry and Conservation Association blamed everyone but operators for fires, including auto-driving tourists, poor educational programs for children, the state for not committing more resources to fighting fire, and workers for not tending the engines or tossing cigarette butts aside carelessly.[24]

What timber executives did not do was blame the political ideology of workers for fires. That changed in World War I. The IWW had a self-inflicted reputation for sabotage, calling at its 1914 convention for "all speakers to be instructed to recommend to the workers the necessity of curtailing production by a means of 'slowing down' and sabotage."[25] However, actual evidence of sabotage in the timber camps remains elusive. When Calson & Callow Company's mill burned in 1917, *West Coast and Puget Sound Lumbermen* claimed it was "thought to be the work of the I.W.W."[26] When fires got out of control, employers blamed Wobblies for intentionally not putting them out.[27]

Wobblies objected to these claims. Striking Wobblies near Eureka, Montana, left their pickets during the strike to fight fires with two dying on the fire line.[28] As the IWW Press Committee said of the Wobblies' firefighting efforts, "while they [the capitalists] destroy our property, we are out protecting theirs."[29] It accused newspapers and insurance companies of promoting the arson myth, noting stories on Wobbly fire threats with insurance advertisements on the same page.[30] Attempts to harass Wobblies through sabotage accusations often fell apart. William Amey was charged with willful destruction of property when a donkey engine

[24] "Forest Fire Conference on Canadian Soil a Brilliant Success," *The Timberman*, December 1913, 32A–32CC."

[25] McClelland, *Wobbly War*, 27. See Eric Thomas Chester, *The Wobblies in Their Heyday: The Rise and Destruction of the Industrial Workers of the World during the World War I Era* (Santa Barbara, CA: Praeger, 2014) for a comprehensive discussion of how IWW rhetoric around sabotage laid the groundwork for their own destruction.

[26] "Late Grays Harbor News," *West Coast Lumberman*, August 15, 1917, 27. See, e.g., *Little Logged-off Lands*, June 1912, 4; "Late Grays Harbor News," *West Coast Lumberman*, August 15, 1917, 27.

[27] "Save the Camps and Mills from Fire," *West Coast Lumberman*, June 1, 1918, 1; Charles Howell, Memorandum for the District Forester, September 1, 1919, National Archives and Records Administration – Seattle, RG 95, Records of the U.S. Forest Service, Region 1, Historical Collection, ca. 1905–1990, Box 47 Folder Fire Control Historical Selway Fires, 1906–1964.

[28] "I.W.W. Fighting Fires," *Industrial Worker*, July 28, 1917.

[29] "Friendliness of Labor and Capital," *Industrial Worker*, July 30, 1917.

[30] "Firebugs Busy Again," *Industrial Worker*, February 2, 1918.

was destroyed. But the jury found Amey not guilty after testimony that the engine's oil had not been changed for months.[31]

A more dispassionate view of the strikes came from U.S. Forest Service officials, the government agency most exposed to logging camps. Region 1 supervisor M.H. Wolff wrote an internal report evaluating the labor situation in the forests in northern Idaho. Wolff called Wobbly doctrine "unsound and dangerous," but stated in no uncertain terms that the workers themselves were not striking against capitalism. Rather, as he made clear to federal forest officials, "it is a demand from the men for better conditions of work and more consideration from their employers." He deemed the Wobbly demands, including the eight-hour day, better food, sanitary bunkhouses, and quality medical care, financially feasible for companies, calculating the cost between 25 cents and $1.50 per million board feet and noting that the rise in timber prices during the war made it reasonable at "even twice that much." Wolff dismissed owners' protests that workers only demanded bathhouses to cause problems for the employers and that beds were too expensive to provide.[32]

Despite the power and size of the strike, by the late summer timber operators gained the upper hand. Authorities raided Wobbly halls and arrested organizers in Washington and Idaho in August and September, while an attempt to expand the strike into Oregon stalled. In early September, after ten weeks off the job, the IWW called off the strike and urged workers to engage in "striking on the job," continuing to build worker power while also earning money. This meant quitting work after eight hours and bringing whistles to work to announce the day's stoppage. Such a strategy could do little for the sanitation demands, but it bought time and built worker organization for the next round of strikes planned for 1918.[33]

Over the next several months, Wobbly-dominated camps sporadically shut down operations after eight hours, occasionally walked off the job for better conditions, and highlighted to members where activism had led to sanitation. Wood production plummeted in the face of these strikes,

31 "Lumber Barons' Tools Pull Kidnapping Stunt," *Industrial Worker*, March 6, 1918.

32 M.H. Wolff report on labor conditions, January 1, 1918, NARA, RG 95, Records of the U.S. Forest Service, Region 1, Missoula, Montana, Historical Collection, ca. 1905–1990, Box 1, Folder 1680 History Program NW History Prior to 1933. Emphasis in original document.

33 "Striking on the Job," *Industrial Worker*, September 5, 1917; "Realization of Power Great Result of Big Lumber Strike," *Industrial Worker*, September 5, 1917; "Lumberworkers to Call Strike on Job," *Industrial Worker*, September 19, 1917.

and by the fall mills were producing only half of the ten million board feet demanded by the government each month.[34] Wobblies invited workers to clean camps while warning them to avoid those that were unreformed. One worker reported that a camp in Gold Basin, Washington, had "good grub, good sleeping quarters, boss not bad," and provided information on how to arrive at the camp.[35] As camp conditions improved in response to their activism, loggers celebrated. A Wobbly named Dowling called "the change between now and three months ago in grub, steam and hours, makes it seem as though we had jumped a century ahead."[36] Better fed and cleaner loggers could feel empowerment on their bodies. When loggers struck over unsanitary conditions, such as a Dungeness, Washington, crew did in December 1917, they explained that "the lumberjacks want clean surroundings as much as the eight-hour day and will use the same tactics to get both."[37] This threat was clear to both the industry and the government by the fall of 1917.

FEDERAL INTERVENTION IN THE TIMBER WORKSCAPE

The 1917 strike not only differed from previous Wobbly actions in the forests because of its size; it also attracted federal attention thanks to the development of air power in warfare. Soon after the Wright Brothers first flew off the dunes of Kitty Hawk in 1903, military tacticians began dreaming of the use of the airplane in war and by World War I, both the Allies and Central Powers saw airpower as a vital weapon to win the war.[38] The U.S. military preferred Sitka spruce for planes because of its light weight and good durability. However, the tree only grows in the Pacific Northwest and British Columbia and is not a dominant species in the Douglas fir forests. These enormous trees require extremely moist conditions and usually do not grow in large groves. To produce enough spruce for the nation's airplane needs, employers had to conduct a coordinated effort. Yet the timber industry, as intransigent toward workers as

34 Philip Dreyfus, "Nature, Militancy, and the Western Worker: Socialist Shingles, Syndicalist Spruce," *Labor* 1, no. 3 (Summer 2004): 88–89.

35 "Making Woods Safe for Job Democracy," *Industrial Worker*, October 3, 1917.

36 "Timber! Timber! Hours Coming Down," *Industrial Worker*, November 10, 1917.

37 "Lumberjacks Want Cleanliness," *Industrial Worker*, December 22, 1917.

38 I.B. Holley, Jr., *Ideas and Weapons: Exploitation of the Aerial Weapon by the United States during World War I; A Study in the Relationship of Technological Advance, Military Doctrine, and the Development of Weapons* (New Haven: Yale University Press, 1953). James J. Hudson, *Hostile Skies: A Combat History of the American Air Service in World War I* (Syracuse: Syracuse University Press, 1968).

ever, could not harvest it because of its unwillingness to grant loggers' demands for sanitation and an end to the slow violence grinding down their bodies.[39]

Soon after the United States entered the World War I in April 1917, the Wilson administration set up unprecedented government coordination over the economy in order to facilitate the war effort. It soon turned its attention to the Northwest forests. Wilson created the War Industries Board in July 1917 to streamline war-related manufacturing, while Congress passed the Lever Act in August 1917, giving the president the power to regulate supplies and prices of food and fuel during the war.[40] The Council of National Defense, created in June 1916 to prepare national businesses for war, coordinated industry cooperation after the nation entered World War I. Its subsidiary, the Aircraft Production Board, sent Charles R. Sligh, its lumber subcommittee head, to investigate the timber problem. His report indicated the strike's seriousness and the impossibility of producing the necessary spruce. He emphasized, "it calls for heroic measures … The industry must be largely revolutionized, and this with skill, sureness and justice, else the attempt will fail."[41]

Responding to Sligh's report, in October 1917 General John J. Pershing appointed Colonel Brice P. Disque to find a solution to the labor situation in the Northwestern forests. Disque was a lifetime military officer who enlisted in 1899, playing a role in capturing Filipino freedom fighter Emilio Aguinaldo. He retired from the military in 1916 to take a position as warden of the Michigan State Penitentiary but reenlisted when the

39 Harold Hyman, *Soldiers and Spruce: Origins of the Loyal Legion of Loggers and Lumbermen* (Los Angeles: Institute of Industrial Relations, University of California, Los Angeles, 1963), 44.

40 See Robert H. Zieger, *America's Great War: World War I and the American Experience* (Lanham, MD: Rowman & Littelfield Publishers, Inc., 2000), 64–77, for a good overview of the Wilson administration's mobilization of the economy during the war. Also see Joseph A. McCartin, "Using the 'Gun Act': Federal Regulation and the Politics of the Strike Threat during World War I," *Labor History*, 33, no. 4 (1992): 519–28; Eileen A. Boris, "Tenement Homework on Army Uniforms: the Gendering of Industrial Democracy during World War I," *Labor History* 32, no. 2 (1991): 231–52; William J. Breen, "Industrial Training and Craft Production in World War I: Unions, Employers, and the States, 1917–1919," *Labor History* 37, no. 1 (1995–96): 50–74; Carl R. Weisberg, *Labor, Loyalty, and Rebellion: Southwestern Illinois Coal Miners and World War I* (Carbondale: Southern Illinois University Press, 2005); and Robert D. Cuff, *The War Industries Board: Business-Government Relations during World War I* (Baltimore: Johns Hopkins University Press, 1973) on labor, employers, and government intervention in industry during the war.

41 United States Army and United States Spruce Production Corporation, *History of the Spruce Production Division*, 5.

nation entered World War I. Pershing gave Disque the authority to recruit a division of soldiers to log spruce for the military.[42]

Disque created the Spruce Production Division (SPD), an army unit fighting in the Northwest forests instead of the French trenches. Made up primarily of experienced loggers, the SPD helped the military acquire the necessary wood, placed army men among the radicals in camps, and limited drafted Wobblies from spreading their doctrine into the army mainstream since many radicalized loggers made up the core of the SPD. However, the soldiers could not work directly for the government. There were not enough SPD troops to log all the needed spruce and to do so would have made the military look like a strikebreaking outfit, making the labor problem worse. Troops would be interspersed with civilian loggers but the military would not allow them to live in the conditions that lumber workers endured daily. Getting out the cut required government intervention in the industry's sanitary regime.[43]

Disque initially dismissed sanitation as the reason for the labor problems. He wrote the War Department about the strikes, saying, "I do not believe that the living conditions in the camps are responsible for it because there is a general effort by employers to improve living conditions in every way."[44] He changed his mind after touring the camps. Witnessing housing and toilet facilities and eating with loggers, Disque compared conditions unfavorably to American POW camps in the Philippines, noting, "we treated captured Moros better in the Philippines during a war." After one meal in a camp cookhouse, he remarked, "we could not eat it."[45]

The timber industry was initially suspicious of Disque's presence. Edwin Ames was happy to use federal troops as a strikebreaking force, but resisted further incursions in labor relations. He wrote Disque, "all that is required is for the government to detail a small squad of men to guard each logging operation and sawmill plant manufacturing lumber for government purposes," while calling for limited government interference in his operations.[46] Disque thus had to integrate his soldiers into civilian camps while ameliorating suspicious owners, raising the sanitation standards to those acceptable to the military, convincing workers the troops were not strikebreakers, and getting trees processed for the war

[42] Ibid., 7; Hyman, *Soldiers and Spruce*, 28–34.

[43] Hyman, *Soldiers and Spruce*, 114, 116.

[44] Brice Disque letter to Chief Signal Officer, War Department, November 27, 1917, Brice Disque Papers, University of Washington Special Collections, Box 3, Folder V0257a.

[45] Hyman, *Soldiers and Spruce*, 109.

[46] Ames to Disque, October 30, 1917, UW Box 17, Folder 9.

effort. To accomplish this Herculean task, Disque and his advisors, particularly labor economist Carleton Parker, convinced the timber operators to place their labor problems in Disque's hands in February 1918, promising an end to strikes and consistent production.

Disque then announced the Loyal Legion of Loggers and Lumbermen (Four-L), which became the nation's first government-sponsored company union. The Four-L required a loyalty oath and banned active IWW members from work, but guaranteed the eight-hour day, steady work, and improving conditions. In return for meeting workers' demands, the Four-L insisted that workers not strike during the war and consider it a mediating organization between themselves and their employers. This led to a major victory for workers, but a complete defeat for the IWW.[47]

In March 1918, Disque issued an order that laid out the environmental improvements the industry must make. In addition to enforcing an eight-hour day and setting minimum wages for each job in the camps, this order demanded that camps provide real bedding to their workers, including mattresses, pillows, blankets, and sheets. He also sent subordinates to inspect mess halls and renovate "the entire physical conditions under which the lumber workers lived."[48] The camp operators had to undergo government inspections of their camps with enforcement power from the military. This ensured that labor tumult would not result from the government-employed soldiers.[49]

Military repression went far to ensure worker participation. A SPD officer made an impassioned speech to convince loggers to join the Four-L. Most signed up but when George Harper refused, some workers threatened to tar him. After the lieutenant worried about the bad publicity of such an act, the workers beat Harper and evicted him from camp.[50] "C.C." was not a Wobbly but was disgusted by the pressure to join the Four-L. He took a position with the Admiralty Logging Company, where he faced a vermin-infested bed and poor food. Five days later, a SPD officer came into sign up the camp for the Four-L. Of the 190 workers present, 120 signed cards after a rousing speech, but C.C. and others did

47 Hyman, *Soldiers and Spruce*, 179.

48 United States War Department, Office of the Secretary, *A Report of the Activities of the War Department in the Field of Industrial Relations during the War* (Washington, D.C.: Government Printing Office, 1919), 45–46.

49 United States Army and United States Spruce Production Corporation, *History of Spruce Production Division*, 18.

50 "Knock Their Blocks Off!" *The Industrial Worker*, January 5, 1918.

not, instead "debating on a man's rights in a free country." He quit, but this pressure forced most loggers, even most radicals, to accept it.[51]

The quasi-military organization of the forests had long-term effects upon the workscapes of the timber industry. First, it effectively ended the iron control of operators over their camps. One employer confessed to a government investigator that the strikes had convinced him to provide decent bunkhouses, but not until he had eliminated the IWW because "he was not going to allow those fellows to tell him what he had to do."[52] Disque intervened in this standoff, building upon health measures the military adopted in the Spanish-American War and the Philippines and was implementing during World War I, as well as the broader emphasis on cleanliness among middle-class reformers in the 1910s.[53] The SPD ordered seven changes to an Aloha Lumber Company camp, including placing the toilets farther away from the kitchen and keeping them clean, providing shade for the meat house so the food did not spoil, and working to keep flies out of the mess house.[54] Military sanitation inspectors challenged timber operators on many of the same issues as the Wobblies. Paul E. Page protested an order that he clean up his company's water supplies. He used its log pond for its camp drinking water and an inspector worried that the men would defecate in the water, leading to a "serious epidemic." Complaining that an inspection of his camp was "unfair and unreasonable," he placed the water system in his camp within the context of the entire industry, arguing that "if the entire water supply west of the Cascades is to be condemned for the reason that some log may be pulled through human excretia and come in contact with some brook that supplies drinking water, we are certainly in a bad way."[55]

51 "A Soldier Writes," *The Seattle Union Record*, January 7, 1919.

52 C.M. Plummer to C.C. McEachran," March 1, 1918, Ames Papers, Box 17, Folder 43.

53 Vincent J. Cirillo, "Fever and Reform: The Typhoid Epidemic in the Spanish-American War," *Journal of the History of Medicine and Applied Sciences*, 55, no. 4 (2000): 363–97; Nancy K. Bristow, *Making Men Moral: Social Engineering during the Great War* (New York: New York University Press, 1996); David J. Pivar, "Cleansing the Nation: The War on Prostitution, 1917–1921," *Prologue* 12 (Spring 1980): 29–41; and Douglas Habib, "Chastity, Masculinity, and Military Efficiency: The United States Army in Germany, 1918–1923," *International History Review* 28, no. 4 (December 2006): 737–57. On the middle class and cleanliness, Suellen Hoy, *Chasing Dirt: The American Pursuit of Cleanliness* (New York: Oxford University Press, 1995), especially 87–123.

54 John E. Stansbury to Commanding Officer, 45 Spruce Squadron. Aloha Lumber Company Papers, University of Washington Special Collections, Box 1, Folder P1319-4b.

55 J.W. Sherwood report, July 23, 1918; J.W. Sherwood to Frank Scott, August 15, 1918; Paul E. Page to C.F. Stearns, August 9, 1918, RG 18, Box 88, Folder Spruce Production Division, Correspondence – Suregon."

Improving conditions meant happier workers and higher production. One Four-L report compared the worker dissatisfaction in one camp because of bad water, biting insects, and a lack of bathing facilities to a nearby camp without union problems which had already provided bathing facilities. This report requested that the War Department appoint men to make camp inspection tours as a way to enforce these changes.[56] Disque also rejected attempts by companies to get around the new mandates. When the Puget Mill Company requested workers labor after their mandated eight hours to make repairs, Disque refused, calling the eight-hour day an "iron-clad rule."[57]

Continued Wobbly agitation made Disque's actions necessary. Loggers continued striking into 1918. Workers at a Wenatchee, Washington, camp walked out that winter for a new cook and the eight-hour day; winning, it forced non-Wobblies to quit. In February, the IWW announced that on May 1, loggers would burn their bedrolls and go on the largest strike in the industry's history to force companies to provide beds and sheets. It openly publicized the plan, worrying Disque and the timber industry.[58] One government investigator urged operators to "pull the teeth of this proposition by doing away with blanket carrying by the first of April."[59] When the Four-L announced beds and sheets in all camps in March 1918, the IWW crowed, "Damn it all, it seems the I.W.W. can never get what it wants" because every time it fought for something, the government "'voluntarily' grants what we were fighting for and had got in shape to take."[60] In this new atmosphere of reform, loggers kept winning their demands. When Wobblies working for the Mineral Lake Lumber Company held a meeting in March 1918 and demanded a bathhouse, the company immediately complied.[61]

From the IWW's perspective, workers' activism created these changes. Forrest Edwards, a twenty-year veteran of lumber camps, reflected on what the IWW had accomplished. He bemoaned the terrible food quality

[56] Minutes of the Convention of the Inland Empire Division of the Loyal Legion of Loggers and Lumbermen, 13–14, Brice Disque Papers, University of Washington Special Collections, Box 3, Folder V0257a.

[57] Ames to Disque, March 6, 1918; C.P. Stearns to Puget Mill Company, March 12, 1918. Ames Papers, Box 17, Folder 45.

[58] "All Bundles Will be Burned on May First," *The Industrial Worker*, February 9, 1918; "Won in a Walk Out," *The Industrial Worker*, February 9, 1918; "We Claim Credit in Advance," *The Industrial Worker*, March 16, 1918.

[59] "C.M. Plummer to C.C. McEachran," March 1, 1918, Ames Papers, Box 17, Folder 43.

[60] "Steal Our Thunder and It Looks Like Rain," *The Lumberjack*, March 23, 1918.

[61] "Got Their Bath House," *Industrial Worker*, April 13, 1918.

but noted, "Just as I.W.W. propaganda has brought springs and mattresses, shower baths, better bunkhouses," it would also bring better food and the eight-hour day.[62] When Disque established the eight-hour day, *The Industrial Worker* credited "the I.W.W. through its open strike and the strike on the job, brought the lumber interests to time." Dismissing the Four-L as an organization with no worker voice, it bragged, "the I.W.W. got the eight-hour day for the lumberjacks of the Northwest." Its next goal was to change the "camps where the food is so rotten that milady's dog would turn up its nose in disgust at the nauseating mess" and the "camps where the sleeping accommodations are not fit for pigs."[63]

However, Four-L repression and the granting of Wobbly demands led to the union's rapid decline. By the spring of 1918, a minority of loggers identified with the IWW. Only nine of forty-two loggers at a Simpson camp in Shelton and about one-fourth of the seventy-five in St. Paul's camp in Orting, both in Washington, were union members. The Day Lumber Company in Big Lake, Washington, had no Wobblies and an organizer described the workers as "hostile" to the IWW.[64] The IWW exhorted workers to remember why their lives had improved, urging them not "to lay down when things are coming our way; that is the time to keep on the hustle."[65] But by April, talk of the May 1 walkout had disappeared, replaced by detailing the state repression and mob violence against Wobblies. In Spokane, Aberdeen, Anacortes, and Astoria, Wobblies were arrested, beaten, and tarred and feathered.[66] Attacks upon IWW halls made organizing more difficult, leading to a call for workers to commit themselves to passing along all IWW literature to other workers in order to "show the capitalist that the closing of our halls only serves us to make us more active on the job."[67] The Spokane office opened to coordinate Northwest timber strikes closed in April 1918 because money was needed to fight for the release of the class war prisoners.[68]

The IWW's rapid decline reflects both government repression and the union's tenuous hold on loggers. When the government met their concerns

[62] Forrest Edwards, "The Lumber Workers and Their Success," *Industrial Worker*, February 2, 1918.

[63] "I.W.W. Forces Eight-Hour Day in Northwest, *Industrial Worker*, March 9, 1918.

[64] Untitled reports, *Industrial Worker*, March 9, 1918.

[65] "Steal Our Thunder and It Looks Like Rain," *The Lumberjack*, March 23, 1918.

[66] For example, Tom L. Thurman, "Doesn't Sound Like Desertion," *Industrial Worker*, March 30, 1918. On repression, see a number of articles from *Industrial Worker*, April 13, 1918.

[67] "Make Our Literature Count," *Industrial Worker*, April 20, 1918.

[68] "Lumber Workers Move to Chicago," *Industrial Worker*, April 20, 1918.

about the camps and made work dependent upon leaving the IWW, most abandoned a union that endangered their jobs. Like many workers during World War I, "they would take the concrete benefits and let the ideological loyalties go," as David Brody has stated.[69] Improved health and comfortable housing meant more for many loggers than abstract revolutionary goals. Even committed Wobbly organizers such as Ern Hanson recognized this fact, remembering, "the bulk of the membership were just card carriers and would fight for higher wages and better conditions but had a pretty vague idea about syndicalist organizations and revolution."[70]

For the federal government, the SPD and Four-L was a success. Disque established 234 SPD camps around the Northwest that included 27,661 enlisted men and 1,222 officers, working in camps with around 125,000 Four-L members in approximately 1,000 camps and mills. Disque estimated that job turnover in lumber dropped from 600 percent per year in 1917 to 25 percent by the fall of 1918 because of the Four-L's influence, transformed camp sanitation, and improved food. Spruce production skyrocketed from 2.887 million board feet in November 1917 to 22.145 million board feet in October 1918. Fir production also rose and nearly 145 million feet of aircraft stock was produced over the year.[71] While the Four-L was a disaster for the IWW, for rank and file loggers its legacy is more complex. Their own activism led to military intervention to make a decisive turn in logging workscapes. The future of camp sanitation was hardly written at the end of 1918, but for the first time, loggers could expect clean sheets, sanitary toilets, decent food, and a bunkhouse that would protect them from heat, cold, rain, and vermin. This came at a harsh cost for radicals, but for many loggers, the cost was worth it.

INSTITUTIONALIZING THE SANITARY REVOLUTION

Soon after World War I ended in November 1918, the federal government withdrew from regulating the timber industry. The SPD disbanded and Disque resigned as Four-L head in December. Employers chose to

[69] David Brody, *Workers in Industrial America: Essays on the Twentieth-Century Struggle* (New York: Oxford University Press, 1980), 40.

[70] Bert Russell, ed., *Hardships and Happy Times in Idaho's St. Joe's Wilderness* (Caldwell, ID: Lacon Publishers, 1978), 108.

[71] General Comments, 14. Disque papers, Box 1, Folder V0257a; Untitled Report, 22. Brice Disque papers, University of Washington Special Collections, Box 4, Folder V0257b; United States Army and United States Spruce Production Corporation, *History of the Spruce Production Division*, 5, 114.

continue the organization on a voluntary basis, hoping that their example would set wage and sanitary standards and achieve labor peace throughout the industry. Government intervention during the war limited employers' options after its conclusion.[72] They could not reinstate the system of unsanitary housing and transient labor because of loggers' higher expectations of their working and sanitary conditions. When workers did face bad conditions, they again struck, as did a crew in May 1919 when the company did not provide clean bedding.[73] Labor's fight for industrial democracy during World War I may have failed to unionize American workers, but its influence became enmeshed in corporate welfare and company unionism through the 1920s.[74]

Although the Four-L became a civilian organization, its goals changed little. By eradicating environmental reasons for unrest, it hoped to eliminate any reason for workers to revolt. A September 1921 *Four-L Bulletin* front-page story argued that workers must have hope in their lives and jobs in order to forestall revolution.[75] It wanted to give workers just enough hope to accomplish this task without surrendering any actual control over the day-to-day operations of its industry. Camp sanitation would continue to evolve but under the direction of companies, not unionists.

Four-L-affiliated companies worked to institutionalize sanitary changes. The St. Paul and Tacoma Lumber Company reported in 1920 of changes made in three camps, including steel bunks, screened cook houses to keep out flies, new toilets, chlorinated water, drinking water piped from a nearby spring, electric lights, and new dishes in the cookhouses.[76] Wobblies continued taking credit and pressed for new aims that reflected the victories loggers had achieved. Meeting in Tacoma in July 1919, IWW loggers set new demands that included the six-hour day to improve on the eight, plus "blankets of pure cotton and wool ... at least 64 by 80 inches in size" in addition to clean bedding, no more than four men in a room instead of just

[72] See Susan Eleanor Hirsch, *After the Strike: A Century of Labor Struggle at Pullman* (Urbana: University of Illinois Press, 2003), 100–28 for a discussion of this in the railroad industry.

[73] "Fortine Strikers Stand Unbroken Resist Greed of Lumber Trust," *New Solidarity*, May 17, 1919.

[74] Joseph A. McCartin, *Labor's Great War: The Struggle for Industrial Democracy and the Origins of Modern American Labor Relations, 1912–1921* (Chapel Hill: University of North Carolina Press, 1997).

[75] Norman F. Coleman, "Primary Needs of the Worker," *Four-L Bulletin*, September 1921, 1–2.

[76] St. Paul and Tacoma Lumber Company to T. Tharaldsen, August 21, 1920, St. Paul and Tacoma Lumber Company Papers, University of Washington Special Collections, Box 5, Folder Loyal Legion of Loggers 1920.

sanitary housing, as well as hot and cold water and "good accommodations for washing."[77]

The IWW had few members in the 1920s. However, employers knew their workers had once been Wobblies. So they worked to place their sanitary reforms in a nest of the paternalistic labor relations frequently employed by corporations in the 1920s.[78] George Cornwall had long talked in this language, referring to loggers as "the child of the forest," needing direction to avoid radicalism.[79] In February 1926, *The Four L Lumber News* ran a story about an Eastern European immigrant logger named Gus, who had a wife in his homeland. Due to the United States' restrictive immigration policies, she could not join him. She made it to Canada, but faced deportation. So Gus went to visit the boss, who then pulled strings and Gus' wife joined him. Sadly, American loggers would never see their boss in this light because "the American workingman … learns an ideal of independence in his first school days. So, even if he is of the first generation of American-born in his family, the idea of the feudal system, which we call paternalism today, soon becomes obnoxious to him." But for the writer, the Four-L could change this because it allowed workers to feel they had a voice while still relying on beneficent employers.[80] The Four-L would have to create conditions that led to compliant loggers since those workers would not naturally look toward the companies with gratitude.

77 "Preparing for Control of Lumber Industry on Puget Sound," *New Solidarity*, July 19, 1919.

78 On paternalism, Stanley Buder, *Pullman: An Experiment in Industrial Order and Community Planning, 1880–1930* (New York: Oxford University Press, 1967); Lisa M. Fine, The Story of *Reo Joe: Work, Kin, and Community in Autotown, U.S.A.* (Philadelphia: Temple University Press, 2004); Douglas Flamming, *Creating the Modern South: Millhands and Managers in Dalton, Georgia, 1884–1984* (Chapel Hill: University of North Carolina Press, 1992); Jacquelyn Dowd Hall, James Leloudis, Robert Korstad, Mary Murphy, Lu Ann Jones, and Christopher B. Daly, *Like a Family: The Making of a Southern Cotton Mill World* (Chapel Hill: University of North Carolina Press, 1987); Gunther Peck, *Reinventing Free Labor: Padrones and Immigrant Workers in the North American West, 1880–1930* (New York: Cambridge University Press, 2000); Andrea Tone, *The Business of Benevolence: Industrial Paternalism in Progressive America* (Ithaca: Cornell University Press, 1997); and Mary Lethert Wingerd, "Rethinking Paternalism: Power and Parochialism in a Southern Mill Village," *Journal of American History* 83, no. 3 (1996): 872–902.

79 George Cornwall, "Your Country and Mine," *The Timberman*, July 1917, 1.

80 James Stevens, "Why Did Gus, Immigrant Laborer, Go Directly to the President of the Company, When He Needed Help?," *The Four L Lumber News*, February 1926, 6–7; For responses, see David C. England, "Gus Had the Right Idea," *The Four L Lumber News*, March 1926, 6 and various letters about the article, same issue, 6, 30.

The IWW had long warned workers of employers trying to buy them off with a few camp improvements, noting in 1916, "it is in their interests to make the slaves believe that instead of organizing and doing something for themselves they must look to the masters to do things for them."[81] That is indeed what the companies hoped. Attempting to convince workers of its beneficence, the Four-L heavily publicized the companies creating sanitary and comfortable working and living spaces. As early as December 1919, the *Four-L Bulletin* proudly talked of the disappearance of unsanitary camps, noting that permanent movable structures had begun replacing the temporary dwellings thrown up during the war.[82] The Inman-Poulsen Lumber Company camp in Kelso, Washington, told employees they would never again carry their beds on their back. Now, each worker would receive his own bed with a mattress and blankets. The company even painted the buildings to "give the camps a very attractive appearance."[83]

Companies framed granting sanitation not as a response to radicalism, but to new technologies. Claiming that portable housing on rail cars made it possible for employers to provide quality housing, Four-L employers insinuated that if workers had patience, beneficent bosses would have taken care of workers without the IWW. Companies had long complained that erecting permanent structures made no sense because they moved their operations so frequently, but this had always served as a convenient excuse to cut costs. Now, technological advancements allowed them to invest in their workers. Tom Jones of Potlatch Lumber Company made explicit connections between sanitation and labor stability, noting, "I have always believed that the carrying of blankets was wrong from every standpoint. It helps breed the tramp spirit." Now, Potlatch eliminated flea-infested bedding, providing sheets, pillowcases, and blankets. It purchased electric dishwashers for its camps and hired an outside laundry service it made available to workers.[84] Many camps reported such advances, such as Coats-Fordney, with its rail cars with hot water, a wash room, shower, and dressing room.[85]

Food quality was also approached through a mix of technology and paternalism. By the 1920s, many American companies realized that better

81 "Bosses Can't Crush Lumber Workers," *The Industrial Worker*, December 30, 1916, 4.
82 Thorfinn Tharaldsen, "How Sanitation Has Been Improved," *Four-L Bulletin*, December 1919, 13.
83 "I-P Builds Model Camps," *Four L Bulletin*, September 1919, 12.
84 "Modern Methods Prevail at Potlatch Camps," *The Timberman*, September 1918, 41.
85 "Company Operates Cafeteria," *Four L Bulletin*, November 1923, 13.

fed workers made more productive workers and improved the quality of their offerings.[86] The Four-L encouraged operators to standardize cookhouses and improve food quality in order to create happy workers and increase production.[87] Coats-Fordney camps had two rail cars specifically for cooking. In the first, kitchen workers did preparatory work for meals while the food cooked in the second car. Sanitation improved significantly compared to the log shacks that housed kitchens before the war. The Four-L also wholeheartedly approved the Pacific Spruce Corporation's idea to serve 450 men a day in a cafeteria-style setup. Workers paid only for what they ate and employers saved money on food often wasted when served on individual tables.[88] Four-L writers cited scientific studies on what loggers should eat, telling camp cooks, "it is a mistake to think that meat is the most nourishing food. It is not, and unless it is supplemented with green vegetables such as spinach, carrots, peas, salad, and cabbage, and such starchy foods as potatoes, spaghetti, and rice, the diet is one-sided and unhealthful."[89] Four-L writers touted how workers deserved to eat like kings, claiming, "camp workmen should not be too severely censured for expecting better food."[90] Workers had known this for years, but the Four-L co-opted the idea.

The company union framed these reforms as coming from generous employers who cared about safety, health, sanitation, and food, with careless loggers needing guidance from experts. Paternalistic employers saw workers as messy children who needed the sharp guidance of a parent on how to keep a bunkhouse clean. Dr. Thorfinn Tharaldsen complained that workers "demand a modern sanitary camp from their employer and still seem unwilling to do their part in maintaining the camp in first class condition. They resent, as an infringement on their personal liberties, any attempt to enforce local rules and regulations governing individuals, in the maintenance of a sanitary camp."[91] Such attitudes were common among sanitary reformers in the 1910s and 1920s, ignoring the fact that working Americans had become much cleaner in recent years to chastise them for not being clean enough.[92]

[86] Nikki Mandell, *The Corporation as Family: The Gendering of Corporate Welfare, 1890–1930* (Chapel Hill: University of North Carolina Press, 2002), 2–3, 54–58.

[87] W.C. Ruegnitz, "Standard System for Management of Messhoues," *The Timberman* November 1921, 34–39.

[88] "Company Operates Cafeteria," *Four L Bulletin*, November 1923, 13.

[89] "Health Problems of the Workers," *Four L Bulletin*, December 1923, 46–47.

[90] Charles Sharkey, "Department of Camp Cooking," *Four L Bulletin*, April 1919, 18.

[91] "How Sanitation Has Been Improved," *Four L Bulletin*, December 1919, 13.

[92] Hoy, *Chasing Dirt*, 141–42.

This attitude extended to the jobsite. When workers died at work, companies defended themselves by blaming sloppy, careless workers. First-aid and safety courses attempted to avoid employer liability, assuming that the onus for safety fell on workers, not employers.[93] R.A. Mullenger, safety engineer for the Bellingham Safety Council, commented that companies needed to educate workers on safety's value: "It requires constant hammering to get into the minds of men the necessity for caution."[94] A first-aid instructor employed by the Washington Department of Labor emphasized selling safety to loggers using modern advertising methods. Safety officers should "impress workmen with sincerity" and to "put it over with the men." Duncan assumed loggers would not implement safety programs on their own merits; rather, one had to appeal to their emotion and collective mentality to break through to them.[95]

However, without mandated safety changes, the toll of the timber industry was still terrible. Between 1918 and 1923, at least 912 people died in logging accidents in the state of Washington alone. Falling trees or branches caused 200 of these deaths, rolling logs 165, while flying logs attached to machinery that pulled them out of the ground killed 78.[96] In November 1923, at least 22 people died or suffered serious injury in the woods.[97] When injury or death occurred, worker compensation programs kicked in. Idaho reported that 30.8 percent of compensation claims between November 1, 1919, and July 31, 1920, came from timbering, for a total of 1,117 claims costing employers $177,799.19.[98] Many timber operators resented the system. A.W. Cooper, secretary-manager of the Western Pine Manufactures' Association, claimed loggers took advantage of the system all the time. He wanted workers to receive no benefits if they missed less than five days of work to stop lazy men from getting paid for lying around the house. He maintained, "these cases are so numerous that while the amount paid out is small, they increase the cost of administering the law and interrupt employment."[99]

93 See, e.g., Robert P. Duncan, "Teaching Safety to Industrial Workers," *The Timberman*, May 1922, 100, 102, and "Complete First-Aid Course Attracts Many Loggers and Sawmill Workers," *Four L Lumber News*, February 1, 1931, 24.

94 "Meeting Washington Loggers' Safety Committee," *The Timberman*, July 1921, 68.

95 Robert P. Duncan, "Teaching Safety to Industrial Loggers," *The Timberman*, May 1922, 100, 102.

96 "Fallers Top List of Fatal Accidents," *Four L Bulletin*, March 1924, 40–41.

97 "Fatal Accidents," *Four L Bulletin*, December 1923, 34.

98 "Can Logging Accidents Be Reduced?," *The Timberman*, October 1920, 78.

99 "The Oregon Compensation Law," *Four L Bulletin*, January 1923, 10, 36.

Sometimes the programs functioned smoothly. But injured loggers and their families found themselves fighting for fair compensation. E.S. Gill, supervisor of the Washington Industrial Training program, wrote to the Aloha Lumber Company complaining of the poor treatment of a fatally injured worker and his family. E.E. Thomas died from a crushed spine while logging. Washington law demanded a critically injured worker receive his own hospital room, something that Aloha ignored. In addition, it forced Thomas' brother-in-law to pay $110 for medical services. Gill requested Aloha repay the money. However, Aloha had limited incentive to follow the law. It received no fine or sanction from the state, nor did Gill threaten additional action if they did not pay. Gill only asked for Aloha's cooperation in the matter.[100]

The workers' compensation system made little difference in many injured workers' lives. Charles Roberts suffered a compound fracture of his right ankle while he loaded logs in 1919. It took eleven hours to get him to the nearest hospital. He had hobbled on the leg all day, making it worse. Then, the doctor did not set it right. Writing in old age, Roberts complained that he had had trouble with it for the rest of his life. Roberts also suffered an accident while hauling a water pipe up a steep incline in a push car. When the brakes failed, Roberts was thrown into the tracks and then run over. After several months in the hospital, the state gave him six hundred dollars in compensation, but no disability pay, despite injuries from which he never fully recovered.[101]

Despite the continued safety problems in the forests, the Four-L tried to foster an environmental memory among loggers, reminding them of their terrible lives a few years earlier. In doing so, the Four-L celebrated its own achievements, telling workers of the pointlessness of radicalism. In 1925, W.A. Kennedy wrote in the *Four L Bulletin* about his experiences before World War I, noting the exposure to the elements, lack of bathing facilities, and vermin-infested beds. Typically, he also focused heavily on the food, remembering "when the food was the cheapest, and poorly prepared; when real butter of milk was never seen, and fresh vegetables and eggs but seldom; and when . . . the cockroaches contended with the men for the food on the tables." Kennedy's lesson was that thanks to the Four-L, his memories were becoming relics of a distant

[100] E.S. Gill to Aloha Lumber Company, November 25, 1922, Aloha Lumber Company Collection, University of Washington Special Collections. Box 1, Folder P1319-4b.

[101] Charles C. Roberts, "The Luck of the Seventh Son" Unpublished Autobiography, Polson Museum, Hoquiam, WA, 16, 20–23.

past.[102] As late as 1958, timber executive George Lincoln Drake stated, "the Wobblies, of course, always claimed all the credit but I don't think that's right," instead crediting the government for the reforms.[103] Yet, for other observers of the forest, the IWW still received credit for the changes. The forester Robert Marshall, working in Idaho in 1925, observed that the improvements in camp life "can fairly be attributed to the I.W.W . . . they forced a revolution in sleeping quarters and today the dirty wooden bunks of yore have given place to iron cots and clean bedding."[104]

By 1924, the U.S. Forest Service (USFS) employees had begun comparing their own working conditions unfavorably with logging camps. Elers Koch, assistant district forester for USFS Region 1, wrote angrily to his bosses about the USFS' penny-pinching ways and the declining working conditions for its employees. He noted the great night of sleep he received in a comfortable logging camp that provided a good mattress and clean wool blankets. The next night, at the ranger station, he cursed his bed without a mattress and pillow and noted that such conditions were causing high rates of labor turnover.[105]

Four-L conditions may have generated jealousy from other forest workers, but environmental paternalism was only one strategy to undermine worker radicalism. Timber companies began experimenting in the 1910s with "gyppoing," or contracting out logging operations to independent operators, to get loggers to buy into production by giving them incentives as self-employed men. The Hill Logging Company made it clear to employees that it provided only a low base wage and that workers' real earnings were based on how hard they worked to produce more timber.[106] Companies immediately saw its advantage in undermining labor radicalism. Oregon's Clear Lake Lumber Company hired gyppos at its mills explicitly to undermine the IWW, even paying them so much "it nearly ruined us."[107]

102 W.A. Kennedy, "Early Days in a Sawmill," *Four L Bulletin*, April 1925, 12. See "The Lumberjack Returns," *Four L Lumber News*, January 1936, 28–29 for another excellent example of this genre.

103 Elwood Manuder interview with George Lincoln Drake, Forest History Society, November 10, 1958. University of Oregon Special Collections, 14.

104 Quoted in Paul S. Sutter, *Driven Wild: How the Fight against Automobiles Launched the Modern Wilderness Movement* (Seattle: University of Washington Press, 2002), 205.

105 Ellis Koch, "Memorandum for D," November 14, 1924, NARA, USFS Region 1, Box 1 Folder 1680 History Program NW History Prior to 1933.

106 "Bonus System Employed," *The Timberman*, July 1914, 48K.

107 Huntington Baylor to W.C. Rugenitz, December 5, 1936, Ruegnitz Papers, UW Box 1, Folder 14.

Gyppoing's anti-union implications quickly became clear. An underworld dictionary from 1927 defined gyppo as "a piece worker. A gyppos a goddam skunk what's too goddam mean to join a union."[108] By 1919, IWW bulletins referred to them as "scab jypos."[109] Ralph Winstead wrote, "the effects of gypoing are the same as those of scabbing. The only difference is that they are worse" because even union members saw it as a way to make money rather than viewing it as destroying solidarity. He challenged gyppos' masculinity, writing, "if there is a single spark of manhood in your over-worked carcasses ... pay attention to these words ... Right now is the time to quit. Don't be a gypo; be a man."[110] By 1925, the IWW blamed gyppoing for dividing workers. J.J. Dunning, president of the Wobbly loggers union, described the problem: "But the sound feeling of the more class conscious workers could not stop the practise [sic], and more and more men left the union of their class and followed after the gods of the petty bourgeois – each hoping to chop his way through the 'gypoed' forests to a home."[111] Many companies subcontracted their entire tree falling operations by the 1940s. The International Woodworkers of America, a CIO union created in 1937, wanted to organize gyppos, but found them unreceptive.[112] After World War II, unions mostly gave up on organizing gyppos. Whereas radicalism centered in the woods in the 1910s, by the 1930s the success of gyppos meant unions were largely a phenomenon of the timber mills.[113]

Promoting family was the third strategy to undermine radicalism. The Four-L consciously connected family and labor stability through constructing sanitary housing. University of California economist Cloice Howd encouraged the Four-L in this mission, identifying "better provision for family life in the camps" as the best way to end labor migration and radicalism.[114] The Puget Sound Lumber Company, near Twin, Washington, combined "livable" structures for workers' families with a

108 Elisha K. Kane, "The Jargon of the Underworld," *Dialect Notes*, Vol. 5, Part 10 (New Haven, CT: American Dialect Society, 1927), 449.

109 Strike Bulletin, October 13, 1919, Broussais C. Beck Papers, UW Box 2, Folder 14.

110 Ralph Winstead, "Chin-Whiskers, Hay-Wire and Pitchforks," *One Big Union Monthly*; found in Luke May Papers, Box 1, Folder 2, University of Washington Special Collections.

111 J.J. Dunning, "The Lumber Industry: Will Its Workers Awaken," *Industrial Pioneer* February 1926, 6–8.

112 "Hartung Calls on Unions to Go After 'Gypo' Mills, *Labor Newdealer*, January 27, 1939.

113 Denny Scott speech to Society of American Foresters, October 5, 1977, IWA Box 106, Folder 7.

114 Cloice Howd, "What Kind of Man Are You?," *Four L Bulletin*, July 1922, 10–11.

company store, a privately run movie house, a recreation room, and even a public school building for local children. The same company had another camp six miles away that had no female residents except for kitchen workers, no recreation facilities for loggers, and no modern camp facilities. YMCA observer Worth Tippy saw those workers spending their free hours lying on their filthy bunks, fighting, playing cards, and acting obscene. The difference was stark to Tippy, who recommended investing in family housing and closing these old camps.[115]

The Four-L created a short-lived auxiliary for its eastern Washington and Idaho camps. The Ladies Loyal Legion hoped to link families, stability, and labor cooperation, although it faded quickly when companies found it too expensive.[116] Companies also hoped hiring more women would tame their loggers. The Four-L's ideal female worker was Celia Pease, a nurse at the Snoqualmie Falls Lumber camp. Before Pease came on board, men took care of each other when injured, with blood poisoning a likely result. But a woman like Pease, who was "courteous and gracious with a personal charm that makes a visit to her little red and white, two-room hospital an event to be remembered," could take care of an injured man and nurse him back to health with a woman's touch.[117] For lumber executives, the presence of women meant they had won a major battle in the spatial revolution. C.C. McLean argued, "women make the beds in our camps, and I think that women in logging camps are an influence for good. They have a great influence on camp morals, making for cleaner language and better social conditions. A man will try to keep his bed in a better condition if he knows that a woman is going to clean up after him."[118]

American industries in the 1920s, such as Reo Motors in Lansing, Michigan, forged links between work, family, and masculinity in order to create a harmonious workplace where production and workers' living standards grew together.[119] By talking of logging in the woods as a "he-man's occupation" or through defining highclimbing, the job of climbing to the tops of trees to cut them off, as something that "lily-fingered college dudes" could never do, the Four-L appealed to loggers'

[115] Worth Tippy, *Report on the Logging Camps of the Pacific North West with Recommendations* (New York: Joint Committee on War Production Communities, 1919), 5.

[116] "Doings of the Three L," *Four L Bulletin*, June 1921, 30.

[117] "Miss Pease Takes Care of Injuries," *Four L Bulletin*, January 1921, 11.

[118] "McLean Favors Eight-Hour Logs," *Four L Bulletin*, November 1921, 4.

[119] Fine, *The Story of Reo Joe*, 38–61.

pride in the danger and physicality of their daily work, not as collective workers, but rather special individuals.[120] Charles O. Olson's poem "The Highclimber," printed in the *Four L Bulletin*, demonstrates how it united masculinity and the dangers of forest labor. After accomplishing his task, the highclimber bounds down the tree victoriously. There was a melody in his heart: "Bold as his courage and will/Fierce as his toil and its thrill/ Voice of the savage lust of strife." Why? Because he survived: "See him smile as he strides away!/He gambled with death and won – today."[121] The highclimber has a "the savage lust of strife," but he turns that lust against the tree rather than the employer. His manhood remained unquestioned so long as he directed his passions toward conquering nature instead of class warfare. Not only did the highclimber risk his life every day for his employer, but he also served as a model for others to follow in his masculine sacrifices for his work. Such constructions allowed companies to naturalize risk as manly while fighting against workers' demands for government intervention to protect their bodies from the hazards of the job.[122]

Companies worked to build these ideas of manhood in the aftermath to the Centralia Massacre. On November 11, 1919, the first anniversary of Armistice Day, the town of Centralia, Washington, celebrated with a parade. The local American Legion post, led by Warren Grimm, a former University of Washington football player, local lawyer, and veteran of World War I and the military mission against the Bolshevik Revolution, decided to turn the parade into an attack upon the IWW union hall.[123] This was the not first time that Centralia citizens had used violence against the Wobblies. In February 1915, citizens evicted forty Wobblies from town. In May 1918, marchers in a Red Cross parade destroyed the IWW hall. But the Wobblies kept returning. Throughout the summer and fall of 1919, the *Centralia Daily Chronicle* whipped up an anti-IWW frenzy, asking Centralia citizens whether the country would "go into a program of revolution ... or shall it remain American?"[124] The

[120] W.A. Kennedy, "Early Days in a Sawmill," *Four L Bulletin*, April 1925, 37; "Highclimbing" *Four L Bulletin*, September 1925, 12.

[121] Charles O. Olson, "The Highclimber," *Four L Bulletin*, May 1922, 11.

[122] Edward Slavishak, *Bodies of Labor: Civic Display and Labor in Industrial Pittsburgh* (Durham: Duke University Press, 2008), 5.

[123] See Stephen H. Norwood, *Strikebreaking and Intimidation: Mercenaries and Masculinity in Twentieth-Century America* (Chapel Hill: University of North Carolina Press, 2002), 15–33 on the relationship between college students and strikebreaking in the early twentieth century.

[124] "Propaganda of Class Hatred," The Centralia Daily Chronicle, July 25, 1919.

Legion planned to parade to the Wobbly office and tear the place apart, showing the radicals once and for all they were not welcome in Centralia.

The IWW learned of the impending attack and prepared to fight back, believing they had the legal right to defend their property. When the approximately fifty uniformed members of the American Legion reached the hall, they embarked upon their plan. Behind the door stood Wesley Everest and Rayfield Becker, both armed. Everest had organized loggers into the IWW since at least 1914, when he was arrested and jailed in a vigilante roundup of labor activists while working in a Coos County, Oregon, logging camp. As the marchers charged in, they fired into the crowd. On Seminary Hill, one quarter of a mile away, Wobbly shooters poured lead down from afar. Grimm was gunned down immediately from inside the hall. As Everest ran away, he shot Ben Casagranda, a shoeshine parlor owner, in the stomach, killing him. Arthur McElfresh had spent eighteen months in the army in France and managed a drugstore. He took a bullet in the brain. Everest ran toward the Skooumchuck River. Unable to cross due to high water, he waited for his pursuers. Among them was Dale Hubbard, a University of Washington graduate and former member of the Tenth Army Engineers. Everest shot Hubbard dead before the attackers overwhelmed him.[125] The Legionnaires beat Everest severely and threw him into a prison cell with other arrested Wobblies. That evening they took him from his jail cell and hanged him from a bridge. A jury found eight Wobblies guilty of second-degree murder and they received sentences ranging from twenty-five to forty years at the Washington State Prison in Walla Walla. Their cause served as a rallying cry for an increasingly marginalized IWW over the next twenty years.[126]

The Centralia Massacre became not only an excuse to crack down on radicalism, but also a rhetorical site where constructions of the meanings of work, nature, patriotism, and masculinity were publicly debated. Condemnations of the IWW after Centralia focused on the perceived differences between the union and the American Legion during wartime. For the Legion's defenders, Northwestern loggers had two options during the war: go fight in France or work diligently to cut down the trees necessary to destroy the Kaiser's forces. IWW members had done neither.

[125] Tyler, *Rebels of the Woods*; McClelland, *Wobbly War*; Tom Copeland, *The Centralia Tragedy of 1919: Elmer Smith and the Wobblies* (Seattle: University of Washington Press, 1993); *Seattle Post-Intelligencer*, November 12, 1919.

[126] Walker C. Smith, *Was It Murder? The Truth about Centralia* (Northwest District Defense Committee, 1922).

As the SPD's official history said, "this Northwest woods has become a field of honor; without the heroics, but not without the heroic ... There is the thrill of achievement; of men battling with Nature, with Nature's forces, and Nature's seeming whimsicalities."[127] But only certain men had the gumption to take up the battle with nature and they were not striking Wobblies.

The Centralia and Tacoma American Legion posts hired Ben Hur Lampman to write a pamphlet titled *Centralia Tragedy and Trial*. A nature writer for the Portland *Oregonian*, Lampman admitted writing propaganda, though he claimed that his work differed from that of the Wobblies because he wrote "the propaganda of truth."[128] Lampman continued impinging the manhood of the Wobblies. Because the IWW placed snipers on the hills around town and did not all face the Legionnaires straight on, they "violated the principles of manhood and self-defense ... and coolly butchered four followers of the flag."[129] They fired bullets from the hills "that plunged spitefully through the throngs of women and children on the gala streets ... As each hidden rifle cracked it spoke the welcome of radicalism to men who had returned from peril overseas." Despite their treasonous sabotage during the war, Wobblies wanted the full protections of the Constitution after the Centralia Massacre, something that Lampman wanted to deny them.[130]

In response, Wobbly defenders reminded their enemies of why loggers joined the union. According to radical writer Anna Louise Strong, Centralia prisoner Bert Bland became a Wobbly because of his experience in an overcrowded bunkhouse in a camp near Raymond, Washington. He could not stand it and "The bad conditions drove me/From camp to camp/Twenty-two different ones/In a single year/And only one of them all/Had a BATH!"[131] The IWW directly connected the massacre to the timber industry's unwillingness to allow loggers a decent life, noting in *The New Solidarity*, "when the lumber barons refused to grant decent wages and conditions to the workers, the latter organized and took these things," outraging the timber industry.[132]

[127] United States Army and United States Spruce Production Corporation, *History of the Spruce Production Division*, 117.
[128] Ben Hur Lampman, *Centralia Tragedy and Trial*, 71.
[129] Lampman, *Centralia Tragedy and Trial*, 47.
[130] Ibid., 14.
[131] Joyce Kornbluh, ed., *Rebel Voices: An I.W.W. Anthology*, 273.
[132] "Our Record Is Clean," *The New Solidarity*, November 25, 1919.

In defending the Centralia class war prisoners, the IWW built upon its prewar attempts to define loggers as a masculine proletariat defined by their toil in the forests for capitalists who sought to oppress them. An IWW flyer sent to Centralia citizens stated, "our manhood revolts at mob violence coming from the hands of the lumber barons."[133] Propagandists Ralph Chaplin and Walker Smith led the public defense. These texts relied heavily on constructions of white masculinity based in western nature, ideas the IWW often used in its western campaigns.[134] If the companies refused to provide workers homes worth the name, then they would call the union hall home, where the solidarity of their fellow workers would become their family. In 1918, the Wobblies had allowed Centralia citizens to destroy their union hall without a fight, but Chaplin asked how could men allow villains to attack their home repeatedly? They had the right by law to defend their property from attack and civilized men would not take this right away.[135] Instead, using the rhetoric of Western history, the Wobblies compared themselves to pioneers defending their wagons from an Indian attack. Chaplin equated the mob in Centralia to Indians, arguing that "the painted and be-feathered scalp hunter of the Sioux or Iroquois were not more heartless in maiming, mutilating, and killing their victims than the ... men who conceived the raid on the union hall in Centralia on Armistice Day." Centralia prisoner Eugene Barnett used the same analogy, comparing the raid to a savage Indian attack upon brave white settlers.[136] Walker Smith compared the attack upon the Centralia hall to Indian attacks on colonial American towns, comparing the torture and killing of white prisoners by Indians to the mutilation and death of Everest.[137]

Wobbly propagandists constructed those who had suffered and died fighting for all loggers as idealized masculine figures. Wesley Everest became a proletarian superhero. Wobbly publications described Everest as a "muscular and sun-burned young man with a rough, honest face and a pair of clear hazel eyes in which a smile was always twinkling." According to one document, his closest friends claimed, "he was never

[133] IWW Archive, University of Washington Special Collections, Box 3, Folder 1.

[134] Rebecca N. Hill, *Men, Mobs, and Law: Anti-Lynching and Labor Defense in U.S. Radical History* (Durham: Duke University Press, 2008), 18, 147–48; DePastino, *Citizen Hobo*, 95–126.

[135] Ralph Chaplin, *The Centralia Conspiracy*, 34–35.

[136] Chaplin, *The Centralia Conspiracy, 36; Walker C. Smith, Was It Murder? The Truth About Centralia* (Seattle: Northwest District Defense Committee, 1922), 47.

[137] Smith, *Was It Murder?* 47.

afraid of anything in all his life." When he had no choice but face the mob after failing to cross a river to escape, he turned and in a loud voice, proclaimed his willingness to surrender to any legal authority, which the savage mob ignored. When the crowd captured Everest they beat him and put a rope around his neck in a prelude to what they would do to him that night. Wobbly reports said that Everest simply responded: "You haven't got the guts to lynch a man in the daytime."[138] However, martyrdom made Wesley Everest more than a man. Wobbly songs compared Wesley Everest to the ultimate masculine figure: Jesus Christ. The song "Wesley Everest" began "Torn and defiant as a wind-lashed reed, Wounded he faced you as he stood at bay; you dared not lynch him in the light of day" and ended "A rebel unto Caesar – then as now – Alone, thorn-crowned, a spear wound in His side."[139] By fighting and dying for changes in working and living conditions for loggers, Wesley Everest became the personified idea of anti-capitalist proletarian manhood.

Wobblies constructing Wesley Everest as a masculine ideal contributed to Four-L anti-radical constructions of manhood. It was the idea of the single, masculine logger the company union worked to counter. In 1924, Guy E. Fuller, president of a Four-L local in Bend, Oregon, wrote a poem summing up how the Four-L saw itself breaking from the past of labor strife through employer leadership. The Four-L man worked hard for home and company and through this work, he attained working-class manhood, as opposed to the crazy Wobblies, with their "wild revolts [and] stupid hates." A decade earlier, "men burned the mills/In which they earned their bread/Then famine stalked a stricken land/And filled each home with dread." But then the Four-L revolutionized the workplace. Now "we ask as *man to man*/We believe there is no cleaner wealth/ Than won by work-worn hands/That there is dignity in toil/For this the 4L stands."[140] The IWW believed in dignity in toil as well, but for unionists, the toil was exploitation when it created profit for an employer. The Four-L spent twenty years trying to foster loyalty to employers through toil in sanitary conditions. But even while institutionalizing the sanitary revolution, it largely failed to instill that loyalty.

In 1918, the YMCA sent Worth Tippy to the Northwestern logging camps to understand how church communities could help solve logging

138 Ibid., 47, 64, 65, 38.

139 I.W.W. Songbook, Industrial Workers of the World Archive, University of Washington Special Collections, Box 7.

140 "Where the Four L Stands," *Four L Bulletin*, April 1924, 22. Italics in original.

camp problems. Tippy reported workers' deep distrust of the lumber companies and opposition to the Four-L. He discussed how workers "were solidly against" the Four-L and disbelieved it would maintain the eight-hour day and decent environmental conditions. Workers knew that companies profited unjustly off cheap timber land. Thus any lengthening of hours would "produce an explosion."[141] The federal government and Four-L may have begun to transform the workscape of the timber industry but building loyalty was a much harder project.

Loggers' suspicion of the Four-L did not dissipate over time. A logger calling himself "A wide awake worker" wrote to the "Editor of the Four Hell Lumber News," telling him, "I am a 4L member not because I want to be one, but because I was threathned [sic] with my job if I did not join and jobs being scarce I have to let them rob me out of a dollar every month. I dare not sign my name to this as I might loss [sic] my job."[142] Real worker representation still appealed to many loggers. With the IWW sidelined, the American Federation of Labor's small Timberworkers Union attempted to organize workers but a 1919 strike in Bellingham, Washington, failed. The union claimed that the Four-L sent in its people as strikebreakers. The Four-L denied this accusation but admitted membership had skyrocketed since the strike began.[143]

Despite repression, the IWW still had a presence in the forests, especially in eastern Washington and northern Idaho, where the 1917 strikes had begun. One Wobbly retrospective on the strikes in 1921 blamed the organization growing too rapidly and members falling away once the eight-hour day and better working conditions were achieved. Wobblies continued savaging the Four-L as a cheap company union that was a "direct emulation" of the IWW, granting the Wobbly program without giving workers power.[144] However, IWW publications' conversations about loggers became more vague and disconnected from workers struggles, with no sense of major organizing efforts or significant grassroots support. One article on timber mills in Tacoma noted, "efforts are being made to interest the mill workers in organization," but the article lacked evidence of worker interest or a sense of the

[141] Tippy, *Report on the Logging Camps of the Pacific North West with Recommendations*, 13–14.

[142] "A Wide Awake Worker to the Editor of the Four Hell Lumber News," William C. Ruegnitz Papers, University of Washington Special Collections, Box 2, Folder 50.

[143] "Legion Members Not Used to Break Strike," *Four L Bulletin*, November 1919, 10.

[144] John Hammer, "That Gentling Art," *Industrial Pioneer*, January 1922, 21–24.

strategy.[145] A short-lived Idaho-based strike to free the class war prisoners in 1923 briefly brought the IWW back to employers' attention, but it was quickly rebuffed.[146] While the Wobblies did not disappear from the woods entirely until the late 1930s, most workers did not look to the radical union as the answer to their problems. Perhaps the Wobblies' decline is best summed up in an IWW article by California Publicity Man subtitled, "Saddest feature is the apathy of the workers," blaming company spies for the union's inability to organize the redwood workers.[147]

A few workers maintained a radical stance by operating cooperatively owned mills on socialist principles. One started in Ballard, Washington, in 1917, surviving until 1931. Forty workers collectively ran the mill. Despite their radicalism, they needed loans to operate, which meant they had to rely on a capitalist banking system. They believed they had paid off most of the loan by 1931, but the bank claimed they had only paid the interest and refused to advance them any additional money to buy logs, bankrupting them. One worker wrote that this would never happen under a Soviet system, remarking "this should prove to workers that they can never expect to own anything under the capitalist system. The only way is to take control of the mills, mines, and shops, the whole state and government, and run them in the interest of the workers; not for bosses and bankers."[148]

This radical bent became more pronounced in the industry during the Great Depression, which devastated the timber industry. In 1923, as many as 495,586 people were employed in logging camps and sawmills, but in 1932 this dropped to only 124,997. Wages fell from an average of $19.34 a week in 1929 to $8.40 in March 1933.[149] A 1932 Four-L survey covering 2,320 camps and mills in Oregon, Washington, and Idaho showed that 35,250 workers had full-time employment, 29,263 had to make do with part-time work, and 58,235 were unemployed.[150] Approximately 20 percent of company unions around the nation dissolved between 1929 and

[145] "Organization in the Lumber Industry," *Industrial Pioneer*, August 1921, 23–24; "Tacoma, the Lumber Capital of America," *Industrial Pioneer*, November 1923, 13.

[146] Walter Galenson, *The CIO Challenge to the AFL: A History of the American Labor Movement, 1935–1941* (Cambridge: Harvard University Press, 1960), 382; Robert Ficken, *The Forested Land: A History of Lumbering in Western Washington* (Seattle: University of Washington Press, 1987), 163.

[147] California Publicity Man, "The Tragedy of the Redwoods," *Industrial Pioneer*, April 1924, 19–21.

[148] "Ballard News: Wage Cuts," *Seattle Unemployed Worker*, March 6, 1932.

[149] Ruegnitz to Dr. Isador Lubin, October 15, 1934, Ruegnitz Papers, Box 3, Folder 21.

[150] "4L Employment Letter," *Four L Lumber News*, January 1, 1931, 6.

1932 as companies looked to cut costs and the Four-L struggled to survive as companies withdrew because its wage rates were too high.[151] By the early 1930s, the Four-L had only a few thousand members left after peaking at more than 100,000 at the end of World War I. A major membership push in 1933 tripled the number of affiliated companies to 134, but it quickly declined from there.[152]

With economic hardship, workers increasingly resented Four-L claims to represent them. A Bend local demanded Four-L President William Ruegnitz's resignation in 1933 for telling Secretary of Labor Frances Perkins that he headed a labor organization. It then sent a resolution to all the Four-L locals and insisted upon a 20 percent wage increase for everyone in the industry.[153] Another local insisted that the Four-L reduce hours while keeping wages the same; soon after that same local dropped out of the organization after wages were cut. While Ruegnitz did not resign, and the workers did not receive their wage increase either, these actions suggest that loggers did not trust the Four-L as it stood but at least some sought to make it a real voice for them.[154] Another Four-L committee member slammed the organization in 1934 because they refused to raise wages, telling the organization's field officer, "the President [Ruegnitz] would see that these ... bastards paid a living wage but the 4L couldn't do it when a bunch of fat assed 4L officers and field men sat on their god damned fannies."[155] With workers taking matters into their own hands, the Four-L became increasingly irrelevant.

The Four-L fought this by appealing to workers over its wage and sanitation standards, even publicizing strikes occurring when workers wanted the same conditions the Four-L operations provided, such as a 1922 walkout in southern Oregon and northern California with loggers demanding Four-L standards. By taking on companies that undermined Four-L standards, the company union could reiterate to workers that it stood between them and unscrupulous employers while also sending the message to employers that it could provide labor peace.[156] It also hoped

[151] Jacoby, *Employing Bureaucracy*, 221, 226–27; H.L. Carlisle to W.C. Ruegnitz, May 28, 1935, Ruegnitz Papers, Box 1, Folder 9.

[152] "4L Membership Trebled," *Four L Lumber News*, November 1933, 21.

[153] Floyd Sullivan to All 4L Locals, May 27, 1933; Brooks-Scanlon 4L Local to Four L Headquarters, Ruegnitz Papers, Box 1, Folder 6.

[154] Resolution 83 and 84, Ruegnitz Papers, Box 4, Folder 2.

[155] Report from Field Officer Ford, July 12, 1934, Ruegnitz Papers, Box 4, Folder 12.

[156] "Yesterday and Today," *Four L Bulletin*, March 1923, 19; "Klamath Stakes All On 8 Hours," *Four L Bulletin*, April 1922, 6; "Union Allows Men to Return to Mills at Klamath Falls," *Four L Bulletin*, July 1922, 20.

New Deal legislation would revive the organization. Franklin Delano Roosevelt wanted industry support for his reform efforts and he created a series of labor boards that came close to endorsing company unions in 1934.[157] Four-L leaders believed the National Industrial Recovery Act took its mission from the organization and stated that Frances Perkins "sanctioned the 4L as the proper setup for collective bargaining in the lumber industry."[158] Given that the lumber code developed under the National Recovery Administration lowered hours while increasing wages, restoring the average minimum wage of 1929, it served to reinforce the Four-L's attempt to claim it operated in the workers' interest.[159] However, the Four-L found its optimism misplaced. In 1934, National Recovery Administration head Hugh Johnson called the Four-L a company union in a radio address. Ruegnitz protested it was not a company union but rather an "industry organization," one that happened to set wages and hours for the industry.[160] Its illusions shattered, the Four-L crowed when the Supreme Court ruled the NIRA unconstitutional in 1935.[161]

However, the National Labor Relations Act, passed in response to the Court's ruling, created the National Labor Relations Board, protected workers' right to organize and strike, and guaranteed collective bargaining for union contracts. The Four-L saw its demise at hand: "The Wagner Act as drawn up would lend aid to national unions who would like to destroy the 4L," the *Four L Lumber News* complained."[162] The NLRA also barred company unionism, which meant the end of the Four-L when the Court ruled in favor of its constitutionality in 1937.[163] Timber

157 Nelson Lichtenstein, *State of the Union: A Century of American Labor* (Princeton: Princeton University Press, 2002), 38; Irving Bernstein, *The Turbulent Years: A History of the American Worker, 1933–1941* (Boston: Houghton Mifflin, 1969), 318–39.

158 John F. Buchanan to J.M. Pond and J.E. Hellenius, May 23, 1933, Ruegnitz Papers, Box 4, Folder 20.

159 Rodney C. Loehr, ed., *Forests for the Future: The Story of Sustained Yield as Told in the Diaries and Papers of David T. Mason, 1907–1950* (St. Paul: Minnesota Historical Society, 1952), 99–107.

160 William C. Ruegnitz to General Hugh S. Johnson, March 15, 1934, Ruegnitz Papers, Box 3, Folder 17.

161 "A Death Blow," *Four L Lumber News*, June 1935, 3. See also Bernard Bellush, *The Failure of the NRA* (New York: Norton 1975); Colin Gordon, *New Deals: Business, Labor, and Politics in America, 1920–1935* (New York: Cambridge University Press, 1994).

162 "Disputes or Good Will," *Four L Lumber News*, May 1935, 3.

163 Lichtenstein, *State of the Union*, 37; G. William Domhoff and Michael J. Webber, *Class and Power in the New Deal: Corporate Moderates, Southern Democrats, and the Liberal-Labor Tradition* (Stanford: Stanford University Press, 2011), 104–41.

executives found their control over employees slipping away and were shocked to find that the federal government, which for decades had worked with industry against unions, had seemingly switched sides overnight. The timber industry had used the transformed timber camp landscape to control labor relations, but the Roosevelt administration eliminated that strategy.

Yet while the Four-L failed to build loyalty between workers and employers, it did help transform the filthy workscapes of the 1910s. The slow violence destroying loggers' lives in the filthy camps largely ended. Workers own activism played the vital role by forcing the government to intervene, leading to a company union that sought to buy off their anger through providing a modicum of sanitation. The timber unions that developed to replace the Four-L would have their own environmental critique of the timber industry, but notably sanitation, safe food, clean water, and disease were all off the table in the strikes of the 1930s. Even IWW remnants in Idaho understood the sanitary revolution had settled the issue. A flyer listing demands from a 1936 IWW strike included "the continuation of clean sheets," but no new sanitation issues.[164] The timber workplace remained violent due to the hazards of the job, but the slow violence destroying working bodies through disease, bad food, and a lack of cleanliness had become a relic of the past. The Four-L succeeded in improving the daily life of the timber worker, but completely failed in tampering down worker radicalism, which came roaring back in the 1930s.

[164] Potlatch Forests to R.R. McCartney, August 11, 1936, Ruegnitz Papers, Box 3, Folder 50.

3

Working-Class Forests

In April 1939, Harold Pritchett, president of the International Woodworkers of America, the nation's largest union of timber workers, went on KIRO radio station in Seattle to explain his union's program for forest conservation. Pritchett bluntly attacked the timber industry for its wasteful practices, noting, "under the present policy of timber destruction three feet of Northwest timber is being used for every new foot being grown." Saying the nation's forests were too important to serve corporate masters, Pritchett demanded an aggressive government-led reforestation program that would hire unemployed loggers and recharge the timber resource. He argued for federal policies mandating selective logging rather than the clear-cutting that deforested large patches of forest. Pritchett justified federal intervention by comparing it to the New Deal's expansion of government authority into public utilities, banking, and social security. Only through "initiating a forest program that is based on the needs and also the responsibilities of the forest land owners" under "federal control of forest cutting practices," Pritchett declared, could the forests of the Northwest remain productive for future generations.[1]

From its organization in 1937 through the early 1950s, the IWA articulated a powerful working-class voice for conservation, challenging the timber industry's control over the Pacific Northwest forests. The IWA was the first American labor union to make natural resource planning a

[1] Harold Pritchett, "How Can We Conserve Our Forest Resources," Radio Address on KIRO, April 23, 1939, reprinted in *The Timber Worker*, April 29, 1939.

central policy position.[2] It denounced timber companies for their cut-out and get-out attitude, resistance to reforestation, and indifference to the region's long-term future. It demanded greater government regulation of forests to make them work for laboring people's long-term economic security. In the midst of the Great Depression, Pritchett described an IWA vision for forestry that explicitly connected the work humans did in the forest and the work forests did for humans by providing building materials. Only through controlling both forms of labor could the nation achieve a sustainable timber supply and sustainable rural communities for the future. The IWA made alliances with conservationists that lasted for decades, including union support for early wilderness legislation. No grassroots organization before the environmental movement of the 1970s provided the timber industry with as strident a challenge to its forestry practices than the International Woodworkers of America.

The New Deal era created the conditions allowing for successful union organizing campaigns and facilitated the revival of the timber workers' radical tradition. Beginning with the passage of the National Industrial Recovery Act in 1933, millions of workers walked off the job to demand union recognition, higher wages, and shorter hours. Union contracts provided increased economic security, the definition of which expanded over time, eventually leading many unions to fight for health security through a national health insurance plan.[3] Security was even more

[2] Scott Dewey, "Working for the Environment: Organized Labor and the Origins of Environmentalism in the United States, 1948–1970," *Environmental History* 3, no. 1 (January 1998): 45–63, makes the argument that organized labor's entry into what he calls "proto-environmentalism" began after the Donora Fog of 1948, but the case of the IWA shows at least one union exploring these questions a decade earlier.

[3] Key overviews on the New Deal include William E. Leuchtenburg, *Franklin D. Roosevelt and the New Deal, 1932–1940* (New York: Harper & Row, 1963); Alan Brinkley, *The End of Reform: New Deal Liberalism in Recession and War* (New York: Knopf, 1995); Eric Rauchway, *The Great Depression and New Deal: A Very Short Introduction* (New York: Oxford University Press, 2008); Anthony J. Badger, *The New Deal: The Depression Years, 1933–40* (Chicago: Ivan R. Dee, 2002); David M. Kennedy, *Freedom from Fear: The American People in Depression and War* (New York: Oxford University Press, 1999); Ira Katznelson, *Fear Itself: The New Deal and the Origins of Our Time* (New York: Liveright, 2013). On the expansion of organized labor in the 1930s, see Irving Bernstein, *The Turbulent Years: A History of the American Worker, 1933–1941* (Boston: Houghton Mifflin, 1969); Lizabeth Cohen, *Making a New Deal: Industrial Workers in Chicago, 1919–1939* (New York: Cambridge University Press, 1990); Nelson Lichtenstein, *Walter Reuther: The Most Dangerous Man in Detroit* (Urbana: University of Illinois Press, 1997); Robert H. Zieger, *The CIO, 1935–1955* (Chapel Hill: University of North Carolina Press, 1995); Elizabeth Faue, *Communities of Suffering and Struggle: Women, Men, and the Labor Movement in Minneapolis, 1915–1945* (Chapel Hill: University of North Carolina

tenuous in rural America. A century of land mismanagement undermined the ability of farmers and natural resource industry workers to make a respectable living. Millions of rural people moved to the nation's cities in the early twentieth century, with the cities holding a majority of the nation's population by 1920. New Deal conservationists such as Secretary of Agriculture Henry Wallace, U.S. Forest Service Chief Ferdinand Silcox, and Soil Conservation Service head Hugh Bennett saw a denuded landscape stripped of its nutrients that led to interconnected natural and human disasters, most notably in the Dust Bowl. They sought to use state power to prevent future disasters, hoping to conserve both humans and nature through federal land management programs. Agencies such as the Soil Conservation Service, Civilian Conservation Corps and Resettlement Administration worked to stabilize both people and land. By the late 1930s, the growing science of ecology began influencing New Deal land managers. Ecologists such as Bennett and Paul Sears sought to bring "permanent agriculture" to the soil through the application of ecology to agriculture. Wallace and Silcox roiled the timber industry by pressing for public regulation of private forests, the expansion of national forest lands, and limiting clearcutting.[4]

Press, 1991); Rosemary Feurer, *Radical Unionism in the Midwest, 1900–1950* (Urbana: University of Illinois Press, 2006); David F. Selvin, *A Terrible Anger: The 1934 Waterfront and General Strikes in San Francisco* (Detroit: Wayne State University Press, 1996); Janet Irons, *Testing the New Deal: The General Textile Strike of 1934 in the American South* (Urbana: University of Illinois Press, 2000).

4 See Neil M. Maher, *Nature's New Deal: The Civilian Conservation Corps and the Roots of the American Environmental Movement* (New York: Oxford University Press, 2008), 43–55, 159–61. Other important work on the environment and the New Deal includes Sarah T. Phillips, *This Land, This Nation: Conservation, Rural America, and the New Deal* (New York: Cambridge University Press, 2007); Paul Sutter, *Driven Wild: How the Fight against Automobiles Launched the Modern Wilderness Movement* (Seattle: University of Washington Press, 2002); Sara M. Gregg, *Land Use Planning, the New Deal, and the Creation of a Federal Landscape in Appalachia* (New Haven: Yale University Press, 2010); and Randall S. Beeman and James A. Pritchard, *A Green and Permanent Land: Ecology and Agriculture in the Twentieth Century* (Lawrence: University Press of Kansas, 2001). On the Tennessee Valley Authority, see Philip Selznick, *TVA and the Grass Roots: A Study in the Sociology of Formal Organization* (New York: Harper and Row, 1966); Michael McDonald and John Muldowny, *TVA and the Dispossessed: The Resettlement of Population in the Norris Dam Area* (Knoxville: University of Tennessee Press, 1982); William U. Chandler, *The Myth of TVA: Conservation and Development in the Tennessee Valley, 1933–1983* (Cambridge, MA: Ballinger Publishing Company, 1984); Nancy L. Grant, *TVA and Black Americans: Planning for the Status Quo* (Philadelphia: Temple University Press, 1990). On the Soil Conservation Service, R. Douglas Hurt, "The National Grasslands: Origin and Development in the Dust Bowl," *Agricultural History* 59 (April 1985): 246–59; and R. Douglas Hurt, "Dust Bowl: Drought, Erosion, and Despair on the Southern Great

This chapter explores how the IWA combined the radicalism of left-leaning labor unions with conservationists' critique of corporate despoliation of natural resources in order to fight for community stability in an ecosystem threatened by rapacious private forestry. Its leaders believed stabilizing communities through sustained-yield forestry with government assistance to small operators would create working-class security and a permanent industry. In 1945, the union hired a professional forester named Ellery Foster to push its agenda in Congress. This ended in disappointment when federal agencies and corporate interests combined by the 1950s to increase logging rates, leading the Northwest on an IWA-predicted path to liquidate its timber by the year 2000.[5] Growing anti-union and anti-radical sentiment after World War II, a more conservative Congress, and the return of the presidency to Republicans in 1953 led to dashed hopes of an expanded New Deal state, national health insurance, and the application of ecological principles to land management. It also doomed the IWA attempt to make forest policy serve the Northwest's working class.

CONSERVATION AND THE INTERNATIONAL WOODWORKERS OF AMERICA

The West Coast had long seen union battles between radicals and political conservatives. The American Federation of Labor's opposition to Industrial Workers of the World activities in the West mirrored its actions around the nation, and the AFL helped facilitate official repression of the IWW during the Red Scare. The New Deal's pro-labor legislation spurred a new round of organizing in the West,

Plains," *American West* 14 (January 1977): 22–27, 56–57; Neil Maher, "'Crazy Quilt Farming on Round Land': The Great Depression, the Soil Conservation Service, and the Politics of Landscape Change on the Great Plains during the New Deal Era," *Western Historical Quarterly* 31 (Summer 2000): 319–39.

[5] On the New Deal push for working-class security are Cohen, *Making a New Deal; Lichtenstein, The Most Dangerous Man in America; Jennifer Klein, For All These Rights: Business, Labor, and the Shaping of America's Public-Private Welfare State* (Cambridge: Harvard University Press, 2003); Roy Lubove, *The Struggle for Social Security, 1900–1935* (Cambridge: Harvard University Press, 1968); James Patterson, *America's Struggle against Poverty, 1900–1994*, 3d edn. (Cambridge: Harvard University Press, 1994); Gail Radford, *Modern Housing for America: Policy Struggles in the New Deal Era* (Chicago: University of Chicago Press, 1996); Landon R.Y. Storrs, *Civilizing Capitalism: National Consumers' League, Women's Activism, and Labor Standards in the New Deal Era* (Chapel Hill: University of North Carolina Press, 2000).

rejuvenating these battles between powerful unions, perhaps most famously with Harry Bridges International Longshore and Warehouse Union against Dave Beck's International Brotherhood of Teamsters.[6] These divides would also help define the timber unionism spurred by the New Deal. The United Brotherhood of Carpenters (UBC) claimed jurisdiction over timber workers and 100,000 loggers became UBC members between 1935 and 1937, after the Great Strike of 1935 forced recalcitrant companies to the bargaining table. However, the Carpenters did not grant full union rights to the loggers. Politically conservative UBC President Bill Hutcheson worried about the effect that thousands of ex-Wobblies and communists would have on his union's politics. Loggers grew restless over having no voice in their union. Many wanted the industrial unionism model of the newly created Committee for Industrial Organization (soon to be the Congress of Industrial Organizations).[7]

In 1937, dissenters created the International Woodworkers of America, led by Harold Pritchett, a Canadian shingle weaver and communist, and affiliated with the CIO. The IWA and UBC spent the next four years in a jurisdictional war. UBC members picketed IWA mills and its Teamsters allies refused to move IWA processed timber.[8] By the end of 1941, the IWA represented about 100,000 loggers centered in western Oregon and Washington, as well as semi-autonomous Canadian locals.[9] The UBC had 35,000 timber workers, dominating northern California's redwood forests in particular. These two unions were fundamentally oppositional in political leanings, leadership structure, and environmental policy. The IWA would be nearly torn apart by communism, with the Oregon locals revolting against the Canadian communist Pritchett, leading to John L. Lewis sending Adolph Germer, his chief anti-communist troubleshooter, to the Northwest. Combined with the U.S. government denying Pritchett an entry visa in 1940, a series of anti-communist presidents took over union leadership. Yet

[6] Jennifer Luff, *Commonsense Anticommunism: Labor and Civil Liberties between the World Wars* (Chapel Hill: University of North Carolina Press, 2012); Richard White, *"It's Your Misfortune and None of My Own": A New History of the American West* (Norman: University of Oklahoma Press, 1991), 488–91.

[7] Melvyn Dubofsky and Warren Van Tine, *John L. Lewis: A Biography* (New York: Quadangle Press, 1977), 211–21.

[8] Bruce Nelson, *Workers on the Waterfront: Seamen, Longshoremen, and Unionism in the 1930s* (Urbana: University of Illinois Press, 1988), 224.

[9] While it would be an interesting case study to compare IWA forestry policy in Canada and the United States, for the purposes of this book, Canada is outside its purview.

while political divisions roiled the IWA in its early years, none of this significantly affected its environmental policy.[10]

In March 1938, Franklin Roosevelt toured western Washington, which faced severe timber depletion after decades of heavy logging. During his trip, Roosevelt called the nation's disappearing timber resources "a matter of vital national concern." He expressed dismay over lax reforestation efforts and erosion and urged legislation to increase land acquisition for the national forests, provide funding for fire suppression, and create employment through reforestation, leading to the Joint Congressional Committee on Forestry in the early 1940s.[11] The IWA used Roosevelt's speech to launch its own forestry program based upon its vision of an activist government creating working class security through full employment,

[10] On the battles between communists and anti-communists within the IWA, see Jerry Lembcke & William M. Tattam, *One Union in Wood: A Political History of the International Woodworkers of America* (New York: International Publishers, 1984). On the Great Strike of 1935, see Irving Bernstein, *The Turbulent Years: A History of the American Worker, 1933–1941* (Boston: Houghton Mifflin, 1969), 624–32. On communism during the 1930s, see Randi Storch, *Red Chicago: American Communism at Its Grassroots* (Urbana: University of Illinois Press, 2007); Harvey Klehr, *The Heyday of American Communism: The Depression Decade* (New York: Basic Books, 1984); Mark Solomon, *The Cry Was Unity: Communists and African-Americans, 1917–1936* (Jackson: University Press of Mississippi); Robin D.G. Kelley, *Hammer and Hoe: Alabama Communists during the Great Depression* (Chapel Hill: University of North Carolina Press, 1990); Bert Cochran, *Labor and Communism: The Conflict That Shaped American Unions* (Princeton: Princeton University Press, 1977); Vernon Pedersen, *The Communist Party in Maryland, 1919–57* (Urbana: University of Illinois Press, 2001); Roger Keeran, *The Communist Party and the Auto Workers Unions* (Bloomington: University of Indiana Press, 1980); Fraser Ottanelli, *The Communist Party of the United States: From the Depression to World War II* (New Brunswick, NJ: Rutgers University Press, 1983); Paul Buhle, *Marxism in the USA from 1870 to the Present Day* (London: Verso, 1987); Mark Naison, *Communists in Harlem during the Depression* (Urbana: University of Illinois Press, 1983); Joshua Freeman, *In Transit: The Transport Workers Union in New York City, 1933–1966* (New York: Oxford University Press, 1986); Vernon H. Jensen, *Lumber and Labor* (New York: Farrar and Rinehart, 1945), 164–85; Walter Galenson, *The United Brotherhood of Carpenters: The First Hundred Years* (Cambridge: Harvard University Press, 1983), 256–66; Zieger, *The CIO, 1935–1955*; Lisa Philips, *A Renegade Union: Interracial Organizing and Labor Radicalism* (Urbana: University of Illinois Press, 2013).

[11] Franklin D. Roosevelt, *The Public Papers and Addresses of Franklin D. Roosevelt 1938* (New York: *The MacMillan Company*, 1941), 144–50. See also, "F.D. Talks Turkey On Need to Check Depletion in U.S.A.," *The Timber Worker*, March 26, 1938. On FDR's interest in forestry, see Thomas W. Patton, "Forestry and Politics: Franklin D. Roosevelt as Governor of New York," *New York History* 75, no. 4 (October 1994): 397–418. On the Joint Congressional Committee on Forestry, see William Robbins, *American Forestry: A History of National, State, and Private Cooperation* (Lincoln: University of Nebraska Press, 1985), 133–34.

income redistribution, and the end of corporate control over the landscape. Although nearly silent on forestry issues before Roosevelt's visit, immediately after it became a central concern for the union, suggesting that IWA leaders saw conservation as a hammer to use against the timber companies rather than an ideological commitment, at least at first. Don Hamerquist, a logger and IWA organizer, wrote in the IWA newspaper *The Timber Worker* that he had given up hope that capitalist timber companies would manage the forests sustainability, stressing "the workers must drive hard for conservation and reforestation before the state is turned into a Gobi desert." He concluded that timber executives should face charges for "conspiracy against posterity."[12] IWA Plywood District Council President W.J. Baker agreed: "The timber barons don't seem to care what the next generations have or what happens to the logger. If we sit down and continue to let these forests go down with no thought of their preservation, we can blame no one but ourselves when the time comes to shut the sawmills down for want of logs."[13]

For the next decade, the IWA tied sustainable forestry with good wages guaranteed by union contracts to create a long-term basis for working-class security in the Northwest forests. Union leadership told its members in 1938, "we shall unite in every honest effort to save the forests. Real conservation, selective logging, sustained yield, reforestation, fire preventions – coupled with union recognition, union wage scales, means sustained prosperity in the lumber industry for all!"[14] Viewing the exploitation of both labor and nature as the result of corporate greed, IWA officials saw the New Deal state as the last best hope to reroute forestry's trajectory in order to prevent a future of deforestation and poverty, erosion, and community instability.

Marshaling union and state power was an immediate concern because communities across the Northwest already felt the impact of deforestation and poor timber management. This was a particular problem in the Grays Harbor region of southwestern Washington. The union counted seventy-six towns in the region that had completely disappeared due to forest depletion and another seventy-seven in decline. The union noted in 1939, "a trip to the Grays-Willapa Harbor country in Washington will show pretty clearly the economic decay and community desolation that await the people of that cut-over forest area, unless some miraculous substitute

[12] Don Hamerquist, "Timber Is a Crop?" *The Timber Worker*, April 16, 1938.
[13] W.J. Baker, "Save Our Forests!" *The Timber Worker*, April 2, 1938.
[14] "Support Grows for Selective Logging," *The Timber Worker*, October 22, 1938.

is discovered. Security and stability – continued existence perhaps – these are the things at stake."[15]

The IWA's challenge to timber capitalism fell within an already existing debate over private forestry. Early twentieth-century conservation efforts led to calls to regulate private forestry as the nation's timber supplies dwindled. In 1919, the Society of American Foresters issued a report urging federal regulations to promote fire protection and reforestation, creating a rift between the society and many of the nation's largest timber operators.[16] The Great Depression's environmental crises provided openings for broader participation in natural resource debates. The Roosevelt administration used natural resource agencies to build political support, showing the government providing concrete benefits for land and citizens.[17] The IWA used some of those same agencies to press its own agenda. It could do so because leading conservationists and administration officials also connected poor resource management and community instability, bemoaned the nation's poor conservation record, and sought to use the New Deal state to provide a stable rural economy based on sound land management practices.

Roosevelt naming Ferdinand Silcox as Forest Service chief in 1933 upped the pressure on the timber industry. Silcox had worked in the Northwest since the USFS' first days, and became sympathetic to timber workers' plight.[18] At the 1935 Society of American Foresters conference, Silcox told the timber industry to choose between its current exploitative path and federal regulation of private forestry to stabilize communities. This outraged timber executives, who responded by trying to undermine Silcox in the media, halls of Congress, and Roosevelt administration, referring to his plan as socialism.[19] Silcox gained an ally in the IWA. After a mill in Malone, Washington, shut down in 1938, the IWA used it as an example of the irresponsibility of private forestry. Depleted of

[15] Proceedings of 3rd Constitutional Convention, 1939, International Woodworkers of America Papers, Special Collections, University of Oregon (hereafter IWA except where specified) Minutes of the Executive Board Meeting, 18 October 1936), Box 25, Folder 3.

[16] Harold K. Steen, *The U.S. Forest Service: A History*, Centennial edn. (Seattle: University of Washington Press, 2004), 177–79.

[17] Phillips, *This Land, This Nation*, 3.

[18] E.I. Kotok and R.F. Hammatt, "Ferdinand Augustus Silcox," *Public Administration Review* 2, no. 3 (Summer 1942): 240–53.

[19] Robert Ficken, *The Forested Land: A History of Lumbering in Western Washington* (Seattle: University of Washington Press, 1987), 217–18; David Clary, *Timber and the Forest Service* (Lawrence: University Press of Kansas, 1986), 70, 104–07.

timber supplies because of "unbridled greed," the union fretted that much of southwest Washington could soon follow it into oblivion. Only working-class pressure on Washington to insist "on the New Deal conservation policies as expressed by Chief Forester F.A. Silcox" could save towns like Malone.[20]

The IWA used the history of forestry to contextualize its apocalyptic vision of the corporate logging future, with deforested mountainsides, erosion, and widespread unemployment. When corporations deforested a region, they could pick up and move operations to a new forest, as they had moved from Wisconsin and Michigan to Oregon and Washington.[21] Loggers who had followed the timber industry from the Great Lakes to the Northwest remembered the environmental destruction of migratory capital. G.D. Meek reminded his union brothers how the timber industry destroyed the forests of his beloved Michigan, and that it was a "duty to our children" to protect the Northwest from the same fate.[22] When Silcox publicly warned of the Northwest becoming the next deforested and impoverished Great Lakes cutover, the IWA agreed, pointing to the region "as an example of timber butchery."[23] The USFS continued to help the IWA build these connections. In 1939, future USFS Chief Lyle Watts spoke to the IWA annual convention, explaining, "there is still time to avoid the mistakes made in the forests adjacent to the Atlantic Seaboard, in the Appalachians, and in the Lake States," but only if loggers "are willing to take remedial action."[24]

The IWA took up Watts' challenge, urging members to see the specter of the capitalist despoliation of the landscape for themselves. Rain and snowmelt washed soil from deforested mountains into the Puget Sound in the spring of 1938, causing it to turn brown near the shoreline. A *Timber Worker* editorial blamed the erosion and brown water on private forestry,

[20] "Ghost Town Follows Boss Greed," *The Timber Worker*, August 19, 1939, 4.

[21] On the timber industry in the Great Lakes region, see William Cronon, *Nature's Metropolis: Chicago and the Great West* (New York: Norton, 1991), 148–206; Charles E. Twining, *Downriver: Orrin H. Ingram and the Empire Lumber Company* (Madison: State Historical Society of Wisconsin, 1975); Robert F. Fries, *Empire in Pine: The Story of Lumbering in Wisconsin, 1830–1900* (Madison: State Historical Society of Wisconsin, 1951); Willard Hurst, *Law and Economic Growth: The Legal History of the Lumber Industry in Wisconsin* (Cambridge: The Belknap Press of Harvard University Press, 1964).

[22] G.D. Meek, "Conservation – A Duty to Posterity," *The Timber Worker*, April 9, 1938.

[23] "Chief Forester Warns of Wood Famine," *The Timber Worker*, January 28, 1939.

[24] Speech of L.F. Watts, October 19, 1939 IWA, Box 25, Folder 3.

calling corporate leaders "criminally guilty of causing floods. Their reckless depletion of the Northwest's greatest natural resource has recently been scathingly criticized by President Roosevelt."[25] As fires consumed the forest that summer, union writers accused companies of allowing them "to burn a little, or much, rather than take precautionary steps."[26] The Northwest reeled from many large fires in the 1930s, including the Tillamook Burn of 1933, which torched 311,000 acres of prime timberland in northwest Oregon. *Timber Worker* articles on fires repeatedly made the point that fires equaled unemployment and undermined communities' futures. One writer noted that 250 acres of timber would keep a logger employed for one year and that when a fire burned it, "someone has the right to get good and mad. There went a job."[27]

Ultimately, the future of the forests and the Northwest's working class was at stake. A 1938 IWA editorial lambasted the timber industry's lackadaisical approach to preserving community stability through reforestation, noting that nature might reforest logged-off lands, but the industry neglects to "think of the children of those lumber workers, who cannot wait until the year 2000 before they get their first pay check off those 'fairly well-stocked' areas."[28] To ensure community security, the IWA would seek to influence national forestry legislation.

OLYMPIC NATIONAL PARK

In 1938, Monrad Wallgren, a New Dealer congressman from Washington, introduced a bill to create Olympic National Park. The bill added 400,000 acres to the current national monument boundaries to construct a 900,000-acre park with some of the last old-growth, low-elevation forests in western Washington.[29] While many in Washington

[25] "When Puget Sound Is Muddy," *The Timber Worker*, April 30, 1938.

[26] "Who Will Stop the Fires," *The Timber Worker*, July 30, 1938.

[27] "Forests and Jobs," *The Timber Worker*, June 22, 1940, 4. On the fires of the 1930s, see Gail Wells, *The Tillamook: A Created Forest Comes of Age*, 2d edn. (Corvallis: Oregon State University Press, 2003); Nancy Langston, *Forest Dreams, Forest Nightmares: The Paradox of Old Growth in the Inland West* (Seattle: University of Washington Press, 1995), 248.

[28] "Pacific Logging Congress: An Editorial, *The Timber Worker*, October 29, 1938.

[29] The most comprehensive study of Olympic National Park's creation is Carsten Lien, *Olympic Battleground: The Power Politics of Timber Preservation* (San Francisco: Sierra Club Books, 1991). See also Ben W. Twight, *Organizational Values and Political Power: The Forest Service versus the Olympic National Park* (State College: The Pennsylvania State University Press, 1983); Paul Hirt, *A Conspiracy of Optimism: Management of the National Forests since World War Two* (Lincoln: University of Nebraska Press), 37–38;

supported a mountain and glacier park, including commercially viable timber caused consternation. The USFS opposed the loss of control over the area while local newspapers attacked Wallgren and Secretary of the Interior Harold Ickes, the park's most powerful supporter in Washington. The editor of the *Forks Forum* charged Wallgren with caring more about New York tourists than the people of his home state and the Roosevelt administration of trampling on the rights of local people to develop land.[30] The Hoquiam Chamber of Commerce requested an investigation of Ickes from Martin Dies' House Un-American Activities Committee, accusing administration officials of tying up the peninsula's resources to serve America's enemies.[31]

The IWA invited Wallgren to pen an editorial for *The Timber Worker* explaining the bill. Calling the park a magnet for "increased tourist travel from California," he promoted tourism as a job creator in a forest whose long-term sustainability remained in question, creating a diversified Northwest economy that would provide economic stability if the timber industry cut the rest of the forest. The IWA lauded the bill as "a move to conserve the timber and other natural resources from greedy and rapid depletion," and noted that local residents would make more money on the tourist industry over the long run than through logging the forests.[32]

However, the IWA also faced resistance in its claim to speak for loggers about conservation. The United Brotherhood of Carpenters offered a very different view in the first major policy battle between these unions. The UBC claimed to support conservation. It favored reforestation and fire suppression, but also called for the mass poisoning of all chipmunks for eating tree seeds that challenged maximum forest production.[33] Reflecting the UBC's distrust of the New Deal, it believed the federal government had too much control over the forests and that labor should restrict collective

Gerald W. Williams, *The U.S. Forest Service in the Pacific Northwest: A History* (Corvallis: Oregon State University Press, 2009), 126–27.

30 "Hoh River News," *Forks Forum* June 2, 1938; "Hoh River News," *Forks Forum* November 30, 1939.

31 "Hoh River News," *Forks Forum* November 3, 1939.

32 Minutes of the Executive Board Meeting, October 18, 1936. IWA Box 14, Folder 1; Minutes of the Executive Board Meeting October 31, 1937, IWA Box 14, Folder 2; Mon C. Wallgren, "The Wallgren Bill," *The Timber Worker*, April 9, 1938.; "Timber Barons Use Censorship in Effort to Kill Wallgren Bill," *The Timber Worker*, May 28, 1938; "Bosses Would Carve Up New Olympic Park; U.S. Wouldn't," *The Timber Worker*, October 29, 1938.

33 "Real Reforestation Program Needed to Perpetuate Forests," *The Union Register*, October 27, 1939.

bargaining to wages, hours, and working conditions while trusting industry directives on forestry.

The UBC rejected the IWA's environmental critique of corporate forestry as another front in the CIO's attempt to bring communism into the United States. E.A. Stewart wrote in December 1939 that the IWA focused on conservation to cover up its failed communist policies. With the "unexpected alliance of Joe Stalin and his comrade in arms and ideologies Adolf," Stewart wrote that IWA morale had collapsed. To distract its members' attention, IWA leaders "now pose as conservationists deluxe, and are pointing the way to the salvation of the lumber industry in North America," Stewart sarcastically proclaimed.[34] The Carpenters claimed the park would throw 12,000 loggers out of work. It called the idea to include large amounts of timber in the park "asinine" and mocked the arguments of Wallgren and the IWA of building a tourist economy, noting of a poorly attended 1937 trip to the Olympics, "how ridiculous it is to lock up enough timber to perpetually employ ten thousand men in order that thirteen people annually can make pilgrimages through virgin timber."[35]

In June 1938, Roosevelt signed the bill that created Olympic National Park. Although smaller and including less timber than Wallgren and the IWA hoped, it gave the president authorization to expand the park after a year, which Roosevelt did in 1940 and again in 1943 to protect the forests cut out of the original legislation.[36] The IWA celebrated the protection of rare virgin timber for the future enjoyment of its members and noted it would protect the famous herds of Roosevelt elk, "where these magnificent animals will be protected against further slaughter."[37] Congressman John Coffee reported to the 1938 IWA Convention that the union had endeared itself to Ickes "because it had the intestinal fortitude and temerity to stand up and fight for conservation of the most beautiful things that God ever created – and that's an old-growth virgin fir tree."[38]

The union's success in pushing for Olympic National Park was a successful trial run for its effort to wrest natural resource policy away from the timber companies and create a more sustainable economy and

[34] E.A. Stewart, "Conservation Being Used by IWA to Cover Up Fast Falling Morale," *Union Register*, December 15, 1939.

[35] "Plan Threatens Harbor Mills," *Union Register*, February 25, 1938; "Park Threatens Future Logging," *Union Register*, March 4, 1938; "Local Unions Urged to Send Resolutions against Park Proposal to Congress," *Union Register*, March 18, 1938.

[36] Lien, *Olympic Battleground*, 167–212.

[37] Olympic Park is Assured by Solons," *The Timber Worker*, July 2, 1938.

[38] Proceedings of 2nd Constitutional Convention, 1938, IWA Box 25, Folder 2.

forest for the future. In the following decade, the IWA would make conservation central to its mission, providing the strongest working-class challenge to corporate forestry in the Northwest's history.

IWA FORESTRY

As the United States prepared to fight World War II, the IWA worried about its implications for natural resource policy. World War I had led to a rapid increase in timber production for airplanes. In 1940, Wilson Compton of the National Lumber Manufacturers Association called for five billion board feet of lumber for national defense. The IWA fretted about the long-term effects private control would have on the forests when regulation took a back seat to war production. But when Henry Wallace supported a more sustainable cut of spruce than World War I, the IWA thought a war might leave forests in shape to build sustainable forestry after its conclusion.[39]

Like the rest of organized labor, the IWA gave the war effort its full support when the United States entered the war in December 1941, agreeing to a no-strike pledge and putting its conservation agenda aside for the duration. Yet environmental concerns did not disappear. IWA District 2 worried about "reactionary forces" attempting to reduce forestry appropriations, placing the need for conservation in terms of "the fire hazard that can and may be created by Axis invaders."[40] However, when an Anacortes, Washington, local wrote a resolution in 1943 opposing a state bill to place state timber lands in the hands of industry without public input on forestry practices and called for state conversation through an elected board, the international declined to act on it.[41]

As the war neared its end, the IWA refocused on forestry policy, believing its conservation plan had a key role to play in the postwar world. The 1944 IWA Convention Officers' Report proclaimed, "following the war we can

[39] For the full text of the Wallace letters, see Henry Wallace to John Boettinger, August 20, 1940, NARA Seattle, RG 95, Records of the U.S. Forest Service, Region 1, Missoula, MT, Historical Collection, ca. 1905–1990, Box 8, Folder, Direction – Historical Nat'l Forest Program, 1940–42. See also "Five Billion Board Feet of Lumber For Defense," *Timber Worker*, August 17, 1940; "Excess Private Control, Cut-Out Get-Out Policy Major Timber Problems," *Timber Worker*, August 31, 1940; "More Public Ownership Needed to Solve Timber Problem," *Timber Worker*, September 7, 1940; "National Defense Must Mean Forest Defense," *Timber Worker*, September 7, 1940.

[40] Proceedings of 6th Annual Convention Northern Washington District Council No. 2, 1942, IWA Box 27, Folder 11.

[41] "Subject: Protection of State Forest Lands," IWA Box 37, Folder 1.

have an expanding economy and stability in the forest industry only by rebuilding and improving the forest resources and regulating their exploitation."[42] The 1944 CIO Convention passed a resolution supporting the public regulation of private forestry with major union leaders such as the United Auto Workers' Richard Frankensteen speaking publicly of labor's newfound interest in sustainable forestry. The CIO assigned Assistant General Council Anthony Smith to support its new forestry resolution in Washington. Smith, who later served as head of the National Parks and Conservation Association, became an important ally for the IWA.[43]

Most importantly, the IWA named forester Ellery Foster the head of its newly created Research, Education, and Statistical Department in 1945. Foster was the first professional forester ever employed by an American labor union. Foster had worked for the USFS in the 1920s and 1930s and was Minnesota State Forester from 1937 to 1939 before being forced out for publicly denouncing Governor Harold Stassen's forestry policy. He later headed a committee to remember the legacy of recently deceased foresters Robert Marshall and Ferdinand Silcox.[44] During World War II, Foster worked with the Lumber Division of the War Production Board, resigning to work for the IWA after CIO official Leo Goodman introduced him to IWA leaders.[45] Foster provided needed expertise and credibility to the union view that corporate control over the land and labor was destructive. Foster helped bridge the IWA's and CIO's notion of economic and social security for the American working class with conservationists' concerns with American land and resources that lacked a strong connection to populist impulses. However, with Foster's hiring, the IWA forestry plan would be funneled almost entirely through him, making this program a top-down exercise that did not engage the rank and file.

[42] Proceedings of 8th Constitutional Convention, 1944, IWA Box 25, Folder 5.

[43] Proceedings of 9th Constitutional Convention, 1945, IWA Box 25, Folder 6; Richard T. Frankensteen, "Labor's Interest in Forestry," *Journal of Forestry* 42, no. 11: (November 1944): 805–07.

[44] Raphael Zon to Ellery Foster, June 12, 1939, Folder Correspondence and Other Papers, April-July 1939, Raphael Zon Papers, Minnesota Historical Society, Box 10. Officers Report to the 9th Constitutional Convention of the IWA Box 37, Folder 7; Foster to Zon, June 14, 1940, folder Correspondence and Other Papers, June–Sept 1940, box 11; Foster to Zon, October 27, 1940; Zon to Foster, November 6, 1940; Zon Papers, both folder Correspondence and Other Papers, Oct–Dec 1940, Box 11. On Zon, see Norman J. Schmaltz, "Raphael Zon: Forest Researcher," *Journal of Forest History* 24, no. 1 (January 1980): 24–39.

[45] Lembcke, *One Union in Wood*, 123.

The fight for sustainable forestry dominated postwar IWA political action. The nation needed between 3.5 and 5 million new homes to replace its dilapidated housing stock. The government created incentives for single-family housing over the next decade through Federal Housing Administration mortgage insurance, GI Bill benefits, and the Interstate Highway Act of 1956, connecting suburban housing to jobs in the cities. The Department of Veterans Affairs guaranteed 2.5 million home mortgages between 1944 and 1952, and between 1945 and 1966 the FHA and VA insured half of California's new home mortgages.[46]

For this timber, the nation relied on an industry that mismanaged its land. By hiring Foster, the IWA tapped into professional discontent at a time when the union movement entered new policy debates. The CIO had supported "slum clearance" and federal housing from its beginning. Good housing was central to working-class security and the lynchpin to the IWA's role in creating the postwar consumers' republic. The IWA congratulated itself at its 1946 Convention for not joining other unions in that year's strike wave, "despite the fact that almost every provocation to strike was thrown at us", choosing instead to remain at the bargaining table with employers and produce housing for American workers.[47] As the suburbs grew, jobs for woodworkers became plentiful. But without sustainable forestry, loggers could measure the time trees would exist for those jobs at a few decades.[48]

Foster first articulated a detailed union forestry agenda at the 1945 IWA Convention. It included federal regulation over all private forests on fire control, reforestation, conservation, and logging methods, and federal acquisition of non-producing lands that could be reforested. It called for government assistance to small landowners to develop their timber, employment programs in conservation, and wood efficiency programs to maximize resource use.[49] To accomplish these goals, the IWA needed to harness federal power to shift forest control away from corporations. Foster had a Jeffersonian vision of "dirt foresters,"

[46] Lizabeth Cohen, *A Consumer's Republic: The Politics of Mass Consumption in Postwar America* (New York: Alfred A. Knopf, 2003), esp. 73–75, 121–22, 141, 152–68.

[47] Proceedings of 10th Constitutional Convention, 214, IWA Box 25, Folder 6.

[48] IWA Report to the 10th Constitutional Convention, 1946, 14–16, IWA Box 37, Folder 10.

[49] IWA Executive Board Meeting, January 29–31, 1945, IWA Box 14, Folder 12. Foster developed a similar program that explained to the forestry profession in Ellery Foster, "Lumber Snafu," *Journal of Forestry* 44, no. 6 (June 1946): 393–400.

assisted by government forestry experts, producing sustainable wood products for the American working class.[50] The idea of dirt forestry became powerful within the union leadership. For example, IWA executive J.E. Fadling wrote in 1946 of "dirt foresters" plowing their profits back into sustainable forestry practices to stabilize communities and create regional security.[51]

This farming rhetoric fit a period when labor and conservationists tried to build alliances to extend the New Deal state.[52] In 1946, the IWA issued an "open letter to farmers," noting that the IWA forestry program would shift taxes away from them and onto timber companies. Foster also spoke on the Oregon Farmers' Union Program, a radio show broadcast from Corvallis, arguing that the farmers and loggers could only prosper with government experts guiding them.[53] The Forest Service had long thought of forestry as agriculture.[54] However, as the IWA noted at its 1945 Convention, "all the work of Nature and of man in growing a forest can be wiped out in a few weeks of destructive logging," making government regulation of forestry more important than traditional agriculture.[55]

In 1946, Foster carried the IWA standard in three battles to provide environmental and economic security for its members. First, it played a major role in the opposition to the Sustained-Yield Forest Act of 1944, through which the federal government signed 100-year contracts with private timber corporations, giving them exclusive access to large tracts of the national forests. Second, Foster attacked corporate forestry at the American Forestry Congress, outraging industrialists who saw union involvement in forestry as impertinent. Third, the IWA attempted to implement its forestry program in Congress through the Resource Conservation and Development Act. Ultimately, these battles would show the limitations of organized labor's ability to challenge corporate control of the nation's natural resources.

[50] See Ellery Foster, "Trees Good Crops," *International Woodworker*, January 15, 1947.

[51] J.E. Fadling to Oregon Wood Industries Outlook, July 17, 1946. IWA Box 343, Folder 17.

[52] See for example, P. Alston Waring and Clinton Strong Golden, *Soil and Steel: Exploring the Common Interests of Farmers and Wage Earners* (New York: Harper Brothers, 1947).

[53] "An Open Letter to Farmers," IWA Box 344, Folder 4; "Conservation for Peace and Plenty," IWA Box 344, Folder 4.

[54] Clary, *Timber and the Forest Service*, 75, 180–88.

[55] Proceedings of 9th Constitutional Convention, 1945, IWA Box 25, Folder 6.

THE CONTESTED MEANINGS OF SUSTAINED-YIELD FORESTRY

Concerns about how to sustain struggling logging communities not only concerned the IWA; the problem also occupied the minds of New Deal forest officials, who sought to implement the practice of sustained-yield forestry as a solution. Broadly defined as balancing harvesting and growth to ensure production in perpetuity, sustained-yield forestry had its roots in the early years of the Forest Service. But its practical definition remained contested. The lack of functional knowledge about forest ecosystems, even within the USFS, led to a great deal of guess work as to what level of harvesting constituted sustained-yield forestry. The timber industry believed sustained yield meant the sustainability of the industry more than the resource. Corporations pushed to expand sustained-yield numbers based upon projected future growth, maximizing short-term production with the hope that long-term management would make up the difference. The industry argued that sustainable forestry was best accomplished through clearcutting, or the harvesting of all trees on a tract of land. Industry journal *The Timberman* asserted that clearcutting could create a sustainable crop because the profitable Douglas fir regenerated in direct sunlight: "Nature pointed the way to scientific forestry by indicating that mature Douglas fir forests should be clear-cut to allow all new trees an even chance for sunlight as they grow." Moreover, forests' natural regeneration meant corporate investment in artificial reforestation was an unnecessary expense.[56] Logging every tree was efficient, profitable,

[56] "Tip from Nature: Fires Prove Clear-Cutting Value," *The Timberman*, July 13, 1951, 12. For a similar argument, H.H. Chapman, "Is Selective Cutting a Panacea for Forest Regulation," *Journal of Forestry* 42, no. 5 (May 1944): 345–47. For a professional defense of selective cutting, see William E. Cooper, "In Defense of 'Selective Cutting'" *Journal of Forestry* 43, no. 9 (September 1945): 638–39. The most detailed recounting of clearcutting is Richard A. Rajala, *Clearcutting the Pacific Rain Forest: Production, Science, and Regulation* (Vancouver: UBC Press, 1998), 91–153. See also David A. Clary, *Timber and the Forest Service* (Lawrence: University Press of Kansas, 1984), 46–50. On sustained yield forestry and its definitions, see Hirt, *A Conspiracy of Optimism*, 39–41; Langston, *Forest Dreams, Forest Nightmares*, 168–74; Johannes H. Drielsma, Joseph A. Miller and William R. Burch, Jr., "Sustained Yield and Community Stability in American Forestry," in Robert G. Lee et al., *Community and Forestry: Continuities in the Sociology of Natural Resources* (Boulder, CO: Westview Press, 1990), 55–68. See also Rodney C. Loehr, ed., *Forests for the Future: The Story of Sustained Yield as Told in the Diaries and Papers of David T. Mason, 1907–1950* (St. Paul: Minnesota Historical Society, 1952) for the development of the idea of sustained yield forestry in the work of one leading forester.

and destructive, leading to erosion, fires, and watershed degradation. Clearcutting had also liquidated many private timber stocks by the 1940s, leading to increased corporate demands on the national forests.

The IWA disagreed sharply with the industry on both its definition of sustained-yield forestry and the acceptable logging practices to ensure it. Critics said that clearcutting destabilized communities by wiping out local timber harvests for decades, and that avoiding manual reforestation doomed the forests to wasteland. Henry Wallace and Ferdinand Silcox had proposed federal leadership on sustained-yield forestry since 1930, with Wallace calling clearcutting "completely unsocial."[57] Ellery Foster agreed, writing that only "the weight of the CIO, added to that of other groups that have long deplored the recklessness with which we permit our forests to be destroyed, may turn the tables in the long struggle to curb needlessly destructive logging."[58]

Progressive foresters such as Robert Marshall argued instead for selective cutting, where foresters chose only mature trees to cut and left the rest of the forest intact for future harvests. Selective cutting would foster the growth of shade-tolerant new trees, while keeping watersheds healthy and recreational opportunities plentiful.[59] The IWA suggested using Caterpillar tractors that could reach individual trees. Foster claimed "it can produce twice as big a sustained yield of logs as hundred-year cycles of clear-cutting."[60] A number of northern California firms experimented with selective logging during the 1930s; a 1938 report optimistically found larger tree rings over the past seven years for recently cut trees.[61] However, most companies believed that selective logging damaged young timber because of falling trees and damage from machinery. They also bemoaned its lower profit margins. They questioned whether the nation could meet its postwar timber needs if it ended the most efficient way

[57] Henry Wallace to John Boettinger, August 20, 1940, NARA Seattle, RG 95, Records of the U.S. Forest Service, Region 1, Missoula, MT, Historical Collection, ca. 1905–1990, Box 8, Folder, Direction – Historical Nat'l Forest Program, 1940–42. See also, Drielsma et al., "Sustained Yield and Community Stability in American Forestry," in Robert G. Lee, Donald R. Field, and William R. Burch, *Community and Forestry: Continuities in the Sociology of Natural Resources* (Boulder, CO: Westview Press, 55–68).

[58] Foster, "Woodworkers and World Forestry" *Unasylva* 1, no. 3 (November–December 1947).

[59] "Editorial: Selective Logging," *Journal of Forestry* 28, no. 3 (March 1930): 271–72.

[60] "Monopoly Timber Interests Scheme Looting of Public Domain, Foster," *International Woodworker*, May 11, 1949.

[61] Emanuel Fritz, "The Growth of Redwood Trees Left after Selective Logging," *The Timberman*, June 1938, 14–16, 53–55.

known to harvest large patches of forest.[62] For the IWA, this missed the point. Denuded forests threw lives into turmoil. George Prokopovich, an IWA millworker at a Bend plant, killed himself after his mill shut down. Tim Sullivan, his district president, blamed it on a lack of selective logging and used the suicide as an example of clearcutting's toll on workers.[63]

Still, the IWA had to take industry concerns about producing enough timber through selective cutting seriously. Foster urged government leadership on four programs to develop the forests responsibly. First, it should invest in forest roads. For decades, timber companies opposed logging the national forests because they saw it as competition for their own private stocks. Congress provided only limited funding for forest roads. Millions of acres of virgin timber remained inaccessible. When the USFS did sell timber for logging, private companies built roads and deducted the cost from the purchase price of timber, effectively a federal subsidy of private forestry. The timber industry thus opposed public construction.[64] With private timber stocks in decline, industry officials wanted the national forests opened, but only so long as they continued to see the benefit.

The USFS lobbied for increased congressional funding for public forest roads to both provide timber and democratize access. Earl Mason, an Oregon forester and IWA supporter, told union members that private roads incentivized clearcutting and encouraged "a type of logging that customarily is incompatible with sustained yield forestry."[65] Over time, Mason argued, private companies would eat up government timber just as they had done to their own lands. To combat the relationship between road building and monopoly forestry, the IWA passed a 1946 resolution in favor of a federal forest road system based on farm-to-market road programs that would open all the timber up at once, allowing for small foresters to compete with large companies.[66]

Public forest roads would only serve sustained-yield forestry if the federal government managed logging operations, Foster's second demand. Government foresters would visit all logging operations and

[62] Hirt, *A Conspiracy of Optimism*, 245; Williams, *The U.S. Forest Service in the Pacific Northwest*, 137–38; Ficken, *The Forested Land*, 201–02.

[63] "IWAer's Suicide May Be Related to 'Slash and Get Out Policy,'" *International Woodworker*, February 28, 1951.

[64] Steen, *The U.S. Forest Service*, 283–84; Hirt, *A Conspiracy of Optimism*, 78.

[65] "Letters," *International Woodworker*, September 28, 1949.

[66] IWA Report to the 10th Constitutional Convention, 1946, 14–16, IWA Box 37, Folder 10; Resolution No. 15, Box 37, Folder 17.

tag trees the companies could take. This would make selective logging national policy. As Foster said in a 1946 talk, "piddling regulation calling merely for a few seed trees to be left" can never "safeguard our forests and bring security to communities which depend on wood industries for job and income." Instead, foresters would implement a strict construction of sustained-yield forestry, making sure that trees could not be cut at any rate faster than the forest grew. To industry officials who dismissed these ideas as utopian, Foster replied, "we don't believe sustained yield and competent marking is as tough a job as organizing the mass production industries was," which makes connections between the current forestry campaign and the larger trajectory of CIO victories clear.[67] To pay for the foresters, the IWA called for a federal tax on cut timber levied on timber companies.[68]

Even with an expansion in forest roads, eliminating clearcutting could cause short-term timber shortages. Fighting these threats made up the last two facets of Foster's program. He argued for robust federal funding for a wood utilization program that would use every scrap of wood cut. Both wood utilization and the fourth IWA demand, fighting fire and insect infestations, were far less controversial. Nearly every stakeholder in the forests believed in the complete suppression of fires and using whatever tools available to fight against insects, fungus, and other threats to forest production. The USFS had conducted research into wood utilization going back to the Gifford Pinchot era, while timber companies and forestry departments at universities also explored these options. By the 1940s, researchers developed products using previously wasted wood scraps. Foster urged greater investment in wood utilization, pushing for science to discover "how to use wood to make food, clothing, motor fuel, plastics and countless important chemicals."[69]

However, the IWA believed that private forestry threatened these goals. Union President Claude Ballard said the IWA had to fight an industrial alcohol monopoly "that can only be broken when the public is fully informed as to the advantages of utilizing this wood waste."[70] Instead, wood utilization should create jobs in small mills, with independent

[67] From Brief for Presentation at American Forestry Congress, October 9, 1946, IWA Box 344, Folder 6.

[68] Resolution 12, 1951 IWA Convention, IWA Box 39, Folder 3.

[69] Ellery Foster, "Wood versus the World's Want," *International Woodworker*, June 8, 1949.

[70] IWA Executive Board Meeting, January 29–31, 1945, IWA Box 14, Folder 12.

operators sharing a common pool of raw materials.[71] Foster lambasted corporate concerns about paying for fire protection, comparing it to putting a price on the air people breathe and saying "the market value of trees standing in the woods is no suitable measure of what it is worth to protect a forest from burning up."[72]

The contested meanings of sustained forestry became crucial when the USFS implemented the Sustained-Yield Forest Management Act in 1946. This law, originally passed in 1944, directed the Departments of Agriculture and Interior to grant access to government timber to a single company with sustainable harvesting regulations while its own land reforested. Less than a week later, the Simpson Timber Company, one of Washington's largest employers with over 6,000 workers, applied for a 270,000-acre sustained-yield unit combining private and federal lands.[73]

In September 1946, Chief Forester Lyle Watts selected Simpson's application as a test of the law. Simpson signed a 100-year contract that combined private and federal land and that allowed for heavy forestry until 1956, when sustained-yield practices would take over.[74] The next year, the newly created Bureau of Land Management implemented the O&C Lands Act of 1937 to create the Mohawk River Sustained Yield Agreement, granting exclusive logging rights on an Oregon and California Railroad Land Grant parcel to the Fischer Lumber Company near Marcola, Oregon. The O&C Lands Act directed the states to log the land on a permanent basis using sustained-yield forestry. These low-elevation, high-production lands were some of the most valuable old-growth timber remaining in the Northwest. The

[71] Ellery Foster, "Wood versus the World's Want," *International Woodworker*, June 8, 1949.

[72] Ellery Foster, "Let's Talk about Adequate Forest Fire Protection," *International Woodworker*, December 11, 1946.

[73] Steen, *The U.S. Forest Service*, 225–28; Clary, *Timber and the Forest Service*, 85–91; Drielsma et al., "Sustained Yield and Community Stability in American Forestry," 55–68; Roy O. Hoover, "Public Law 273 Comes to Shelton: Implementing the Sustained-Yield Unit Forest Management Act of 1944," *Journal of Forest History* 22, no. 3 (April 1978): 86–101. For a contemporary description of the law, see C.M. Granger, "The Cooperative Sustained Yield Act," *Journal of Forestry* 42, no. 8 (August 1944): 558–59.

[74] Clary, *Timber and the Forest Service*, 126–46; Clary, "What Price Sustained Yield? The Forest Service, Community Stability, and Timber Monopoly Under the 1944 Sustained-Yield Act," in Char Miller, ed., *American Forests: Nature, Culture, and Politics* (Lawrence: University Press of Kansas, 1997), 209–28; Steen, *The U.S. Forest Service*, 251–52; Williams, *The U.S. Forest Service in the Pacific Northwest,* 185–87; Hirt, *A Conspiracy of Optimism*, 40–41; Hoover, "Public Law 273 Comes to Shelton."

law sat unused until the USFS implemented its own sustained-yield agreements.[75]

These agreements spawned widespread opposition. C.C. Crow, publisher of *Crow's Pacific Coast Lumber Digest*, a journal representing small timber operators, and a virulent anti-communist, blamed "forest dictators from Washington" operating "in a parlor-pink haze," who wanted to centralize timber resources in the hands of the few.[76] Many shared Crow's opinions, if not his rhetoric. Owners of small logging operations organized through the Western Forest Industries Association and vigorously protested to the Oregon congressional delegation to reject the plan.[77] The Carpenters opposed the monopoly contracts, which it called "abhorrent to the very basis of our democratic principles as a nation." Conservationists also protested. The Eugene-based chapter of the Izaak Walton League noted the Mohawk River Agreement lacked any protection for clean streambeds necessary for salmon spawning. It asked, "How in the world did this weak-kneed abortion get as far as a public hearing?"[78]

The IWA joined the opposition. Although sustained-yield units set the precedent for limited federal regulation over private forests, they were an extension of the forest road problem: monopoly capitalism's control over the forests made true sustained forestry unlikely. Testifying against the O&C plan before a BLM hearing in January 1948, Foster called it "a betrayal of democracy and conservation." He instead urged the BLM to create small parcels for different companies in competitive bidding contracts in order to spread production, jobs, and wealth around the region. This would spur "a maximum of freedom and a minimum of monopoly."[79] IWA members testified on how monopoly agreements would

[75] Elmo Richardson, *BLM's Billion-Dollar Checkerboard: Managing the O&C Lands* (Santa Cruz, CA: Forest History Society, 1980); Williams, *The U.S. Forest Service in the Pacific Northwest*, 32–33, 90–91, 134. On the BLM, James R. Skillen, *The Nation's Largest Landlord: The Bureau of Land Management in the American West* (Lawrence: University Press of Kansas, 2009).

[76] "Forest Plan Measures Argued," *Crow's Pacific Coast Lumber Digest*, February 5, 1948, 8–9; "The Sustained Timber Grab," *Crow's Pacific Coast Lumber Digest*, March 18, 1948.

[77] Walter Swenson and Helga Swenson to Julius Krug, April 14, 1948; Ernest Wooley to Wayne Morse, January 14, 1948, Wayne Morse Papers, University of Oregon Special Collections, Series J, Box 2, Folder Agriculture Forest Service, 1948–49.

[78] O&C Sustained Yield Hearing Minutes, January 21–22, 1948, 386–89, 399–405, IWA Box 284, Folder 10. On the Izaak Walton League and Forestry, see William Voigt, Jr., "The Izaak Walton League of America," *Journal of Forestry* 44, no. 6 (June 1946): 424–25.

[79] Ellery Foster statement, January 21, 1948, IWA Box 344, Folder 2.

affect their jobs. Mark Culbertson of Local 5–2523 in Westport, Oregon, noted that if one company controlled the timber, "how are we in the timber industry, where the timber is already gone and no industry to take its place, going to survive?" Howard Mallory, president of the IWA local in Woodleaf, California, said a proposed sustained-yield contract with the Sacramento Box and Lumber Company would doom his own mill and many others who might have access to some of that timber under a more democratic plan.[80]

Lyle Watts had little sympathy for these arguments. He, like many New Deal land managers by the late 1940s, believed that too many small mills and farms led to intensified competition over scarce resources and most rural people would be better off moving to the cities and working in a factory. Watts wrote to Oregon Senator Wayne Morse, "excess installed sawmill capacity must be reduced to the timber growing capacity of our forest lands, with consequent community disruption," while the agency admitted that most forestry dependent communities would disappear.[81] Sustained-yield units betrayed IWA principles of proper federal regulation, but they better represented New Deal agricultural programs than did its vision of small farmers and small foresters. Rather than prop up small farmers, the Agricultural Adjustment Act and other legislation centralized agricultural production in the hands of large farmers. Tenant farmers' displacement in the late 1930s was a consequence of these policies; increasingly, so was the decline of small Northwestern lumber towns.[82]

The widespread opposition caught USFS and BLM officials off guard. In June 1948, the vociferous opposition to the Mohawk River unit led to new regulations that guaranteed recreational access and limited the volume of government timber that could be included, but the BLM

80 R. Mark Culbertson to Wayne Morse, September 2, 1952. Morse Papers, Series J, Box 3, Folder Hood River Sustained Yield Unit.

81 Watts to Morse, April 29, 1948, Morse Papers, Series J, Box 2, Folder Agriculture Forest Service, 1948–49.

82 On AAA and the effects of New Deal agricultural policy, Keith Joseph Volanto, *Texas, Cotton, and the New Deal* (College Station: Texas A&M University Press, 2005); Neil Maher, "'Crazy Quilt Farming on Round Land': The Great Depression, the Soil Conservation Service, and the Politics of Landscape Change on the Great Plains during the New Deal Era," *Western Historical Quarterly* 31 (Summer 2000): 319–39; Hurt, "The National Grasslands," 246–59; R. Douglas Hurt, "Prices, Payments, and Production: Kansas Wheat Farmers and the Agricultural Adjustment Act, 1933–1939," *Kansas History* 23, no. 1 (May 2000): 72–87; Deborah Fitzgerald, *Every Farm a Factory: The Industrial Ideal in American Agriculture* (New Haven: Yale University Press, 2003); Shane Hamilton, *Trucking Country: The Road to Wal-Mart's Economy* (Princeton: Princeton University Press, 2008).

sustained-yield units never gained final approval.[83] The USFS only created five sustained-yield units due to continued resistance to the monopoly provisions. The IWA lauded the victory as the beginning of a new era of forestry that would include alliances between farmers, small business, and organized labor. The Washington State Grange had played a leading role in fighting the Shelton agreement and Foster hoped that the different constituencies would build on their alliance and "learn to work together on other projects where the interest of the respective groups is in harmony and in the public interest."[84] But future IWA efforts to shape forestry policy would lack broad-based alliances, suggesting the limits of organized labor in shaping natural resource planning.

THE LIMITS OF IWA FORESTRY

In October 1946, the American Forestry Association sponsored the American Forestry Congress to promote its "Forest Resource Appraisal," which blamed the federal government for timber depletion because it did not contribute enough to the nation's timber supply and rejected all public regulation. The FRA was key to the timber industry's shift from keeping public timber off the market to demanding access to it as private reserves disappeared. The AFA report ignored critiques of private forestry practices, leading Watts to criticize it as "studded with allegation and innuendos" toward the federal government. Striking back, the USFS issued its "Report to the Chief" before the conference. It called private timber practices as poorly managed, with significant problems of erosion and reforestation that would require public regulation.[85]

The gathering promised to be a contentious battle between the Forest Service and industry, but in fact the government took a mostly conciliatory tone, as Watts began to steer the agency away from the heated rhetoric of the 1930s, leading it on a path toward postwar cooperation with private owners. Ellery Foster showed less restraint. His AFC speech began by demanding that the industry take loggers' concerns about their

83 "Interior Department Announces New Sustained Timber Policy," *International Woodworker*, June 9, 1948; "Big Operators' Monopoly Tactics Aired by Editor," *International Woodworker*, April 25, 1951.

84 Hoover, "Public Law 273 Comes to Shelton"; "The New Policy," *International Woodworker*, June 9, 1948.

85 Hirt, *A Conspiracy of Optimism*, 53–57; Steen, *The U.S. Forest Service*, 256–59. For a broad statement of opposition to federal regulation of forestry, see G.F. Jewett, "Why I Oppose Federal Regulation," *Journal of Forestry* 42, no. 7 (July 1944): 483–88.

future seriously. He accused the industry of "butchering" the nation's forests and noting that if he had been asked to prepare a statement to protest the timber industry's lack of concern for the future, he "would look upon the appraisal's remarks on regulation as a gold mine of ideas." He connected the industry's low wages to its opposition to sustainable forestry, arguing both reinforced monopoly capitalism. Pressing for "sustained yield forestry on a community basis" to separate the IWA from USFS sustained-yield agreements, Foster's speech took on a threatening tone. He told the gathering, "we believe a comprehensive national program of assistance and *of control over commercial logging* is the only feasible way to get community sustained yield."[86]

The CIO's Anthony Smith gave an even more strident address, a tone fitting one of the most militant years in the history of American labor. He justified the federal regulation of private timber by claiming that the National Labor Relations Act's authority to allow the federal government to intervene in the workplace gave it the power to regulate all forestry lands engaged in interstate commerce. Smith called for "criminal penalties" for sustainable forestry enforcement. He warned the timber industry that acceding to the IWA plan was the only way "to avoid rapid and sweeping federal condemnation and purchase of timber lands on a nationwide scale. The mass economic organizations of this country, including the CIO, possesses ample machinery for bringing full information on these issues to the people, and I think they can be counted on to do so."[87] Smith castigated the AFA for a "hypocritical resolution" marking Gifford Pinchot's death, since they had opposed the regulation he sought for four decades. After the AFC ended, Foster bitterly dismissed it, calling the timber industry "sinister forces" and even wondered about "international intrigue ... using its influence to take the American public off the scent of our dangerous national timber shortage."[88]

Industry leaders preferred to ignore labor's opinion on forestry entirely. There is little evidence employers ever took the IWA critique of their methods seriously, except after the AFC. Foster and Smith's language forced them to respond. *The Timberman* lauded the spirit of cooperation that permeated the AFC with one great exception: "Labor representatives,

86 From Brief for Presentation at American Forestry Congress, October 9, 1946, IWA Box 344, Folder 6. Emphasis in original.

87 Statement of CIO at American Forestry Congress, 1946, IWA Box 343, Folder 22.

88 Ellery Foster, "The American Forestry Congress," *International Woodworker*, October 30, 1946.

on the other hand, were liberal in characterizing industry as selfishly destructive and in need of strong federal control."[89] The AFA offered its official response through the pages of the *Longview Daily News*. In a long front-page editorial, the AFA's John Woods rejected the IWA's intrusion into forest policy. Woods countered labor's analogy between farming and forestry by rejecting all New Deal land-management planning. Bemoaning federal agricultural programs as burdensome to property owners, Woods pushed for state regulation, where legislators had much closer ties to the timber industry than it did to most members of Congress.[90] Both conservationists and timber operators understood state regulation as industry control. Foster noted that the industry wanted state control because state foresters' "strongest ties are with the lumber companies who have always tried to get the farmer's trees at the lowest possible price," as opposed to federal foresters with broader social and ecological concerns, and bluntly said that AFA supported state regulation because "the lumber lobby is stronger in state legislation than it is in the national congress."[91]

The IWA and CIO never believed that the timber industry would accede to labor's demands on forestry. Foster told union members that they should "keep right on getting more and more people to understand and fight for the Hook Forestry Bill."[92] The IWA had found a champion in Representative Frank Hook of Michigan. A former logger, Hook was a committed conservationist motivated by the timber industry's deforestation of his home state. Hook introduced the bill that created Isle Royale National Park in Michigan in 1940. He was also one of the CIO's strongest congressional supporters. An enemy of Dixiecrats, Hook publicly accused Martin Dies of fascism while John Rankin physically attacked him during a shouting match over the CIO. In Hook, the IWA found a dedicated, if controversial, defender of sustainable forestry.[93]

On April 30, 1946, Hook introduced the Forestry Conservation and Development Act. The Hook Bill, as it became known, attempted to

89 "Conference Reviews National Forestry Affairs," *The Timberman*, November 1946, 96.

90 "Is More Federal Control Answer to Lumber Industry Improvement?" *Longview Daily News*, September 25, 1946.

91 Ellery Foster, "Program with Booby Traps," *International Woodworker*, February 26, 1947.

92 Ellery Foster, "The American Forestry Congress," *International Woodworker*, October 30, 1946.

93 Mary Louise Hook Allen, *Fightin' Frank: The Biography of Upper Peninsula's 12th District Democratic Congressman* (M.L.H.Allen, 2004).

codify much of Foster's forestry program. Small foresters would receive conservation payments and credit aids similar to those paid to farmers under AAA. The government would provide technical assistance in the managing and marketing of forest crops and build logging roads to help farmers get the trees to market. Government foresters would choose the individual trees to log on federal land. Finally, a flat rate of 2 percent of the appraised value of national forest land would fund county governments reliant upon timber taxes for their budgets. Hook believed his bill would create long-term security for both the forest and the communities that relied upon it.[94]

Passing the FCDA became the IWA's sole legislative goal in 1946. Foster urged members to share his union newspaper articles with friends and neighbors to "start a grass (and tree) roots movement to put such a Bill over in the next Congress."[95] He wrote a pamphlet intended for widespread distribution in favor of the FCDA entitled, "America's Logjam and How to Break It." This pamphlet took workers step by step through the problems with the timber industry, and how the IWA forestry program and Hook Bill would solve them. Reminding readers how the timber industry had despoiled the nation's forests, Foster wrote, "now the only sizable tracts of virgin forests are left on the Pacific coast. If they go, there just won't be any more." Foster used an idyllic vision of domesticity and family to make his arguments, urging readers to think about forestry as central to their children's futures. As forests preserve soil and water, he wrote, "our forests that mean the difference between plenty and scarcity for your kids and their kids – are being cut and burned and wasted." Forcefully stating that it is the government's business that this not happen, the pamphlet urged readers to support the Hook Bill and grant the government "police powers to protect forest land."

The benefits to the people were not just conservation, but recreation. Foreshadowing the rapid growth in visitation to the forests with returning prosperity and middle-class growth in the 1950s, Foster wrote that the government would develop facilities with picnic tables, hiking trails, and wading pools. Finally, Foster tied the FCDA to the New Deal, making the case that the IWA plan was not a radical attack on private ownership, as

[94] "IWA-CIO Forestry Program Is Answer to Hook Opponents," *International Woodworker*, October 30, 1946. A good summary of the bill breaking down what the timber industry saw as controversial is at "Editorial: Private Forestry at Public Expense," *Journal of Forestry* 44, no. 8 (August 1946): 547–48.

[95] IWA Report to the 10th Constitutional Convention, 1946, Box 37, Folder 10.

the timber industry claimed, but rather simply applied a well-established precedent of regulation and promotion of working people's economic prospects to a new industry. In case the connections to the history of conservation remained unclear, the pamphlet closed with a quote from Gifford Pinchot congratulating the IWA for taking up the question of sustainable forestry.[96]

Hook tried to build support for his bill by reading a piece from Foster into the Congressional Record in April 1946 that claimed lumber shortages would prevent the nation from solving its housing crisis.[97] But the FCDA never even reached a vote. Accusing Hook of attempting to socialize the forests, Michigan forestry interests used the bill to defeat Hook in the Republican landslide of the 1946 congressional elections.[98] The IWA called for the bill's reintroduction as the next step in its forestry program. It claimed the liberals' defeat was an aberration and the imminent return of New Deal liberalism that would make national forestry legislation possible. However, the passage of the Taft-Hartley Act in 1947 changed the playing field for labor politics. Repealing it became the IWA's primary legislative goal and a forestry bill a secondary concern.[99]

Foster also represented an increasingly unfashionable position in a forestry profession that had long cooperated with the timber industry before the strained relations of the Roosevelt administration. Foster's frustration over his struggle to influence policy came out frequently after 1946, complaining for instance that "the blindness to monopolistic dangers on the part of government foresters reminds us of the enthusiasm with

[96] Ellery Foster, "America's Logjam and How to Break It," 11. IWA Box 344, Folder 4.

[97] Congressional Record, April 13, 1946; copy in IWA Box 344, Folder 23.

[98] "IWA-CIO Forestry Program Is Answer to Hook Opponents," *International Woodworker*, October 30, 1946.

[99] Resolution No. 17, 1946 IWA Annual Convention, Box 37. Folder 8; Ellery Foster to the 1947 IWA Annual Convention, p. 318–21, IWA Box 37, Folder 13. On the backlash to organized labor after World War II, see Elizabeth A. Fones-Wolf, *Selling Free Enterprise: The Business Assault on Labor and Liberalism, 1945–1960* (Urbana: University of Illinois Press, 1994); Judith Stein, *Running Steel, Running America: Race, Economic Policy, and the Decline of Liberalism* (Chapel Hill: University of North Carolina Press, 1998). On the rise of conservatism and early Cold War culture, see Stephen J. Whitfield, *The Culture of the Cold War* (Baltimore: Johns Hopkins University Press, 1991); Elaine Tyler May, *Homeward Bound: American Families in the Cold War Era* (New York: Basic Books, 1988); Kenneth T. Jackson, *Crabgrass Frontier: The Suburbanization of the United States* (New York: Oxford University Press, 1985); James T. Patterson, *Grand Expectations: The United States, 1945–1974* (New York: Oxford University Press, 1996); David M. Oshinsky, *A Conspiracy So Immense: The World of Joe McCarthy* (New York: Free Press, 1983).

which German foresters are reported to have cooperated in Hitler's ruthless forestry and wood utilization plans."[100] Despite Foster's connections with USFS reformers, Pinchot's support before his death, and Silcox's calls for regulation before the war, the USFS distanced itself from the IWA. Foster resigned from the union in 1948.[101] He informally advised the union on forestry but after 1951 disappears from union publications entirely. He later worked for U.S. government development projects overseas. In his later life, Foster became a back-to-the-land proponent in Minnesota, hosting two different communal groups on his farm, and becoming known within regional countercultural circles for his essays on individual empowerment, nonviolence, atheism, and celibacy. Anthony Smith left the CIO soon after it merged with the AFL in 1955 and became president of the National Parks and Conservation Association in 1958.[102]

Perhaps Foster deserves some blame for the program's decline. After 1945, forestry and Foster were synonymous in the union. He asked nothing of workers except to follow his directives. The IWA instructed locals to distribute Foster's materials to members, lobby politicians, and spread his talking points on forestry in their communities.[103] However, union member O.O. Womack of Klamath Falls, Oregon, challenged this passive reception of forestry knowledge from the union office. Womack wrote that the union needed to teach members how to access scientific knowledge in order to check their own observations. This could have democratized the forestry program and empowered workers at the worksite. Instead, Foster was "tending to treat us as children needing tutelage." Foster rejected this, saying only professional foresters could carry out the union program and comparing himself to a doctor. "You have to take a lot on faith alone," Foster wrote, "because a layman can't be an expert on medical science."[104] The union's forestry program had roots in the union's prewar radical culture, but without empowering the rank and file in day-to-day forestry or taking into account their own observations in the forest, it became the

[100] Ellery Foster, "Forest Service Report," *International Woodworker*, February 12, 1947.

[101] Ellery Foster resume, Ellery Foster Papers, Minnesota Historical Society Special Collections, Box 1, Folder 4.

[102] See Ellery Foster Papers, MHS; esp. Box 1, Folders 7–8, 12; "A Way to Cope with Greed," *High Country Anvil*, April–May 1973, 13; "Resurrection in the Whole Self," *High Country Anvil*, June–July 1973, 48–49; "The Gandhian Way," *High Country Anvil*, October–November 1973, 46–47; Denny Scott to Ellery Foster, April 3, 1977; Foster to Scott, April 9, 1977, IWA Box 300, Folder 25.

[103] IWA 1946 Convention Resolution No. 17, IWA Box 37, Folder 8.

[104] Ellery Foster, "The Scientific Approach," *International Woodworker*, March 5, 1947.

program of one union officer. Perhaps there were more workers like Womack who wanted to democratize the forestry program and empower workers to challenge employers on site, but we will never know because Foster was uninterested. When Foster left, the union still broadly supported sustainable forestry but the political will within the union to prioritize it disappeared. The timber industry faced no legitimate challenge to its environmental practices for another twenty years.

WORKING CLASS LEISURE

The IWA continued attempting to influence regional natural resource planning. It provided support for the proposed Columbia Valley Authority in the late 1940s, hoping that public power would prove more popular than public timber and lay the groundwork for another push on the forestry program. The union connected deforestation and erosion to the flooding that wiped out the Kaiser company city of Vanport, Oregon, in 1948. It cited a USFS report which said that fifteen days after the Vanport flood, snow still existed in timbered lands while logged-off lands were bare, and noted that poor logging practices made the flood worse. Erosion clogged stream channels and degraded watersheds, creating a disaster.[105] An IWA radio broadcast said harvesting the river was necessary so it would "serve us and never hurt us again."[106] But the CVA failed too. The timber industry joined with private power to oppose further federal jurisdiction over natural resources. Timber magnate Charles Weyerhaeuser sent a letter to stockholders and employees, ironically urging them to oppose the "huge monopolistic corporation" that would ensue from government ownership[107] Rising conservative opposition led even the powerful Oregon senator Wayne Morse to fear a primary challenge and thus oppose the plan, leading President Harry Truman to give up on it. The fight for purely public power ended in the Northwest.[108]

105 "Northwest Floods Left New Forest Fire Danger," *International Woodworker*, August 4, 1948. On Vanport, see Robbins, *Landscapes of Conflict*, 66–70.

106 "River Control Calls For Land Management as Well as Dams Says IWA Vancouver Broadcast," *International Woodworker*, July 7, 1948.

107 Charles Twining, *Phil Weyerhaeuser: Lumberman* (Seattle: University of Washington Press, 1985), 311–12.

108 On the CVA and the battle over public power, Gerald H. Robinson, "The Columbia Valley Administration Bill," *The Western Political Quarterly* 3, no. 4 (December 1950): 607–14; Charles McKinley, *Uncle Sam in the Pacific Northwest: Federal Management of Natural Resources* (Berkeley: University of California Press, 1952), 644–53; William Lang, "1949: Year of Decision on the Columbia River," *Columbia Magazine* 19, no. 1

The IWA included at least one forestry-related resolution at nearly every convention during the 1950s and 1960s, but they changed little year to year and had little practical application in the union's political activities. When the union talked about natural resources, it increasingly framed its support for conservation in terms of leisure time for its membership, a fitting policy during a time when Americans began using the public lands in record numbers after World War II. Historians have increasingly discovered working-class support for environmental protection when it benefitted their leisure activities. Between 1945 and 1955, annual visits to national forests increased from 16 to 40 million. Fishing-license sales rose 43 percent and hunting licenses 30 percent between 1948 and 1958. Moreover, the late 1940s saw the once-militant CIO turn from challenging the tenets of capitalism to framing their members as middle-class consumers, which could include the consumption of America's recreational spaces. Organized labor had moved toward a consumerist view of nature based upon working-class recreation going back to the 1920s, and the IWA saw a good life of outdoor recreation as central to its vision in the 1950s.[109] Union newspapers began printing stories of members hunting and fishing. In 1956, union President Al Hartung expressed disappointment with the AFL-CIO for not taking conservation seriously. He decried that "we are so lax in protecting the one natural resource that's going to keep your lakes full of water and your homes supplied with water ... a place for recreation where you can get away from the city streets and get out in the shade and into the green of your timbers. These are some of the things that for some reason seem to steel and auto unimportant."[110]

(Spring 2005): 8–15; Karl Boyd Brooks, *Public Power, Private Dams: The Hells Canyon High Dam Controversy* (Seattle: University of Washington Press, 2009).

109 Lawrence Lipin, *Workers and the Wild: Conservation, Consumerism, and Labor in Oregon, 1910–1930* (Urbana: University of Illinois Press, 2007), 117–52; Karl Boyd Brooks, *Before Earth Day: The Origins of American Environmental Law, 1945–1970* (Lawrence: University of Kansas Press, 2009), 97; Lisa M. Fine, "Workers and the Land in US History: Pointe Mouillée and the Downriver Detroit Working Class in the Twentieth Century," *Labor History* 53, no. 3 (August 2012): 409–34; Cohen, *A Consumers' Republic*, 152–65; Andrew Hurley, *Environmental Inequalities: Class, Race, and Industrial Pollution in Gary, Indiana, 1945–1980* (Chapel Hill: University of North Carolina Press, 1995), 77–110. For a broader discussion of the growth of recreation even before World War II, see Paul Sutter, *Driven Wild: How the Fight against Automobiles Launched the Modern Wilderness Movement* (Seattle: University of Washington Press, 2002).

110 Proceedings of 15th Annual Convention, 91–93. International Woodworkers of America Papers, University of Washington Special Collections, Box 10.

Even without federation support, the IWA played an important role in the Northwest's environmental politics in order to provide recreational spaces for its membership. In the 1950s, environmental groups began pushing for the protection of roadless areas. The IWA provided vital working-class support from workers directly affected by the withdrawal of timberlands from production. When the timber industry fought once again to reduce Olympic National Park boundaries in the late 1940s and early 1950s, the union publicly opposed it, although over the objections of its own locals in the region. Hartung justified the IWA's position by calling the park "some of the most magnificent recreation country on the North American continent," and noting that its old growth "will soon be one of the few remaining stands accessible for public recreation."[111] The IWA's support for the Olympics pleased environmentalists such as Wilderness Society head Howard Zahniser, and raised hopes for more labor support for wilderness protection.[112] The IWA also gave support to protections for what became the Three Sisters Wilderness.[113] When Hartung testified before the Senate Committee on Interior and Insular Affairs in support of a 1958 wilderness bill, he articulated an expansive vision of postwar prosperity. Envisioning a future where a growing population combined with technological innovation and a federal commitment to full employment, he saw no alternative but a shorter workweek. Wilderness gave workers a place to enjoy their expanding free time. Hartung argued that a failure to act would cause the nation's children to "hold us responsible for having cheated them of part of their birthright as Americans."[114]

The government did protect some of the future generations' birthright through the 1964 Wilderness Act, which the IWA supported. Consuming nature spoke to the real lives of union members who hunted and fished in their off hours and wanted protection for their leisure activities. However, the IWA's attempt to create working-class forests mostly failed. The new

[111] Resolution No. 17, 1942, IWA Box 37, Folder 17, Con Recs – Call, Committees, 1948; Proceedings of 12th Constitutional Convention, 1948, IWA Box 25, Folder 7; Al Hartung, "Statement on Olympic National, Park," September 25, 1953, IWA Box 280, Folder 43.

[112] Mark Harvey, *Wilderness Forever: Howard Zahniser and the Path to the Wilderness Act* (Seattle: University of Washington Press, 2005), 127–28.

[113] Kevin Marsh, *Lines in the Forest: Creating Wilderness Areas in the Pacific Northwest* (Seattle: University of Washington Press, 2009), 28–29.

[114] Hartung Statement in Support of the Wilderness Bill, November 7, 1958, IWA Box 280, Folder 47.

era of forestry was not one of intensive government regulation to ensure timber supplies, employment, and ecological integrity in perpetuity. Instead, the timber industry set the national forestry agenda. The principle of multiple use that dominated the USFS's early decades transformed into an almost singular focus on timber management. Between 1946 and 1952, timber harvests on USFS land expanded from 2.47 billion to 4.52 billion board feet.[115] Sustained-yield forestry became "maximum sustained yield," with foresters using fantastical predictions about future harvests when making decisions about current harvests. Clearcutting became standard practice. The government did increasingly provide recreational facilities for tourists, but recreation was a secondary mission within the USFS, a distraction from getting out the cut.

The government may have provided some protection for Americans' birthright to the forests, but the IWA believed in a second birthright: stable employment and economic security. Postwar forestry ignored these principles. Between 1948 and 1962, 85 percent of small mills in Oregon closed, compared to only 33 percent of large mills, dooming many one-mill towns to oblivion.[116] Still, more than any union in the United States, the IWA connected conservation and work, seeing sustainable forestry and the federal regulation of all logging as the clearest path to forest management for working-class interests. The IWA channeled fears of unemployment and community instability into concrete policy goals that sought to force the timber industry to give up much of its autonomy and instead prioritize communities over profit.

Moreover, the IWA offered a powerful critique of forest practices that presaged the environmental movement forty years later, even if this history was lost to environmentalists. The Great Depression opened rare space in American society not only to critique the actions of American capital but also to fight at the highest levels of government for meaningful change. The IWA foresaw the future of the Pacific Northwest timber industry as its past: cut-out and get-out. Its timeline proved accurate; a half-century after its creation, the Northwest forests would face a crisis due to overcutting and a lack of reforestation, among other issues. Like the rest of radical labor within the CIO, by the time the IWA organized itself into an effective force, the nation was on the brink of World War II. The possibility for radical change died in the conservative turn after the

[115] Clary, *Timber and the Forest Service*, 125.

[116] Young and Newton, *Capitalism and Human Obsolescence: Corporate Control vs. Individual Survival in Rural America* (Montclair, NJ: Landmark Studies, 1980), 32.

war. The timber industry's victory in the battles over forest regulation had immense implications upon workers, forest ecology, and the future of the Pacific Northwest. In 1938, the union newspaper told IWA members that the industry would die by 2000 if the timber industry did not change its ways.[117] It was right.

117 "Pacific Logging Congress: An Editorial, *The Timber Worker*, October 29, 1938.

4

The Total Work Environment

In 1985, the International Woodworkers of America, in coalition with several partners that included the Oregon Environmental Council, lobbied the Oregon state legislature to pass House Bill 2254. This bill would strengthen so-called "right-to-know" regulations, obligating employers to inform workers of the chemicals they handled on the job. For Morris Sweet, an IWA member from Molalla, Oregon, and "a sawmill worker who has had my health severely damaged by toxic chemicals in the work place," the passage of this bill was of the utmost importance. Sweet worked for thirteen years in sawmills. Eight months after he started work in 1969, he woke up with the skin on his nose split open. A test revealed exposure to pentachlorophenol, a dioxin-based chemical frequently used in wood preservation after World War II. Sweet continued at the job for another twelve years, suffering rashes and cramps. Sweet did not know what was happening to him, but "the thing I noticed is that I always felt sick." Finally, he filed a workers' compensation claim in 1981 for penta exposure, which was rejected by the state. Although the right-to-know bill failed, the testimony of workers like Sweet provided powerful first-hand narratives that made unsafe working environments a central point of contention between IWA members and timber employers in the 1970s and 1980s. Like in the 1910s, timber workers used their union to fight to protect their bodies from the hazards of industrial forestry.[1]

[1] Morris Sweet letter to the editor, *The Oregonian*, March 11, 1985, found in IWA Box 310, Folder 7; "The Penta Problem," *The Oregonian*, September 8, 1984, found in IWA Box 311, Folder 34.

Whereas forest policy primarily engaged union officials, workplace health placed power into the hands of workers to evaluate their own workplaces and shape the environment in which they labored. The timber industry remained one of the nation's most dangerous industries throughout the twentieth century. Protecting members from illness, injury, and death was a central mission of the IWA from its founding. Yet between 1970 and 1979, 1,372 timber workers died in California, Oregon, and Washington.[2] To fight this death toll, in the 1970s the IWA drew from the language of environmentalism to promote health and safety for workers. Conceptualizing the workplace as a corporate-created environment helped the IWA to become a national leader among unions on workplace health. Union leaders investigated the toxicity of the chemicals their members used daily, the noises that reduced members' hearing, and the wood dust that limited breathing capacity. In doing so, the IWA empowered workers on the shop floor to demand safe conditions, stop work if they felt unsafe, and use the nation's new workplace safety regulatory structure as a way to channel the unrest that affected much of the nation's working class in the 1970s into productive action.[3]

The environmental movement becoming a national political force was a necessary ingredient to the IWA workplace safety program. Early-1970s environmentalism was a complex set of movements that together focused both on land preservation and the daily environmental problems Americans experienced, ranging from air pollution to toxic waste. Earth Day in 1970 announced mass-movement environmentalism to the public, contributing to groundbreaking legislation in the 1970 Clean Air Act amendments, the 1972 ban on DDT, and the 1973 EPA decision to phase out leaded gasoline. From the Cuyahoga River fire and Santa Barbara oil spill in 1969 through the Love Canal in 1978 and the creation

[2] Fred Rose, *Coalitions across the Class Divide: Lessons from the Labor, Peace, and Environmental Movements* (Ithaca: Cornell University Press, 2000), 61.

[3] On labor and the 1970s and 1980s, see Joseph McCartin, *Collision Course: Ronald Reagan, the Air Traffic Controllers, and the Strike that Changed America* (New York: Oxford University Press, 2011); Jonathan D. Rosenblum, *Copper Crucible: How the Arizona Miners' Strike of 1983 Recast Labor-Management Relations in America* (Ithaca: Cornell University Press, 1995); Barbara Kingsolver, *Holding the Line: Women in the Great Arizona Miners' Strike of 1983* (Ithaca: Cornell University Press, 1989); Jefferson Cowie, *Stayin' Alive: The 1970s and the Last Days of the Working Class* (New York: The New Press, 2010); Frank Bardacke, *Trampling out the Vintage: Cesar Chavez and the Two Souls of the United Farm Workers* (New York: Verso, 2011); Matthew Garcia, *From the Jaws of Victory: The Triumph and Tragedy of Cesar Chavez and the Farm Worker Movement* (Berkeley: University of California Press, 2012).

of Superfund in 1980, environmentalism that focused on the hazards of industrialization had important working-class support needed to pass legislation and create regulatory structures for the new laws.[4]

The labor movement's relationship with this rising environmentalism was complex, especially after the 1973 oil crisis and recession. Some unions saw environmentalists as job killers, a sentiment encouraged by employers seeking cover for already existing plans to shutter plants and reopen them overseas, a phenomenon becoming all too common by the early 1970s. However, for some unions, particularly those with a left-leaning social agenda, an environmental movement committed to fighting against toxic exposure and for public health provided language to articulate their complaints about unsafe workplaces. Labor and environmental activists formed alliances, sometimes wary, sometimes close, to fight for safe and healthy workplaces, bodies, and homes. Spearheading these ideas was the Oil, Chemical and Atomic Workers (OCAW), which under the leadership of Tony Mazzocchi had led the fight for the Occupational Safety and Health Act of 1970. Mazzocchi, influenced by Rachel Carson's *Silent Spring*, became a national leader on cleaning up the workplace environment, connecting environmental issues to the health and safety of his membership, and forging alliances between environmentalists and labor unions. OCAW was only one of many unions, including the IWA, to center the working environment in its 1970s agenda.[5] Thinking about

[4] *Rachel Carson, Silent Spring, and the Rise of the Environmental Movement* (New York: Oxford University Press, 2007); Linda Lear, *Rachel Carson: Witness for Nature* (Boston: Houghton Mifflin, 2009); Adam Rome, *The Genius of Earth Day: How a 1970 Teach-in Unexpectedly Made the First Green Generation* (New York: Hill and Wang, 2013); Robert Gottlieb, *Forcing the Spring: The Transformation of the American Environmental Movement*, Rev. edn. (Washington D.C.: Island Press, 2005); Kirkpatrick Sale, *The Green Revolution: The American Environmental Movement, 1962–1992* (New York: Hill and Wang, 1993); Philip Shabecoff, *A Fierce Green Fire: The American Environmental Movement*, Rev. edn. (Washington, D.C.: Island Press, 2003); J. Samuel Walker, *Three Mile Island: A Nuclear Crisis in Historical Perspective* (Berkeley: University of California Press, 2006); Lois Marie Gibbs, *Love Canal and the Birth of the Environmental Movement* (Washington, D.C.: Island Press, 2011); Elizabeth D. Blum, *Love Canal Revisited: Race, Class, and Gender in Environmental Activism* (Lawrence: University Press of Kansas, 2008).

[5] Literature on toxicity and the human-centered environment that developed in the 1960s and 1970s include David Zierler, *The Invention of Ecocide: Agent Orange, Vietnam, and the Scientists Who Changed the Way We Think about the Environment* (Athens: University of Georgia Press, 2011); Peter H. Schuck, *Agent Orange on Trial: Mass Toxic Disasters in the Courts*, Rev. edn. (Cambridge: Belknap Press of Harvard University Press, 1987); Mark Hamilton Lytle, *The Gentle Subversive: Rachel Carson, Silent Spring, and the Rise of the Environmental Movement* (New York: Oxford University Press, 2007); Andrew Hurley, *Environmental Inequalities: Class, Race, and Industrial Pollution in*

workplaces as toxic environments gave IWA international officers, local officials, and individual workers a toolbox for to make members safer and healthier. In doing so, the union built on existing relationships it had with the Northwest's environmental organizations, alliances that grew in importance as the Occupational Safety and Health Administration (OSHA) came under attack in the 1980s from an organized business lobby and a hostile Reagan administration.

However, by the 1970s, the American labor movement had begun a multi-decade membership loss that continues today. Labor's campaign to stop widespread capital flight to the lightly unionized American South, Mexico, and Asia proved futile. New organizing efforts in the public sector could not make up for the loss of millions of unionized factory jobs.[6] Timber unions shared the problems of the rest of the labor movement. The IWA saw its numbers decline as automation, the exportation of unprocessed logs to Japan, and capital mobility to forests in the South and abroad undermined timber employment numbers. Companies shut down their unionized mills and kept their non-union operations open. By 1985, less than 10 percent of timber workers in the United States had union representation, although the IWA and Carpenters kept union representation in the Northwest at slightly more than 30 percent.[7]

Gary, Indiana, 1945–1980 (Chapel Hill: University of North Carolina Press, 1995); Gottlieb, *Forcing the Spring*; Luke W. Cole and Sheila R. Foster, *From the Ground Up: Environmental Racism and the Rise of the Environmental Justice Movement* (New York: New York University Press, 2000); Robert Gordon, "Poisons in the Fields: The United Farm Workers, Pesticides, and Environmental Politics," *Pacific Historical Review* 68, no. 1 (February 1999): 51–77. On blue–green alliances, see William Brucher, "From the Picket Line to the Playground: Labor, Environmental Activism, and the International Paper Strike in Jay, Maine," *Labor History* 52, no. 1 (January 2011): 95–116; Robert Gordon, "'Shell No!' OCAW and the Environmental–Labor Alliance," *Environmental History* 3, no. 4 (October 1998): 460–87; Richard Kazis and Richard L. Grossman, *Fear at Work: Job Blackmail, Labor, and the Environment* (New York: The Pilgrim Press, 1982); Andrew Szasz, *EcoPopulism: Toxic Waste and the Movement for Environmental Justice* (Minneapolis: University of Minnesota Press, 1994); Fred Rose, *Coalitions across the Class Divide: Lessons from the Labor, Peace, and Environmental Movements* (Ithaca: Cornell University Press, 2000); Brian K. Obach, *Labor and the Environmental Movement: The Quest for Common Ground* (Cambridge: The MIT Press, 2004); Les Leopold, *The Man Who Hated Work and Loved Labor: The Life and Times of Tony Mazzocchi* (White River Junction, VT: Chelsea Green Publishing, 2007).

[6] Jefferson Cowie, *Capital Moves: RCA's Seventy-Year Quest for Cheap Labor* (New York: The New Press, 1999); Erik Loomis, *Out of Sight: The Long and Disturbing Story of Corporations Outsourcing Catastrophe* (New York: The New Press, 2015).

[7] OSHA, "Industry Profile for the Proposed Standard on Logging," March 1985, IWA Box 310, Folder 27.

Responding to the demands of its members to keep their bodies safe from the chemical and industrial hazards of the modern logging workplace, the IWA fought a bitter battle to do so in the face of enormous challenges. Shrinking numbers and the resultant budget crisis made making new demands of employers unusual for many unions in the era, but the IWA responded differently. Although the union spent a great deal of energy fighting losing battles to save its members' jobs, it also took up new battles for workplace health and safety that, although difficult to implement given the union's declining numbers, had the potential to both build important alliances with environmental organizations and acquire new rights at the workplace for workers to control their own bodies.

WORKPLACE HEALTH AND SAFETY BEFORE OSHA

Forestry policy dominated the IWA's legislative goals in the 1930s and 1940s, but for everyday workers, safe workplaces were probably of greater importance. The Industrial Workers of the World had forced sanitary reforms, but workplace safety remained poor in the industry, as it was in blue-collar labor nationally during the 1930s.[8] In November 1936, an Aberdeen union local counted thirty-three members in area hospitals for work-related injuries.[9] At its first convention, the IWA passed a resolution condemning the continued dominance of company-chosen physicians over loggers' health care, particularly in the context of increased technological advancement and the speed-up, or increased pace of work, which it blamed for the industry's high fatality rates. Future conventions would see similar resolutions, as workers sought to use their union to stay alive on the job.[10] The slow violence of loggers seeing their friends die and knowing companies, the government, and the media did not care rankled. An anonymous logger wrote, "a logging accident has as much news rating as a man being bitten by a dog."[11] Floyd Christey of the North Bend Timber Company was a timber rigger, a job that consisted of attaching pulleys to a spar tree used as a base to drag logs to their gathering point. However, North Bend had the timber fallers work too

[8] Martin Cherniack, *The Hawk's Nest Incident: America's Worst Industrial Disaster* (New Haven: Yale University Press, 1989).

[9] "Hospital List," *The Timber Worker*, November 6, 1936.

[10] Proceedings of the Second Semi-Annual Convention of Federation of Woodworkers, Longview, Washington. February 20–22, 1937, IWA Box 25, Folder 1.

[11] "Lumber Has Black Record for Death in Woods, Mills," *The Timber Worker*, October 5, 1940.

close to the riggers and a falling limb killed Christey. His IWA local unanimously pledged to "bend every effort toward seeing that there are no more avoidable accidents."[12] A logging camp near Seaside, Oregon, walked out in 1941 because management ordered them to work cutting trees on a windy day, an extremely dangerous proposition. No one in this unionized crew lost their jobs over this wildcat action.[13]

The IWA blamed the state as much as the employers for this death toll. After 1938 saw 104 deaths in Washington forests, the most since 1930, IWA member Ken Pettus said, "the Department of Labor and Industries' criminal, intentional failure to launch a program of accident program in the logging industry borders on murder," and blamed the agency for licking "timber baron boots."[14] Union member A.R. Thomas suggested the state staff the safety inspectors with "experienced loggers whose integrity is beyond question." Barring that, "if we are to promote a safety campaign in the woods the job is squarely up to the union" because no one else could be trusted to do so.[15] The IWA endorsed Clarence Dill for governor of Washington in 1940 because of his commitment to increasing timber safety inspections. Dill's narrow defeat may not have forestalled a revolution in timber workplace safety, but it helped demonstrate the challenges the IWA would have in electing politicians who prioritized the lives of its members.[16]

Workplace safety is not just about staying alive. It is also about having control over one's own body at work. Washington's low compensation rates for injury and death dehumanized loggers, leading one union editorial to note that employers "have written a price list on human flesh."[17] Timber companies, like many employers, forced workers into employer-sponsored physicals through the mid-twentieth century, facilitating corporate control over the livelihood of the same people who had become sick and injured due to unsafe working practices. American labor had long resented these physicals for their arbitrary nature and the power it placed in employers to intimidate workers.[18] In 1946, a California IWA local went so far as to demand union-owned hospitals where workers hired the

[12] "Logger's Death Laid at Company's Door," *The Timber Worker*, May 25, 1940.
[13] "Loggers Demand Safety for Production," *The Timber Worker*, November 27, 1941.
[14] "Death Stalks Woods," *The Timber Worker*, October 26, 1940.
[15] "Letter," *The Timber Worker*, January 4, 1941.
[16] "Dill Pledges Logging Safety at IWA Parley," *The Timber Worker*, October 12, 1940; "Lauds Plans to Enforce Safety Laws," *The Timber Worker*, October 26, 1940.
[17] "The Price on Flesh," *The Timber Worker*, November 9, 1940.
[18] Christopher Sellers, *Hazards of the Job*, 118–21.

doctors, although nothing came of it.[19] As late as 1955, IWA Local 140 in Reedsport, Oregon, protested against employers using company physicians because it gave companies power to get rid of workers it did not want, incentivized hiring young workers in order to lower insurance rates, and valued single men over men with children because their workers' compensation rates were lower. All told, it showed that "the profit hunger of these large outfits seems to be without limit. The welfare of their employees certainly seems to be considered last."[20]

Like with the decline of its forestry program, the IWA's approach to workplace safety became more cooperative to employers by the late 1940s, focusing on safety committees negotiated in union contracts. Ideally, union–management safety committees met regularly and made recommendations on improvements in safety and health, created worker education programs, made first aid equipment and first aid training for workers available, and convinced companies to supply protective equipment. However, this hardly guaranteed effective safety committees. In 1956, Local 140 was happy that the State Industrial Accident Commission had scheduled safety classes for the mill. But it wondered what good they would be when the company passed around alcohol at safety committee meetings to put workers "in a mellow mood where they would get off onto subjects of fishing, women, etc., and not bear down on safety subjects ... Employers have been bearing down on drinking on the job or coming on the job reeking with drink. We insist that the same rule apply to supervisors that applies to production workers." Workers did not have to imbibe, but this employer-created chummy culture could inhibit the vigorous enforcement of safety standards.[21]

The ultimate fault for unsafe workplaces came from corporate stonewalling over giving up control over the workplace and admitting fault for accidents and illness. Instead, companies sought to shift blame for accidents away from their unsafe workplaces and onto workers. Corporations held to what became known as the "unsafe act theory," which argued that careless workers were responsible for most accidents and thus employers needed to train them to act with caution. The unsafe act theory allowed timber executives to limit their commitment to workplace safety. R.M. Evenden, the director of accident prevention for the Oregon State Industrial Accident Commission, wrote in 1946 to tell owners that their idea that 85 percent of the responsibility for workplace accidents lies with

[19] Resolution No. 12, IWA Box 37, Folder 8.

[20] Local 140 Newsletter, May 31, 1955, IWA Box 275a, Folder 6.

[21] IWA Local 140 Newsletter, February 17, 1956, IWA Box 275a, Folder 6.

employees was "a fallacy." Noting a recent case of a log truck driver killed when a tree next to the road fell on him, Evenden gently told employers that while the driver may have worked too close to the trees, they had a responsibility to cut down trees next to roads because their weakened root systems meant a greater chance of falling. Rather than ask why workers were unsafe, Evenden told them to combine that question with asking why conditions themselves were unsafe. But without a legal reason to do so, companies largely did not take such critiques seriously.[22]

The IWA thus turned to the state to plead for a stronger regulatory framework on workplace safety. In the 1950s and 1960s, the states of Oregon, Washington, and California all held accident prevention conferences where the IWA made its case for a greater government role. Al Hartung told the California Governor's Safety Conference in 1958 that the average union member responds enthusiastically to employer-led safety programs, but employers refused to take worker input seriously or fix problems. When that happened, "then that spirit is dampened and sometimes completely extinguished by the inability to obtain the kind of action or reform that labor knows must be made for the safety program to become effective." Hartung believed only government mandates could make safety programs effective and he encouraged the state of California to improve workers' compensation benefits, charge companies higher rates for accidents, and increase safety inspectors in the field. Hartung made similar arguments to the President's Conference on Occupational Safety in 1960, when he claimed that the real way to improve safety was to make companies pay 100 percent of a worker's salary through worker compensation.[23] With such action not forthcoming, the workplace environment remained an intractable problem for timber workers through the 1960s. By the early 1970s, calls for increased federal interference in workplace safety would come to fruition and help a newly energized IWA empower its workers to keep themselves alive and healthy.

THE TOTAL WORK ENVIRONMENT

Although workplace health and safety did not dominate the agenda of most American unions in the postwar period, by the late 1960s low

22 "Why Do Accidents Happen," *The Timberman*, August 1946, 124–26.

23 "Speech by A.F. Hartung to the California Governor's Safety Conference," IWA Box 280, Folder 9; Hartung, "Address to the President's Conference on Occupational Safety," IWA Box 71, Folder 10.

unemployment and a healthy economy turned the attention of some unions, particularly the Oil, Chemical and Atomic Workers, United Auto Workers, and United Steelworkers of America, toward pushing for regulatory reform that would make American workplaces safer. For the Steelworkers, although not the AFL-CIO, this led to a call for comprehensive reform legislation, while for the Black Lung Associations within the United Mine Workers of America, federal workplace health legislation represented a rebellion against the indifference of workers' own union leadership. By 1968, the AFL-CIO supported an occupational safety bill, which attracted Lyndon Johnson as a way to cement the Democratic Party's increasingly fragile relationship with working-class whites after signing landmark civil rights legislation. While no bill passed in 1968, in 1970, President Richard Nixon signed the Occupational Safety and Health Act after significant lobbying from organized labor. OSHA created a single government agency, housed within the Department of Labor, with the power to set standards on workplace safety for the first time in the nation's history. It also created the National Institute for Occupational Safety and Health (NIOSH) in the Department of Health, Education, and Welfare to manage the federal research effort into workplace hazards. With an enforcement mechanism that included federal workplace inspectors and fines for violations, OSHA was an unprecedented tool to improve working conditions. Like the Environmental Protection Agency, also created in 1970, OSHA sought to regulate and mitigate the effects of industry's environmental impact on the nation.[24]

The IWA played no major role in the creation of OSHA, although union President Ronald Roley said, "we owe a deep debt of gratitude to those fine legislators in the Congress who passed this legislation."[25] OSHA created national injury reporting standards for the first time. In 1976 and 1977 alone, Washington timber workers suffered 3,821 nonfatal accidents. In 1977, workers suffered 928 chainsaw injuries. Falling

[24] David Noble, *Liberalism at Work: The Rise and Fall of OSHA* (Philadelphia: Temple University Press, 1986); John Mendeloff, *Regulating Safety: An Economic and Political Analysis of Occupational Safety and Health Policy* (Cambridge; The MIT Press, 1979); John Wooding and Charles Levenstein, *The Point of Production: Work Environment in Advanced Industrial Societies* (New York: The Guilford Press, 1999), 82–89; Derek Oden, "Selling Safety: The Farm Safety Movement's Emergence and Evolution from 1940–1975," *Agricultural History* 79, no. 4 (Fall 2005): 412–38; Andrew Szasz, "Industrial Resistance to Occupational Safety and Health Legislation, 1971–1981," *Social Problems* 32, no. 2 (December 1984): 103–16. On OCAW's environmentalism, see Gordon, "Shell No!"

[25] Western States Regional Council 1971 Minutes, IWA Box 31, Folder 21.

limbs struck 196 timber workers and logs hit 155. Falling objects, usually at mills, struck an additional 652 workers. Between 1974 and 1977, thirty-six timber workers died in Washington, leaving twenty-nine widows and fifty children. Five more died in the first four months of 1978. One died from a falling limb while falling a tree in the forest. Another fell off a tree he was falling. A third died when a tree dislodged another tree that landed on him. Miscommunication killed a fourth when a falling tree hit a worker who was supposed to be out of the way. The fifth perished after explosives placed under a stump did not explode, leading an unknowing worker to be blown up when he set the primer for another explosion the next day.[26]

Workers' anger over the death and injury of their fellow workers was palpable. Two members of IWA Local 3–101 filed a grievance in 1977 after a piece of lumber fell and injured a worker because a safety railing was broken. The company took the worker to the hospital and then immediately ordered another man to the same position before fixing the safety railing several hours later. The grievers complained that production should have stopped until the railing was fixed. Noting that it was impossible for a worker to do his job and watch for falling lumber at the same time, they asked, "We already had one serious accident. Was it worth the risk of another just for production?"[27]

These workers found champions in the IWA's new leadership. Keith Johnson replaced Ronald Roley as union president in 1972. An Alberta plywood worker who had organized his mill in the 1950s and had risen through IWA leadership, the forty-three-year-old Johnson was one of the AFL-CIO's youngest union presidents. Johnson provided a sharp break from the business unionism of the Hartung and Roley eras. He brought the union back toward its radical roots of the 1930s and 1940s, asserting its right to chart its own path on the region's environmental debates, supporting grassroots activism within the union, and building alliances with political progressives both within the United States and internationally. Johnson sharply disagreed with the AFL–CIO's anticommunist foreign policy, serving on the National Labor Committee in Support of Democracy in El Salvador in the 1980s, an organization deeply critical of the Reagan administration's policies in Central

[26] Occupational Safety and Health Report, March 1976, IWA Box 311, Folder 25; Steve Levette to Ralph Gregor, June 15, 1978, IWA Box 303, Folder 16.

[27] Greg Stevenson and Ed Lawson Grievance, February 13, 1977, International Woodworkers of America, Local 3–101 Papers, University of Washington Special Collections, Box 5, Folder 1. Emphasis in original document.

America.[28] Johnson brought to the IWA a suspicion of unregulated capitalism, a distrust grounded in the effects of industry upon workers' bodies. At the 1979 IWA Convention, Johnson told delegates, "let's face it, profit is money and money is capital and the people who control capital are capitalists. Capitalists do not care if workers are crippled by unsafe plant environments ... Capitalists do not care if the parents of workers must rot with untreated disease, or the children of workers die at birth ... These are harsh words but they are conclusions compelled by the facts."[29]

Johnson's tough words toward a system that killed workers would influence his priorities as union president. He had developed a background in worker health and safety as vice-president, serving as the IWA representative for Occupational Safety and Health after the passage of OSHA. Johnson hired a new research director that would turn the department into an office dedicated to fighting against unsafe workplaces. R. Denny Scott was a labor economist who had worked for the International Association of Machinists and then as research director for the International Printing Pressmen's Union before coming to the IWA. Scott became the IWA point man on researching and crafting policies, reports, and regulations. He also was the point man on answering workers' questions about their workplace environment and aimed to use OSHA to provide workers the tools they needed to ensure safe working environments for themselves.[30]

To accomplish these goals, Scott called for a focus on the "total work environment." Borrowing this language from the nascent environmental movement, Scott meant thinking about the relationship between worker and workplace in a holistic context that considered how the nature of work affected the human body. This could empower workers to see themselves as part of a work ecosystem that could be transformed. It meant workers and their unions should have the full knowledge of the plant environment. Scott wanted companies to open their books about "accidents, toxic materials, environmental monitoring and the cost of safety materials and safety improvements." He demanded that safety committees have the authority to inspect worksites, investigate accidents, and review remodeling and construction projects for potential safety

[28] Roley to George H.R. Taylor, August 31, 1972, IWA Box 98, Folder 1.
[29] 1979 IWA Convention Minutes, IWA, Box 26, Folder 3.
[30] "Scott Joins R&E Staff," *International Woodworker* January 10, 1973.

problems. In short, Johnson and Scott placed the workplace environment front and center in the union's priorities.[31]

However, the IWA faced significant challenges in remaking the workplace environment. First, timber companies had little interest in reforming it. The still-dominant unsafe act theory meant employers saw health and safety as nuisances to be managed, not problems to be solved. Second, creating new OSHA regulations required acquiring medical data about workplace dangers. But timber work received very little attention from mid-twentieth century workplace medical researchers. Workers' anecdotal data meant little in crafting regulations. Before the 1970s, "we relied on suspicion (however well founded) and emotion in trying to make an argument for better working conditions," said a 1981 union report. Instead, the union now worked to gather data from its locals about workplace conditions.[32] While this placed agency over the workplace environment in the hands of workers, the IWA labored at a significant disadvantage in resources and power in comparison to its bosses. Third, OSHA only had a brief period of agency growth before employers organized to attack it. Given that the IWA did not immediately embrace OSHA as a way to empower workers, the overlap between a proactive OSHA and a proactive union was only a few years in the Carter administration. Ultimately, conceiving of the workplace as an environment had great potential to transform the union health and safety program but the structural barriers the IWA faced in implementing it blunted its power.

The IWA fought for reshaping the work environment on several fronts. The most ubiquitous problem was noise exposure. Noise had long affected industrial workers throughout the country. OSHA began working on a noise standard in 1972, but progress was glacial. Employers wanted workers to wear cumbersome safety equipment while workers wanted new engineering standards to reduce noise.[33] IWA members were furious at employers' attitudes toward hearing protection. Logger Jim Menefee supported an anti-noise resolution the IWA passed in 1977, which called timber executives "callous" and "inhumane" because they opposed reducing the noise standard in mills to 85 dba from the common dba of well more than 105, which NIOSH had declared the safety standard

[31] "The IWA Safety Program: Its Past and Its Future," IWA Box 300, Folder 7; 1977 IWA Convention Minutes, IWA Box 26, Folder 2.

[32] "Western States Regional Council No. 3 Officers' Report to the 22nd Constitutional Convention," IWA Box 54, Folder 12.

[33] Steven Kelman, *Regulating America, Regulating Sweden: A Comparative Study of Occupational Safety and Health Policy* (Cambridge: The MIT Press, 1981), 19–30.

for logging. But Menefee could not figure out how to put teeth into such a resolution when companies controlled the testing and monitoring process. Workers took hearing tests and received no information from the companies who would not share noise levels with workers, saying they would have to take the company's word. When employers did do something about noise, it was to force workers to wear uncomfortable hearing mufflers rather than reducing noise emissions. Or, as Joe Wilson put it, "out at my plant the first damn thing is the company comes around with a great big damn thing they stick on your head."[34]

A 1974 compliance abatement agreement between timber employers and OSHA included an agreement for employers to hire an acoustical engineering firm to help reduce noise in mills in exchange for reduced penalties for noise violations. The companies created a noise control guidebook for sawmills in 1977, but the requirements for employer compliance were low and the Carter administration's OSHA pulled back from industry-wide agreements with meaningful compliance regulations.[35] In 1985, Scott noted that no progress had been made on noise reduction in logging since the early 1970s because industry so successfully appealed violations that tests of logging operations ended by the late 1970s.[36] For timber workers, noise was a consistent hazard that neither government nor industry did much to solve.[37]

While the whirring saws and powerful machinery of the timber mill created a noisy environment for mill workers, for loggers, chainsaws damaged hearing. Chainsaws became the dominant technology for logging in the 1940s. In the 1970s, responding to pressures over chainsaw noise from both loggers and consumers buying them for their homes and farms, chainsaw makers began putting mufflers on the machines to help prevent this. However, quieter chainsaws ran at higher temperatures that could start forest fires. In 1978, the U.S. Forest Service issued new chainsaw regulations, limiting their internal temperatures to 450 degrees Fahrenheit. Even with the mufflers, chainsaw noise levels exceeded OSHA

[34] 1977 IWA Convention Minutes, IWA Box 26, Folder 2. See "Industrial Hygiene Section," May 7, 1980, IWA Box 3, Folder 4 for a set of mill dba readings that regularly reached more than 100, and Johnson to Anthony Robbins, May 30, 1979, IWA Box 291, Folder 24 for the 105 decision.

[35] "Noise Control Guidebook Out for Sawmills," *International Woodworker*, October 20, 1976.

[36] Scott to File, July 22, 1985, IWA Box 311, Folder 28.

[37] Andrew Szasz, "Industrial Resistance to Occupational Safety and Health Legislation, 1971–1981," *Social Problems* 32, no. 2 (December 1984): 103–16.

standards; without them, the sound could be deafening, literally over the long term. OSHA standards suggested worker exposure be limited to 105 dba for no longer than one hour a day, but the saws that allowed cutting at USFS-mandated temperatures ranged between 105 and 119 dbas for the entire workday.[38] The IWA could not support damaging workers' hearing in exchange for increased fire protection, telling the Forest Service, "we don't object to preventing forest fires ... but loggers should not be required to lose their hearing in the process."[39] Yet despite the union filing an OSHA protest, the standard held, once again showing the limited power the union to shape its work environment.

Chainsaws could also lead to potentially deadly chainsaw kickbacks. In 1977, consumers filed a lawsuit with the Consumer Product Safety Commission (CPSC) to create a kickback regulation after a homeowner suffered a disfigured face from a chainsaw accident. The chainsaw industry proposed self-regulation. However, its marketing campaign was aimed at the homeowner, not the timber industry. The industry resisted noise restrictions because consumers enjoyed a loud chainsaw.[40] In 1978, over IWA protests and internal division, the CPSC allowed the chainsaw industry to set its own regulations. But the industry never intended to create regulations and saw it as a measure to kill time. It missed the deadline, leading the union to press the CPSC to issue standards for the industry, arguing that "the chain saw manufacturing industry has proven that their economic interest in making and marketing a cheap, lightweight backyard chain saw conflicts with the public's need for an effective safeguard against kickback."[41] The CPSC suspended the effort to work with chainsaw manufacturers on a safety code in February 1980. CPSC Executive Director Richard Gross chastised the industry, noting, "an effort like this requires good faith and I am disturbed that they appear to have held back information."[42] Ultimately, little came of this attempt to regulate an industry that was destroying loggers' hearing.

Chainsaws also gave workers vibration white finger, a form of Raynaud's syndrome that creates discoloration in the fingers and toes, with workers' fingers turning white because of the constant hours of vibration they suffered in cold weather. Numbness and pain were other symptoms and the

[38] Scott to M.R. Howlett, May 8, 1978, IWA Box 311, Folder 19.
[39] Scott to Luigi U. Di Bernando, July 5, 1978, IWA Box 311, Folder 19.
[40] Scott to Jonathan Falk, June 20, 1977, IWA Box 300, Folder 25.
[41] Johnson to Susan King, et al., January 23, 1980, IWA Box 291, Folder 24.
[42] "Safer Chain Saws: 'Makers Not Trying,'" *Longview Daily News*, February 2, 1980.

long-term effects included the loss of hand function, arthritis, and permanent nerve damage. Extreme cases led to amputation. A 1979 IWA survey showed 20 percent of timber fallers suffering permanent disability due to chainsaw injuries.[43] An Oregon timber faller remembered laughing at his partner in the late 1960s for constantly warming his hands over a fire in order to ward off white finger. The partner retorted that his time was coming. As the cutter remembered, "he was right," as he developed the same syndrome in the late 1970s. When one worker found himself unable to use his hands, even to tie his shoes, he knew his time had come. As IWA member John Gregg remembered it, "eventually his partner walked over – and found the younger faller sitting on his haunches, laces loose, hands tight under his armpits, crying."[44]

Although investigators first noticed the problem in the 1910s and European and Japanese loggers had fought for recognition of the problem since the early 1960s, there was little American interest in white finger before 1970. Denny Scott read about these studies and began incorporating the issue into the IWA total work environment program in the mid-1970s, running union newspaper stories on the syndrome to publicize it to members. These led to workers' families writing to the union to express both frustration and relief that they finally knew what happened to the hands of their logger family members. After reading an *International Woodworker* article on white finger, Thelma Walczyk wrote to the IWA in 1978 about her husband, Frank, a logger since 1941 who had to stop work because of the damage to his hands. She hoped for more scientific information, but the IWA simply did not have it and apologized to her, noting it publicized whatever it could learn.[45] The University of Washington's Department of Environmental Health conducted a limited testing program on fifty IWA members to study white finger.[46] However, creating federal standards on white finger proved no more successful than many of the union's workplace safety efforts. Scott noted that the lack of a successful workers' compensation claim for white finger meant that employers had no financial incentive to prevent the condition.[47] Ultimately, attracting federal interest proved unfruitful. The IWA teamed

[43] Johnson to Dr. Pah Chen, February 13, 1981, IWA Box 291, Folder 24.

[44] "Studies Show Power Saws Cause 'White Finger,'" *International Woodworker*, December 15, 1976; "Chain Saw Vibration: Loggers," *International Woodworker*, May 26, 1978.

[45] Thelma Walczyk to Roy Ockert, November 3, 1978 and Ockert to Walczyk, November 29, 1978, IWA Box 300, Folder 21.

[46] Scott to Ted Bryant, October 13, 1978, IWA Box 106, Folder 7.

[47] Scott to Jonathan Falk, June 20, 1977, IWA Box 300, Folder 25.

up with researchers at Portland State University in 1979 to submit a grant for NIOSH funding to develop safeguards for workers using chainsaws. NIOSH rejected the application. Once again the IWA lacked the power to force changes to the workplace.[48]

Loggers' ears and fingers were only two parts of the body that needed protection from the timber mills. A third was the lungs. Although wood dust was long an irritant to mill workers, only in the early 1970s, when studies showed higher incidences of leukemia-lymphoma cancers among loggers, did unions begin taking it seriously.[49] Wood dust was particularly problematic for western red cedar, causing workers allergic reactions, scarred retinas, and cancers. Adenocarcinoma, a cancer of the adenoids, was known to result from wood dust exposure, but it did not appear until forty years after initial exposure and studies lacked on how it affected current timber workers. Other cancers included nasal cancer (the most common), lung cancer, and Hodgkin's disease, where one medical study showed higher mortality rates among Washington pulp and paper workers.[50]

Workers demanded state involvement in wood dust. Local 3–246 in Springfield, Oregon, inquired to the state Accident Prevention Board about using compressed air every seventy-two hours to blow wood dust out of the mill that made particleboard.[51] IWA members requested a NIOSH inspection of a Longview, Washington, mill in 1976. The agency engaged in a full site inspection and tested 250 workers for dust exposure. It found 13.5 percent of workers had developed occupational asthma from breathing in dust with toxic levels of both fir and hemlock dust found that exceeded the 5-milligram-per-cubic-meter standard. Based upon these inspections, in 1979 NIOSH issued recommendations that included pre-employment medical examinations, frequent breathing tests for workers, better dust vacuuming technology and exhaust ventilation, and lowering the dust standard to 2.5 milligrams per cubic meter.[52]

[48] Johnson to Dr. Anthony Robbins, May 30, 1979, IWA Box 291, Folder 24.

[49] Occupational Safety and Health Report, March 1976, IWA Box 311, Folder 25.

[50] John Lund, "Wood Dust: Much More Than a Nuisance," *International Woodworker*, July 25, 1981; "The IWA Health and Safety Program: Its Past and Its Future," IWA Box 300, Folder 7; Denny Scott to Richard Lemen, November 5, 1980, IWA Box 311, Folder 17.

[51] Scott to File, June 19, 1985; Sabra Warford to Dan Solitz, April 26, 1985, IWA 311 Folder 32.

[52] "NIOSH Team Inspects," *International Woodworker*, January 19, 1977; "NIOSH Advice Issued on Wood Dust Protection," *International Woodworker*, January 31, 1979.

However, meaningful reductions in wood dust were difficult to achieve. OSHA only classified wood dust as a "nuisance," meaning it had little regulatory oversight to control it. It took NIOSH more than two years to issue recommendations in the Longview case, which were voluntary. In 1985, both the IWA and Carpenters petitioned OSHA for a new wood dust standard. Johnson argued that only when OSHA mandated ventilation systems with an enforcement mechanism would employers take wood dust seriously. But OSHA mandated few new regulations in the mid-1980s and wood dust regulations remained without enforcement mechanisms.[53]

Finally, the IWA attempted to protect its members from chemical exposure. After World War II, the market for processed wood products such as plywood grew to supply the rapidly expanding housing market. To create and preserve these products from insects and decay, the timber industry used chemicals. Wood preservative containers had labels that described little to nothing about the contents inside. Union safety and health committees in the 1950s and 1960s rarely discussed these issues, but while timber workers had little knowledge about these chemicals, they understood their health enough to strongly suspect the effects of exposure, which often first showed up on their skin. For plywood workers, formaldehyde-based gules and bonding adhesives in the manufacturing process created high levels of dermatitis and caused allergic reactions.[54]

The most important of these chemicals was pentachlorophenol. Created by Dow Chemical and Monsanto in 1936 and widely used after World War II as a wood preservative, it contained dioxin, notorious in the Vietnam War for its use in Agent Orange. By 1977, American manufacturers produced 51 million pounds of penta a year. Its effectiveness in killing a wide variety of insects that feasted on wood products made it popular not only in the timber mills, but for use by contractors in home construction, applying it late in the construction process for decks and other exposed wood. Penta, as it was commonly referred, had known side effects that included sterility and cancer. During the 1970s, Americans became increasingly concerned about the effects of chemicals on their bodies. Influenced by environmentalism, citizen groups questioned the United States' reliance on chemicals untested for their effects on human and ecological health. The connections between penta and Agent Orange became a powerful rhetorical tool during the Vietnam War and demands

[53] Keith Johnson to Robert Rowland, May 8, 1985, IWA Box 310, Folder 25.
[54] Denny Scott to John Couric, July 19, 1978, IWA Box 310, Folder 26.

grew to regulate dioxin waste through the Environmental Protection Agency.

The concern over chemical exposure in the general population was replicated within the IWA, with individual workers calling Denny Scott to ask for research on the chemicals they faced on the job. Workers such as Morris Sweet began chronicling the medical conditions they connected to pentachlorophenol and other chemicals. Engaging in "popular epidemiology" became a common working-class strategy around the country to fight against exposure. Particularly associated with the environmental justice movement, IWA workers also saw this as a useful strategy.[55] Local 3–98 contacted Scott for information on penta, which they then used in negotiations with Simpson Timber Company, pushing the company for a medical monitoring program, and contacted an independent hygienist for advice on how to operate its own monitoring program and even explored the idea of finding funding to pay for it if the company would not. Simpson agreed to have the union give a presentation about the health problems of penta exposure.[56]

Pentachlorophenol had a long history and yet researchers knew little about its health effects. Many chemicals were new, not labeled, and had no scientific studies about their impact. When workers wanted information from the union office about these chemicals, there was none to be had. Denny Scott testified before the Oregon state senate on the lack of any meaningful labeling on packaging for the union "to even *begin* a search."[57] When one local asked for Scott's help in identifying a substance labeled as "Preservative Tetrachloroisohthalonitrile," Scott first went to the NIOSH list of toxic substances, but did not find it there. He then turned to the Oregon State Accident Board for help, complaining, "this is another one of those cases where the chemical manufacturer has coined his own rather meaningless name."[58] After failing to figure out the chemical makeup of something called Chemex 644, Scott finally contacted

[55] Patrick Novotny, "Popular Epidemiology and the Struggle for Community Health in the Environmental Justice Movement," in Daniel Faber, ed., *The Struggle for Ecological Democracy: Environmental Justice Movements in the United States* (New York: The Guilford Press, 1998), 137–58; Phil Brown and Edwin J. Mikkelsen, *No Safe Place: Toxic Waste, Leukaemia, and Community Action* (Berkeley: University of California Press, 1990), 125–63.

[56] Scott to Lund, May 7, 1984, IWA Box 303, Folder 1.

[57] Statement of R. Denny Scott before the Senate Labor Committee Concerning the Toxic Substances Labeling Bill, March 7, 1983, IWA Box 310, Folder 7. Emphasis in original document.

[58] Denny Scott to Mike Rodia, November 7, 1983, IWA Box 310, Folder 12.

the company, which admitted it did not include the chemical names for the toxic substances included on its packaging.[59]

Dealing with this panoply of problems taxed Scott's small research and education staff, which also had to research timber economics, work on contract negotiations, and serve an important role in the union's political strategy. As a union safety and health overview put it, "it's very difficult to keep up with the hundreds of new chemicals introduced to the wood products industry every year."[60] The IWA used a variety of creative strategies to give the workers the tools they needed to be safe. Scott built connections with medical researchers, international timber health experts, government officials, national health and safety specialists, and environmental organizations in an attempt to build the knowledge base necessary to craft new regulations and provide workers with the information they needed to ensure they could recognize an unsafe workplace and act upon it.

Scott leaned heavily for the expertise and training he could not provide on labor education centers. Some were long-standing university labor programs such as the University of Wisconsin's School for Workers. In 1976, the IWA conducted a joint effort with the School for Workers to train union activists on how to apply OSHA to the workplace. Bringing workers to Portland for a week allowed in-depth training of reading state safety code books to apply regulations to the timber industry, specialized instruction in the health hazards of the particular parts of the timber industry where they worked, and discussions of corrective measures to unsafe workplace environments. International Paper and Weyerhaeuser made plants in Longview, Washington, available to workers for a day-long inspection, where they could test their new knowledge. The newly trained union members found several violations at the plants, leading to an immediate meeting between the IWA local and company representatives to agree on a deadline to fix these problems. This latter event provided more training for the attendees, who would take this experience back to their locals.[61] In 1977, the School for Workers produced four pamphlets on OHSA regulations and workplace health for the IWA, including hazards in the forest and in the timber mills, how unions can create a healthy work environment, and on noise. Each plant's safety

[59] Denny Scott to Mike Rodia, October 25, 1983, IWA Box 310, Folder 12.
[60] "The IWA Health and Safety Program: Its Past and Its Future," IWA Box 300, Folder 7.
[61] IWA Press Release, June 14, 1976, IWA Box 306, Folder 3.

committee was offered a complete set of the pamphlets for use in negotiations and member knowledge.[62]

The IWA also worked closely with the Pacific Northwest Labor College. The AFL-CIO started the National Labor College in 1969 to provide education and training to union members, which local labor councils replicated. Created by the Portland Central Labor Council in 1974, the PNWLC, like other labor colleges, offered night and continuing education courses for workers in order to empower them on the job. The organization's health and safety staffer was John Lund. Later to become President Obama's Director of the Office of Labor Management Standards and then Regional Representative of the U.S. Department of Labor for the Pacific Northwest, Lund worked closely with Denny Scott in developing the IWA health and safety program. Lund provided much of the IWA worker education program by writing union newspaper articles and contributing to health and safety trainings. On wood dust, for instance, he summarized the scientific studies and explained the relationship between wood dust and contact dermatitis, helping provide workers with the necessary information to go to the doctor if they feared exposure. Lund also explained a NIOSH study about wood dust in *International Woodworker*, noting that ten of seventy-four workers in a mill producing wood shakes out of western red cedar had tested positive for decreased lung function and occupational asthma due to exposure, with other workers also suffering after exposure to fir and alder dust.[63]

The IWA built upon this information to hold safety and health seminars at its locals around the Northwest. Calling these workshops "our front-line defense in any attempt at which we have gained," they focused on learning workers' rights under OSHA, how to document violations, and engaging in an actual inspection at an employer who agreed to participate, all with the larger purpose of empowering workers to use federal and state regulations to make their own lives cleaner and safer on the timber mill shop floor.[64] A seminar for Port Angeles members included lessons on how to negotiate with management on safety and health committees. Using the current contract language, the union created

62 "Additional OSHA Pamphlets Available from Research Dept." *International Woodworker*, April 20, 1977.

63 John Lund, "Wood Dust: Much More Than a Nuisance," *International Woodworker*, July 25, 1981.

64 "Western States Regional Council No. 3 Officers' Report to the 22nd Constitutional Convention," IWA Box 54, Folder 12; "OSHA Seminar Teaches Worker Rights," *International Woodworker*, August 18, 1976.

different scenarios where people had carpal tunnel syndrome that the fake company handled in different ways to help workers think about strategies for representing members. It provided complex chemical information on the chemicals woodworkers used, including their health risks and treatments for overexposure. In the case of this mill, it focused on sodium hydroxide, used to bleach paper, and toluene diisocyanate, a yellow liquid used in plywood patching compounds that can lead to respiratory problems, as well as provided detailed procedures on how to use pentachlorophenol.[65]

Workers brought the information they gained at the health and safety seminars back to the shop floor. Scott encouraged members to push for chemical safety procedures in their safety committees, as members did at the Everett Mill Company by 1983, where penta procedures included stipulating the wearing of respirators, plastic gloves, and goggles, as well as encouraging workers to wash their hands after using the substance.[66] After a 1980 IWA Work Environment Conference, the Shelton, Washington, local conducted its own seminar and put the workers "in an uproar over pentachlorophenol exposure." The workers conducted their own air sampling and urine tests and found penta. They took this information to the company, surprising their employers who claimed no knowledge about the health effects of the chemical. Workers convinced the company to provide protective gloves and aprons, but the local also demanded a close-ventilated applicator that sprayed the wood at the end of the production process.[67]

Lund and the Wisconsin School for Workers also helped connect Scott with timber health experts from Europe and Japan. Scott saw the IWA as part of a larger world movement of timber workers needing to build on each other to create national protections and he sought to apply the experiences of workers in Japan and Europe to the United States. Scott used the expertise of foreign scientists and workers to present an alternative to IWA members of a healthier and safer workplace. Swedish researchers had investigated ergonomics in timber mills that saw problems at part of a total work environment that needed a complete redesign. The study found that workers were exposed to wood dust that created respiratory discomfort, noise exposure, drafty workplaces, increased use of fungicides, and uncomfortable postures and work movements, all of

[65] Local 3–90 Safety and Health Seminar Tentative Agenda, IWA Box 306, Folder 44.
[66] Penta Safe Handling Procedures, IWA Local 3–101, UW Box 3, Folder 3.
[67] Scott to Hagglund, November 14, 1980, IWA Box 305, Folder 15.

which led to 75 percent of workers finding sawmill jobs unsatisfactory. Scott hoped that creating the ergonomic workplace in American timber mills would not only prevent accidents but create a shop floor that is "not only safe and healthful but more satisfying as well."[68] Citing a report that 35 percent of sawmill injuries came from injuries and sprains and that 12 percent of all mill injuries were to the back, Scott pressed for a "total ergonomic approach to safety and health." He argued that no one knew the conditions of the workplace better than the worker and thus empowered membership to redesign their workplace environment for comfort. This included bringing workers into planning processes for the building and modification of mills, more worker input with companies on job requirements, and greater communication between timber companies, designers of mill equipment, ergonomic experts, and everyday workers.[69]

The IWA brought Bengt Ager and Anders Soderqvist from the Swedish Royal College of Forestry to a 1978 IWA Work Environment conference to conduct workshops on the ergonomic workplace that told workers of the improvements that could be made in their comfort and health on the shop floor.[70] Shortly after, an IWA mill in Coos Bay protested when management removed a chair used by an operator; the Swedes' information on the benefits of changing work postures was used in the grievance procedure filed by the union.[71] A follow-up 1980 IWA Work Environment Conference brought Soderqvist back to discuss further research on ergonomics, where he talked about back problems, arthritis, and tendonitis over a week-long training session.[72]

Scott and a delegation of six IWA members also took a two-week tour of West Germany and Austria sawmills and logging operations in 1980. The delegation found the German works councils, where elected worker committees outside of the union structure had the ability to take any non-core economic concern to binding arbitration, impressive in creating healthier workplaces. Because one third of a company's board of directors with more than 500 employees had to be workers, labor had access to company information. In a U.S. system systemically excluding workers from corporate decision making and a timber industry where the IWA

[68] Denny Scott to Marianne Gilbert, June 1, 1978, IWA Box 300, Folder 25.

[69] Scott, "A Total Ergonomic Approach," IWA Box 300, Folder 15.

[70] "Work Environments and Job Design are Focus of All-IWA Safety and Health Conference," *International Woodworker*, April 26, 1978.

[71] Scott to Ager and Soderqvist, May 9, 1978, IWA Box 306, Folder 7.

[72] "Work Environment Meeting Proves Hard but Worthwhile," *International Woodworker*, September 22, 1980.

desperately tried to find information, this model had great appeal. The works council in one mill had won work stations that protected workers from noise and heat, while the workers in an Austrian logging operation had refused to work until they received better protection from the weather, after making sure that a government inspector would support the cause. This knowledge meant the employer caved before the government had to intervene.[73]

Scott turned to Japan for help with chainsaws. The All Forestry Workers Union of Japan had fought since 1961 to have the Japanese government recognize white finger syndrome as an occupational hazard and create new safety measures. It had succeeded in reducing the use of chainsaws on small trees, receiving government compensation for affected workers, and experimenting in lighter chainsaws. This led to the Japanese union taking their findings to the International Labour Organization (ILO) and urging international action to protect timber workers. Scott hoped for a similar result from the U.S. government and undertook systemic review of how loggers around the world had dealt with the syndrome, noting important references to the problem in Australia, Sweden, the United Kingdom, and Norway.[74] Scott's internationalism led him to ILO and UN conferences, including a 1984 ILO conference in Geneva, Switzerland, that placed the IWA's concerns over worker health, safety issues, and sustainable forestry in an international context. Topics such as the ergonomics of timber mills, skin conditions caused by chemical exposure, high accident rates, improved chainsaw design to limit injuries, and the need for ILO standards agreed to by member states all helped the IWA fight its battles in the United States.[75]

The IWA also worked to make its members available to researchers within the United States, facilitating medical testing to conduct medical tests on workers to acquire the information needed for OSHA regulations. The University of Washington Medical School tested one local's members in 1978 in order to study the effects of vibration white finger in order to create a clear path to worker compensation for injured workers.[76] Mount Sinai Hospital in New York and the IWA joined together for a study on the effects of chemicals in the timber industry after studies showed the

[73] Sicherheit Der Holzindustrie: Woodworker Safety in West Germany and Austria," *International Woodworker*, May 30, 1980.

[74] Denny Scott to Ted Bryant, October 13, 1978, IWA Box 106, Folder 7; "Chain Saw Vibration: Loggers," *International Woodworker*, May 26, 1978.

[75] "Occupational Health Hazards Explored," *International Woodworker*, June 24, 1984.

[76] Denny Scott to Ted Bryant, October 13, 1978, IWA Box 106, Folder 7.

carcinogenic effects of chemicals such as creosote, coal tar, and pentachlorophenol on laboratory animals. This included tracing workers backwards in time to find retired people to study as well as the physical examination and testing of current IWA members.[77] Local 3–101 in Everett worked with Mount Sinai to determine the health effects of a lifetime in the timber mills. The local gave the hospital a list of employees dating back to 1946 that allowed the hospital to access public records including death certificates, worker compensation claims, and Social Security records to follow the health of these workers. Importantly, the local itself was deeply involved in the study's research, with volunteers tracing the information of the former employees. The study aimed to look at the effects of exposure to wood dust, formaldehyde, resins, in-plant smoke, and other chemicals and pollutants.[78]

Ultimately, all of this work intended to make OSHA an activist tool to press the IWA's total workplace environment agenda. In 1977, the IWA requested an OSHA grant to provide funds to promote the union health and safety program. The agency initially declined, not because it opposed the idea, but because it lacked a mandate to promote a specific union's program and because no one had proposed such a thing before. However, Basil Whiting, OSHA deputy assistant secretary, told the 1977 IWA Convention that he thought this policy wrong: "You have been one of the few unions in the United States that has grasped the nettle here, has begun to move forward in terms of developing your own internal capacity to take action in relation to the serious problems of health and safety that are killing off your members." Whiting created an intergovernmental personnel act arrangement to allow station safety engineer Ron Kemp to work with the IWA and Association of Pulp and Paper Workers on a two-year project based out of Portland State University to develop specific safety programs for the timber industry.[79]

But ultimately, OSHA did not have the funding or power to enforce regulations each day at the jobsite. Only an activist membership enforcing regulations could ensure this and Scott encouraged workers to refuse unsafe work. In 1962, the Supreme Court ruled that workers could refuse to work if they feared unsafe conditions, as opposed to an "objective" standard. OSHA guidelines also gave workers rights to refuse hazardous

[77] "Wood Treatment Health Study Set," *International Woodworker*, August 28, 1974.
[78] Occupational Safety and Health Report, March 1976, IWA Box 311, Folder 25.
[79] 1977 IWA Convention Minutes, IWA Box 26, Folder 2; "OSHA Assigns Specialist to See Hazards in Industry," *International Woodworker*, April 26, 1978.

work, which the Supreme Court backed up in the 1978 decision in *Whirlpool Corporation v. Marshall*. Moreover, in 1982, the 8th Circuit Court of Appeals ruled in *NLRB v. Tamara Foods* that employees who left work after suspecting ammonia leaks could not be fired, even though OSHA inspectors had not found any leaks in previous inspections. The fear of leaks was enough.[80] Based upon these court decisions, Lund and Scott trained workers in the proper response to fearing unsafe working conditions. Safety and health workshops included an exercise where participants plotted out strategies where two workers are suspended for refusing to work on a windy, foggy day on a hillside full of snags.[81]

Workers were already acting on their own. Barry Elson was fired in 1976 because his work booth, where he sprayed preservative chemicals on doors, did not have proper ventilation and lacked respirators for comfortable breathing. The union came to his defense, grieving the case.[82] In 1977, Robert Burton, a mill worker at Publishers Forest Products was fired for absenteeism. The union blamed it on the mill environment. The mill's wood dust had triggered Burton's asthma, leading to illness. Burton's own doctor recommended he not work around sawdust, which the company used to justify firing him. The local thought larger issues were involved and were worried about a precedent by which the company could fire any worker who got sick from their mills, calling it "morally and possibly legally wrong." The company finally agreed to suspend Burton without pay until his doctor approved his return to work, which it felt was unlikely to happen. If it did not happen within ninety days, Burton would be terminated. To this, the union agreed, maintaining the principle that the company had responsibility for workers whose health declined in their mills.[83]

Ultimately, the IWA had a limited ability to get companies to take its workplace environmental program seriously. It did alert management to the seriousness of the union's position on these issues, which led some companies to opening their floor to IWA-led inspections. In 1980, Scott Paper allowed union members training on the work environment to inspect the factory, use its operations as a classroom, and presumably create smooth relations with its union workforce. On the other hand,

[80] Nicholas A. Ashford and Charles C. Caldart, *Technology, Law, and the Working Environment* (New York: Van Nostrand Reinhold, 1991), 372–92.

[81] Local 3-265 Safety and Health Workshop Materials, IWA Box 306, Folder 48.

[82] Barry Elson Grievance, IWA Local 3-101, Box 2, Folder Wholesale Door.

[83] Robert Burton grievance and meeting notes IWA Local 3-101, UW Box 3, Folders 3-4.

while Weyerhaeuser had its Director of Health and Safety to speak to one conference and opened its Everett sawmill to a tour for conference attendees, it simply gave them a standard tour that also included actual tourists from West Germany. It assigned a timber salesman rather than a health and safety officer to meet with the union, and ordered foremen to interrupt when conference attendees attempted to talk to workers. The IWA attendees were insulted and to them it demonstrated the company's lack of seriousness about workplace health.[84]

Companies also ultimately controlled most knowledge at the worksite. Only timber companies had access to the injury and illness logs companies had to turn into OSHA. Although some opened their safety records to the union, the majority refused, leading to the union supporting a proposed 1977 OSHA regulation to grant this information to workers. Where acquired, the safety records provided useful. In one California mill that had employees working their eight-hour shift with an immediate overtime eight-hour shift following, the injury log allowed the IWA to monitor if injury rates rose during the second shift.[85] However, this was the exception, not the rule.

Without OSHA threatening to create regulations, the IWA health and safety program lacked teeth. But OSHA was under attack nearly from the moment of its creation. As early as 1974, the House passed a bill reducing OSHA coverage on small businesses. The Senate did not advance the bill, but only after significant protest from labor. Keith Johnson's statement opposing it noted that 60 percent of timber industry workers were in operations employing fewer than twenty-nine workers in an industry with an accident rate 108 percent higher than manufacturing as a whole; only coal mining and warehousing had higher rates in the early 1970s. For Johnson, "these statistics translate into death, broken bodies and great hardship and they should be attacked on all fronts by maintaining full OSHA coverage for all employers – large and small."[86]

The Carter administration initially pursued a more worker-friendly OSHA than the Nixon and Ford administrations. With OSHA granting

[84] "Walk-Around Takes the Classroom to the Jobsite," *International Woodworker*, September 22, 1980; "Work Environment Meeting Proves Hard but Worthwhile," *International Woodworker*, September 22, 1980.

[85] Denny Scott to Theodore Golonka, November 7, 1977, IWA Box 310, Folder 26.

[86] "House Vote to Reduce OSHA Protection Draws IWA Protest," *International Woodworker*, July 24, 1974; "Safety: A Major Concern for the IWA," *International Woodworker*, October 24, 1973; "Senate Nixes House Attempt to Scuttle OSHA Enforcement," *International Woodworker*, October 9, 1974.

workers a right to a workplace "free from recognized hazards," workers, consumers, and environmentalists around the country began organizing for knowledge of their exposure to potentially harmful substances. However, between conservative attacks and a lack of funding, workers found the agency of limited value. The slowness of federal regulations to deal with substances empowered local communities to lobby for changes on the state level instead. Several states created safety and health administrations of their own, allowable if their guidelines were at least as strong as federal regulations. Washington was a leader on this, with the IWA frequently interacting and often arguing with the state workplace safety agency on developing and enforcing standards.[87]

However, workplace safety faced a severe setback with the election of Ronald Reagan in 1980. Reagan's OSHA Director Thorne Auchter, a Florida building contractor and Republican activist, eviscerated OSHA funding's and mission. Auchter reversed one regulation that allowed construction workers to inspect their own medical records for information on toxic exposure, a move that led Johnson to express concern that OSHA was now "siding with employers against the interest of workers."[88] Secretary of Labor Raymond Donovan scuttled a toxic substance identification rule implemented by the Carter administration, leading Scott to say, "waiving the chemical labeling requirement is an insult and denies workers a basic right to know."[89] Reagan's OSHA found itself with a lack of funding, declining staffing numbers, and suffering from regulatory capture. Penalties for violations declined from an average of $558.86 between 1973 and 1976 to $192.63 between 1981 and 1984.[90] Moreover, the 1980 Supreme Court decision in *Industrial Union Department v. American Petroleum Institute* forced the government to take economic considerations into account in creating OSHA regulations, significantly undermining an aggressive regulatory regime and giving the Reagan administration a judicial precedent in reducing OSHA funding and power in the workplace.

[87] See, e.g., Vernon Russell to Jim Lake, June 11, 1984, IWA Box 302, Folder 26.

[88] Keith Johnson statement, October 2, 1981, IWA Box 293, Folder 18; Noble, *Liberalism at Work*, 132–33. 177–96; Andrew Szasz, "Industrial Resistance to Occupational Safety and Health Legislation, 1971–1981," *Social Problems* 32, no. 2 (December 1984): 103–16.

[89] "Administration Scored for Killing Toxic Labeling," *International Woodworker*, April 23, 1981.

[90] Noble, *Liberalism at Work*, 176–206.

Reagan's election and Auchter's OSHA was a wakeup call to the IWA and unions around the country; the IWA increased its coverage of safety and health in the union newspaper in order to provide workers necessary information, telling workers, "it's going to be up to you to protect yourselves."[91] OSHA cuts provided an immediate threat to the IWA health and safety program. NIOSH funding to study the health effects of workers laboring in the forests in the aftermath of the 1980 Mt. St. Helens eruption was cut entirely, although Senator Mark Hatfield and Representative Jim Weaver of Oregon reinstated $2 million to continue it another year. The federal grant for the University of Washington chemical exposure study lost all funding and it ended. Plans to study vibration white finger were shelved.[92] The Pacific Northwest Labor College (PNWLC) largely depended on federal grants for its programs, including John Lund's entire health and safety program. In early 1982, OSHA funding cuts included a complete erasure of all PNWLC funding, and although a last-minute reprieve in February 1982 kept it alive briefly, the PNWLC closed up shop in 1984, leaving the IWA without its primary outside ally in its struggle to remake the workplace environment.[93]

While the IWA borrowed the framework for the total workplace environment from environmentalism, it did not actively work with environmental groups in its implementation. However, it had long-standing contacts with environmentalists and provided labor support to environmentalist measures in order to preserve timberland for its members' recreation, including wilderness legislation. Thus, when the Reagan administration threatened both environmentalists and labor unions, the IWA was well positioned to help build bridges between the two movements. To fight back against the Reagan threats, national labor and environmental groups formed the OSHA/Environmental Network in 1981 to safeguard workplace health and OSHA standards in the face of Reagan's deregulation efforts, with both national and state chapters. Keith Johnson and Oregon Environmental Council President John Charles served as co-chairs of the Oregon chapter. The OEC formed in 1968 and played a central role in key environmental battles from the establishment of the Mount Jefferson Wilderness to Oregon's landmark bottle bill

[91] "Do You Like These Articles?" *International Woodworker*, March 28, 1981.

[92] "Western States Regional Council No. 3 Officers' Report to the 23rd Constitutional Convention," IWA Box 54, Folder 12.

[93] "$56,344 OSHA Grant Saves PNLC's Safety and Health Program from Extinction," *International Woodworker*, February 11, 1982.

legislation. Johnson and Charles framed this alliance in the context of the Reagan administration threatening the common air shared by all citizens. Johnson put this people-centric environmentalism at the forefront of the organization, noting, "we regard OSHA and the Clean Air Act as two sides of the same coin – both affect the environment in and outside the workplace."[94]

Most of the OSHA/Environmental networks faded quickly, as ultimately neither side prioritized the relationship enough to make it work. But in Oregon, as in Wisconsin, it preserved long enough to promote a major legislative effort around a right-to-know bill in the state legislature in 1983. The bill established mandatory annual training for any worker "likely to be exposed to a toxic substance" and required employers to keep records of any toxic substance to which they were actually exposed. This built upon other right-to-know campaigns that both labor and environmental groups crafted during the early 1980s, most successfully in Wisconsin.[95] The bill would have made Oregon one of only six states mandating record keeping accessible by the workforce. Labor and consumers could unite around the lack of knowledge about toxicity and everyday exposure. The IWA led labor's participation, with tacit AFL-CIO support. The Oregon Environmental Council made the bill one of its seven legislative goals for 1983. Both the IWA and OEC expressed great hope for the new alliance, noting "it is possible Salem will witness a seldom seen, but potentially effective, coalition between organized labor and environmental groups at the next legislative session," while Denny Scott wrote, "just as labor has joined in efforts to preserve a credible Clean Air Act, environmental groups have recognized the value of joining with unions to advocate strong 'right-to-know' regulations and laws."[96] That said, the IWA felt the bill weak, because it did not give workers the right to refuse work without punishment if the worker felt unsafe on the job. Scott called this "a more effective means of enforcement" than any government agency or OSHA citations and attempted to see the principle inserted into the bill.[97]

94 "Coalition Formed to Save OSHA, Clean Air Standards" *International Woodworker*, October 22, 1981.

95 Obach, *Labor and the Environmental Movement*, 53, 92–93, 170–72; Samuel P. Hays, *Beauty, Health, and Permanence: Environmental Politics in the United States, 1955–1985* (Cambridge: Cambridge University Press, 1987), 304–5.

96 Denny Scott, "Toxic Chemicals in the Work Place," and "Right-to-Know in Oregon," *Earthwatch Oregon* (November–December 1982): 8–9.

97 Denny Scott to Dick Springer, December 5, 1983, IWA Box 310, Folder 12.

Employers balked at the legislation, claiming it would drive small businesses from Oregon. Timber and agriculture led the fight against the bill, calling the record-keeping provisions too burdensome and time consuming, and soon it was in trouble.[98] As the bill's fate looked grim, its supporters stripped the employer record-keeping provision. But it still failed by a 37–23 vote.[99] The IWA and OEC agreed they had underestimated the opposition of business and had conducted a poor lobbying effort that did not tap into the grassroots strength of both labor and greens. Scott wrote in the OEC journal *Earthwatch Oregon*, "other state legislatures with 'right to know' on their agendas were treated to large demonstrations by workers and environmentalists. Oregon supporters would have been well advised to use the same tactic."[100] Privately, the IWA was shocked by the failure. Writing to State Senator and future Governor John Kitzhaber, a major backer of the bill, Keith Johnson candidly admitted the coalition's failure, admitting, "we, frankly, thought our testimony and that of others supporting SB 294 was sufficient," and apologized for lashing out at Kitzhaber for the failure in the joint committee that stripped the bill of key provisions at the last minute, assuring him that "we have never taken your vote for granted, nor we will in the future."[101] However, a follow-up attempt the next year to pass a similar bill again failed, despite the testimony of workers such as Morris Sweet about how these chemicals had significantly affected their lives.

The pressure to regulate chemical exposure on the job may have failed in the Oregon legislature, but it still contributed to a national effort to make workers healthy. In 1984, the EPA placed new regulations on three chemicals used in the timber industry, including pentachlorophenol, citing studies noting the possible carcinogenic risk to timber mill workers. Manufacturers had to include warning labels and required employers to provide protective clothing and respirators for employees working with penta.[102] Timber industry lawyer John Varnum told companies in the pages of *Forest Industries* to engage in a confidential toxic substance audit and to self-regulate in order to keep expensive EPA fines at bay, noting "it

[98] Linda Keene, "Right to Know: Hazards in the Workplace," *Willamette Week*, May 3, 1983.

[99] John Lund Testimony before Oregon House Labor Committee, May 1983, IWA Box 310, Folder 8; "House Kills Toxic Substances Bill," *The Oregonian*, June 23, 1983.

[100] Denny Scott, "Defeat of Toxic Substances Bill Provides Worthwhile Lessons," *Earthwatch Oregon*, September/October 1983, IWA Box 310, Folder 12.

[101] Johnson to Kitzhaber, July 5, 1983, IWA Box 310, Folder 12.

[102] "3 Preservatives Face Curbs," *The Oregonian*, July 12, 1984.

is much less costly to manage a problem in-house than to have EPA find the problem and manage it for you."[103] In 1987, the EPA banned penta's use entirely except for its use as a wood preservative, continuing the exposure of timber workers, albeit with more restrictions than in the 1970s.[104] Ultimately, like much in the history of timber workers and workplace safety, the IWA could not win outright victories but added to a broader agitation for changes that led to federal action and safer, healthier lives for workers.

THE IWA IN DECLINE

Reagan's business-friendly OSHA frustrated the IWA, who now faced federal stonewalling in its workplace safety program. Johnson complained to Assistant Secretary of Labor Robert Rowland that OSHA was ineffective because of a lack of clear standards regarding timber. Doctors were reticent to connect workplace exposure and health conditions. The complexity of the law led to an underfiling of compensation claims. Worse, the majority of workers who did file for compensation had their claims denied because of the lack of clear-cut evidence that exposure on the job had directly led to these conditions. Without clear OSHA standards explicitly for the timber industry, Johnson did not believe it possible to compensate ill workers.[105] Workers expressed frustration as well, particularly over what they saw as the incompetence of OSHA inspectors who lacked knowledge of the timber industry workplace. An inspector visited one operation where material was falling off machines into the road and workplace. Workers complained that he did not cite the employer for these major violations, but rather for lacking a full fire extinguisher.[106]

The IWA's total work environment program also suffered from worker discontent. While the union wanted to support medical research on its workers, workers themselves often felt like guinea pigs. In 1985 a Kaiser Foundation researcher hoped to conduct research on IWA workers to

[103] John E. Varnum, "'Toxic Waste' Requirements Cover Wood Preservatives," *Forest Industries* (October 1985): 36–37.

[104] Carol Van Strum and Paul Merrell, "Politics of Penta: A Sorcerer's Apprentice at Work," *Journal of Pesticide Reform* 11, no. 1 (Spring 1991): 4–7; Bret Fisher, "Pentachlorophenol: Toxicology and Environmental Fate," *Journal of Pesticide Reform* 11, no. 1 (Spring 1991): 15–18.

[105] Keith Johnson to Robert Rowland, May 8, 1985, IWA Box 310, Folder 25.

[106] 1977 IWA Convention Minutes, IWA Box 26, Folder 2.

determine the effects of chemical exposure on reproductive systems. Scott targeted local 3–246 in Springfield, Oregon, because of that local's concerns about wood preservatives. But the local resisted. Bob Frazier expressed his frustration that the local had participated in three studies in the past, but had never received results from the researchers. Unable to convince the Springfield local or find another willing local, Scott had to deny the request.[107]

Moreover, when the IWA and companies worked together on health and safety programs, each had different aims from the project. The Shelton local entered into a collaborative study with Simpson Timber Company and the University of Washington to explore phenol exposure in mill workers, testing urine samples for traces of tetrachlorophenol and pentachlorophenol. Much to the union's chagrin, even before the study was released, the timber industry proclaimed it as an industry standard, noting the "clean bill of health" of the workers and arguing that exposure regulations were unnecessary. The union criticized the report itself, noting that the sample size was too small; forty-eight workers began the study and only twenty-two completed it. The union dismissed the study for discrepancies between urine levels in tests they saw and the final report and because it made no consideration to correlate the specific job of a worker and exposure level. More outrageous, midway into the study, without the approval of the union, the Western Wood Products Association, an industry group, requested sampling during workers' vacation to create tests without exposure. All of this alienated the IWA, eventually leading to it dismissing the report entirely and condemning the dissemination of the study draft.[108]

Even when the union won hard-fought improvements to worker health and safety, union members themselves sometimes resisted them, particularly when it involved burdensome clothing or a change in work culture. As early as the 1940s, workers resisted the institution of hard hats when the union forced companies to provide them.[109] A 1973 IWA attempt to place an industrial hygienist on a timber cutting job site in order to inspect for white finger failed because timber fallers "were afraid I might

[107] Patricia Kullberg to Denny Scott, September 9, 1985; Scott to Bob Frazier, October 25, 1985; Frazier to Scott, November 4, 1985; Scott to Kullberg, November 25, 1985, IWA Box 303, Folder 7.

[108] "Critique of University of Washington Chlorinated Phenol Exposure Study at Simpson Timber-Shelton, Washington," July 1984, IWA, Box 311, Folder 33.

[109] "Hard Hats Save Lives," *The Timberman*, September 1949, 43; Keith Johnson to James Sullivan, July 30, 1980, IWA 106, Folder 1.

somehow restrict their use of the saw. They accused me of spying," the inspector remembered.[110] For workers desperate for the good wages of timber falling, a union-approved medical expert on the site could be just as great a threat as the company doctors and medical examinations that unions around the country fought against in the mid-twentieth century, with unhealthy workers seeking to shield themselves from any medical expertise that interfered in their need to bring home a paycheck.

Members also clashed with union officers over a 1980 Washington regulation requiring tree fallers to wear leg flaps to protect themselves from chainsaw cuts. Union representatives had served on the advisory board to create the new regulation and anticipated no resistance from members. Locals in Port Angeles and Aberdeen believed the leg guards would reduce their mobility on the steep terrain of the Northwest forests and publicly attacked them. District 3 President Red Russell, who represented the Northwest workers, refused to get involved and would not issue a statement in support of the regulations.[111] Keith Johnson assured the Washington Department of Labor and Industries that the union supported the leg protections and stated that while some workers will always oppose new safety equipment, they will eventually be "accepted by the membership as worthwhile and necessary."[112] The affected locals were furious. Dumpy Taylor wrote to Johnson, claiming he lacked knowledge on the issue and went against the union principle of listening to the workers. He asked, "Who, and I repeat, who has a better concept of danger to themselves than the person doing their job?"[113] The active furor ended relatively quickly with the IWA leadership reiterating its firm stance to protect workers' lives, even if they do not like it, but it also demonstrates the tentative relationship between what the union professionals saw as workplace safety priorities and those of the rank and file.

However, the real problem with the IWA workplace safety program was not the Reagan administration or disaffected workers. It was the collapse of the union. IWA membership numbers plummeted during these years due to a combination of technological automation, resource depletion, export policies, and corporate disinvestment in the Northwest,

[110] John Gregg, "Chain Saw Vibration: Loggers," *International Woodworker*, May 26, 1978.

[111] Denny Scott to Fernie Viala, July 14, 1980; Scott to Johnson, July 25, 1980, IWA Box 300, Folder 7.

[112] Keith Johnson to James Sullivan, July 30, 1980, IWA Box 106, Folder 1.

[113] Taylor to Johnson, August 5, 1980, IWA Box 291, Folder 35.

as will be explored in Chapter 6. In October 1978, IWA District 3, covering the Pacific Northwest, had 36,300 members. By February 1981, that had declined to 22,273.[114] Bob Lloyd, a delegate to the 1982 IWA Convention who was unemployed at the time, said sadly, "when we are down, the boss feels it is his duty to kick the shit out of us and knock us around a bit." But he said this not in a defeatist mode. Rather, Lloyd urged the union to not back down and instead criticized it for a safety resolution that was too soft on companies on health and safety. Urging the union to not "put a price tag on our Brothers and Sisters lives" and to avoid "playing the company game" on health and safety, Lloyd went to so far as to accept his unemployment if it meant that workers still employed were not exposed to chemicals, and urged the union to rewrite the resolution to call for the banning of chlorophenols.[115]

Unfortunately, unemployment would be something far too many workers had to accept. The timber economy that had dominated the Northwest for nearly a century was fading fast. With the declining employment, the concerns of workers for safe work fell in importance to the principle of working at all. Yet there are important lessons in the story of the IWA health and safety program. First, environmentalism had a real influence in union policies and activism during the 1970s, even outside of land management issues. It provided an important language for the IWA's languishing health and safety agenda, helping a new generation of union officials to make it central to union politics. Even though the IWA did not craft its ideas about workplace health in coordination with environmentalists, its relationships with environmental groups meant that when those programs came under threat in the Reagan administration, it had ready allies to fight for them. Neither labor nor environmentalists, either nationally or locally, took alliances with the other movement seriously enough, thus leading to the OSHA/Environmental Network being only a short-term coalition even in Oregon. However, it at least suggests the potential for meaningful cross-movement bridge building to the advantage of both movements. Conceptualizing the workplace as an environment, with environmental problems not unrelated to those of pollution and forestry, helped locals buy into the ideas, demanding information about the poisons they used from the union office and helping to shape legislative responses when that information proved difficult to obtain. A vigorous

114 "Western States Regional Council No. 3 Officers' Report to the 22nd Constitutional Convention," IWA Box 54, Folder 12.

115 Proceedings of the 32nd Constitutional Convention, 1982, IWA Box 26, Folder 4.

workplace health and safety program expands the meanings of environmentalism to include the everyday, yet dangerous, industrial nature experienced by working people. This more inclusive and populist definition of environmentalism has the potential to create a working-class environmental movement with meaningful alliances with green organizations, even if that potential was never quite fulfilled with the IWA.

5

Countercultural Forest Workers

On February 11, 1978, Gail Slentz and her fellow reforestation workers in the cooperative called Hoedads went to plant Douglas fir seedlings on a mountainside near southwestern Oregon's Umpqua River. After four hours of work, Slentz experienced dizziness and quit for the day. The next day, she experienced mid-cycle menstrual bleeding that continued for several hours. The following day, she suffered from raw, swollen gums, and spat out two mouthfuls of blood after brushing her teeth. She felt feverish and tired and began passing blood clots through her urine. Slentz went to the emergency room of a Eugene hospital, where she tested positive for Silvex exposure. Silvex, also known as 2,4,5-TP, was a herbicide frequently used by federal and state forestry agencies to clear red alder and brush out of parcels before replanting Douglas fir. 2,4,5-TP contains traces of dioxin, the major chemical compound in Agent Orange. Tests on her coworkers showed fourteen had experienced signs of herbicide poisoning. Slentz wondered while testifying before the Oregon state legislature about her experience, "how long will these chemicals be stored in my fatty tissue and what will the long term effects of their presence be on my health; or if I ever want to have children?"[1]

Slentz's experience was hardly uncommon for Northwest reforestation workers. The International Woodworkers of America's fight for workplace health had positive effects on workers throughout the industry, but the unorganized faced far greater exposure to unsafe working conditions

[1] Gail Slentz testimony on House Bill 300, April 26, 1979, Hoedads Box 29, Folder 4; Untitled Document from March 21, 1978, Hoedads Box 4, Folder 6; Coos Bay, 22 Acre Hoedad Unit, University of Oregon Special Collections, Hoedads Box 14, Folder 24.

than union members. Toxic exposure was especially pronounced among tree planters. The timber industry and federal government embraced the rapid growth of chemical warfare against insects and plant pests after World War II.[2] Widespread chemical spraying exposed thousands of workers to poisons. Reforestation workers were on the front lines, the first to labor on a chemically treated plot of land. The least organized and most exploited workers in the industry, most tree planters had little recourse to fight toxic exposure. However, Slentz and her fellow Hoedads were a different kind of reforestation worker. Armed with education and access to the political system, they fought back against herbicide exposure.

This chapter explores how herbicide exposure transformed the politics of countercultural reforestation cooperatives that sprung up around the Pacific Northwest in the 1970s. The centrality of work to many members of the counterculture has been understudied.[3] For those who entered the forests to plant trees as a conscious decision to escape traditional work norms, working for oneself to rehabilitate nature was a liberating experience that offered an opportunity to craft an alternative economy based upon sustainability rather than exploitation. Focusing primarily on Hoedads, by far the largest cooperative, it shows how a new class of labor in the forests helped force changes in forestry policy. Empowered by an idea of regenerating the forest through labor, Hoedads found their

[2] Edmund Russell, *War and Nature: Fighting Humans and Insects with Chemicals from World War I to Silent Spring* (New York: Cambridge University Press, 2001); Pete Daniel, *Toxic Drift: Pesticides and Health in the Post-World War II South* (Baton Rouge: Louisiana State University Press, 2005); Thomas Dunlap, *DDT: Scientists, Citizens, and Public Policy* (Princeton: Princeton University Press, 1981).

[3] On the counterculture, see Peter Braunstein and Michael Doyle, eds., *Imagine Nation: The American Counterculture of the 1960s and 70s* (New York: Routledge, 2002); Andrew G. Kirk, *Counterculture Green: The Whole Earth Catalog and American Environmentalism* (Lawrence: University Press of Kansas, 1997);David R. Farber, *Age of Great Dreams: America in the 1960s* (New York: Hill & Wang, 1994); James J. Farrell, *The Spirit of the Sixties: Making Postwar Radicalism* (New York: Routledge, 1997); Thomas Frank, *The Conquest of Cool: Business Culture, Counterculture, and the Rise of Hip Consumerism* (Chicago: University of Chicago Press, 1997); Todd Gitlin, *The Sixties* (New York: Bantam Press, 1987); Jeffrey Jacob, *The New Pioneers: The Back-to-the-Land Movement and the Search for a Sustainable Future* (University Park: Pennsylvania State University Press, 1997); Gretchen Lemke-Santangelo, *Daughters of Aquarius: Women of the Sixties Counterculture* (Lawrence: University Press of Kansas, 2009); Peter Braunstein and Michael William Doyle, *Imagine Nation: The American Counterculture of the 1960s and '70s* (New York: Routledge, 2002). On the Northwest specifically, see Jeffrey Craig Sanders, *Seattle and the Roots of Urban Sustainability: Inventing Ecotopia* (Seattle: University of Washington Press, 2010); Catherine Kleiner, "Nature's Lovers: The Erotics of Lesbian Land Communities in Oregon, 1974–1984," in Virginia Scharff, ed., *Seeing Nature Through Gender* (Lawrence: University Press of Kansas, 2003), 242–62.

bodies all too permeable to the chemicals of industrial forestry. The cooperatives allied with environmental groups to lobby against chemicals in the forest and considered affiliation with the International Woodworkers of America to provide protection for its members. Emerging from the Northwest's robust countercultural movement, cooperatives represent how a new generation of Northwest residents conceptualized the forests as places to labor and to play, where work sought to regenerate rather than degrade the forests. Yet the IWA and cooperatives would have much in common due to the exposure of their bodies to the chemicals of industrial forestry. Their responses to those chemicals would be similar: mobilizing members to fight against employers and in legislative halls to reform forest policy.

However, to unionize a reforestation cooperative meant politicizing work among a labor force that often did not believe they had much in common with other timber workers. The process of politicization suggests both the potential and problems with cross-class alliances between forest workers after 1970. The herbicide fight required a persistent education campaign within Hoedads' constantly churning membership and it divided people who had entered the woods in part as a rejection of traditional politics and labor. For many Hoedads, organized labor and legislative committees were part of what they fled by coming to the forests. Yet as timber industry employment declined in the 1970s, Hoedads also offered a new vision of forestry's future with the potential to bridge divides between environmentalists and traditional forest workers. Understanding the appeal of a healthy forest and viewing the creation of that paradise as a job creator that would construct a permanent forest-based economy both looked forward into the Northwest's future as a recreational paradise and back to the IWA's working-class forestry.

REFORESTATION, ALTERNATIVE WORK, AND THE COUNTERCULTURE

In the 1940s, the IWA had attacked the timber industry for its lack of commitment to reforestation. By the 1970s, reforestation was more widespread because of declining old-growth supplies, but while a few large timber operations ran their private lands as tree farms, most did not take reforestation seriously while Congress consistently underfunded the Forest Service's reforestation budget. Overcutting combined with small reforestation budgets to create severe ecological damage to the forest. Modern logging technologies allowed for the logging of even the steepest slopes of the mountains. But there was no technology for replanting those mountains with Douglas fir seedlings except sending workers scrambling up steep hillsides to plant seedlings in rows as even as possible.[4]

The physicality of reforestation work makes it one of the most difficult jobs in the industry. Planters worked a 10- to 400-acre clearcut with all the brush recently burned off to facilitate replanting. In the ashy residue of a logging site, laborers carried bags made of waterproof canvas carrying 100 to 400 seedlings weighing between twenty and fifty pounds up and down steep slopes while bending over to plant straight rows across mountainous and uneven terrain in an 8×8 or 10×10 spacing grid. They used a curved hoe called a hoedag that dug a 12–15 inch hole where the planter placed the seedling. The condition of trees received from nurseries varied widely. Some nurseries had reputations for providing trees with muddy roots, meaning extra weight for planters and more trips down the mountain for additional heavy loads of trees.[5]

State and federal forestry officials contracted reforestation work to private operators to find the approximately 10,000 workers a year needed to fill planting contracts.[6] Contractors hired transient labor and college students looking for a few extra dollars on their breaks. Many crews were made up of "Burnside Winos," as one worker referred to people recruited off Portland's Skid Row.[7] By the 1960s, many planters were migrant laborers from Mexico often lacking English language skills and working through family units, although the conviction of a contractor for mistreating his migrant crew deterred Latino involvement for a few years in the early 1970s.[8] A lax regulatory environment and weak labor law covering planters meant underpayment, bounced checks from underfunded or corrupt employers, and unsafe working conditions. Camps were little more than temporary tent towns in the forest. Living conditions had more in common with Wobbly loggers of the 1910s than unionized mill workers a few miles away. With work paid by the tree, many planters either buried trees or

[4] Paul Hirt, *A Conspiracy of Optimism: Management of the National Forests since World War II* (Lincoln: University of Nebraska Press, 1994), 94–97, 203–07, 235–41.

[5] Hal Hartzell, Jr., *Birth of a Cooperative: Hoedads, Inc., A Worker Owned Forest Labor Co-op* (Eugene, OR: Hulogos'i Communications, 1987), 27–37.

[6] For the 10,000 number, see Gerald Mackie testimony in *Citizens against Toxic Sprays v. Earl Butz*, Hoedads Box 29, Folder 1.

[7] Hartzell, *Birth of a Cooperative*, 31, 324.

[8] Brinda Sarathy, *Pineros: Latino Labour and the Changing Face of Forestry in the Pacific Northwest* (Vancouver: University of British Columbia Press, 2012); Gerry Mackie, "Success and Failure in an American Workers' Cooperative Movement," *Politics & Society* 22 (1994): 228.

threw them off cliffs. Exacerbating the transiency of the work, tree planting was a seasonal job of the fall, winter, and spring because the heat of summer dried out the soil and made digging holes difficult.

By the late 1960s, planting contractors began hiring young people hanging out around the countercultural center of Eugene, Oregon. In December 1969, two friends, Jerry Rust, a Peace Corps veteran recently returned from working with farmers in India, and John Sundquist, a recent graduate of the University of Oregon, worked on a reforestation job outside of Eugene. Rust and Sundquist wanted to work with their hands outside the corporate rat race while regenerating the forest rather than contributing to its destruction. Forestry agencies contracted out reforestation jobs through small contracts of short duration rarely lasting longer than two months. Sealed bidding on a fixed-price contract under lowest-bid rules opened the process to anyone who could win and then place a bond on the contract.[9] In 1970, Rust, Sundquist, and a small group of their friends won a contract from the Bureau of Land Management for a parcel near Coos Bay. They barely survived the cold, rain, hard work, and low wages from that first job, but survive they did. They received additional contracts through 1971 and the group began to grow. First naming themselves Triads and then Hoedads, a rephrasing of the hoedag replanting tool, the group began to attract members of the area's thriving counterculture, both to the work and to Rust's home outside of Springfield, Oregon, which became the group's informal center.[10]

Far from consisting of a bunch of dropouts as so often stereotyped in the contemporary media, the counterculture in the Northwest and around the nation was filled with people who placed a high value on work, albeit on their own terms rather than in a factory or within a bureaucratic system. Rebuilding a corrupted nation with your own hands, one cheese wheel, geodesic dome, or planted tree at a time, was central to many members of the counterculture, often more so than LSD, marijuana, or free love. This was certainly true in the Northwest, which became a center of the counterculture. Ken Kesey's move to a farm outside Eugene in 1966 helped signify the area as a countercultural mecca. The strong hippie and New Left movements surrounding the University of Oregon in Eugene, the back-to-the-land and intentional communities that dotted the region, including early lesbian communes, and farming and food organizations

[9] Mackie, "Success and Failure in an American Workers' Cooperative Movement," 218–19.

[10] Hartzell, *Birth of a Cooperative*, 39–49.

such as Tilth, promoting local and organic food on a small scale around Washington and Oregon, all helped promote the Northwest's national reputation as a place where alternative lifestyles and modes of work would be welcomed.[11]

In 1973, Hoedads put an ad in a local newspaper for new members and was overwhelmed by the immediate response of over 100 people who found working as tree planters a potential realization of a vision of countercultural work. The rapid expansion of untrained workers created a difficult period of little money earned, high turnover, and tensions between experienced and inexperienced members. Some questioned whether the cooperative would survive, particularly as new members had equal voting rights with founding members. It also forced a greater structure onto a group that now included several semi-autonomous crews sometimes bidding against each other for contracts. In 1974, Hoedads organized itself into a co-op with 150 members, nine crews, and a written constitution. After 1968, cooperatives became a common feature of the countercultural landscape, attracting both hippies and New Left members looking to create a more stable contribution to changing the nation and realizing that immediate revolutionary transformations through direct action were unlikely to succeed in the United States.[12] Like many of such organizations that lasted more than a few years, Hoedads became increasingly professional, with a more stable and experienced membership. Revenues doubled between 1975 and 1976, and by 1977 the group had 350 members in fifteen crews. By 1980, the best workers earned up to $25,000 a year and the group had all the work they could handle between 1978 and 1980.[13] Other cooperative reforestation groups also developed around the region, although they rarely lasted longer than a year or two.[14]

In part, Hoedads subscribed to what historian Andrew Kirk calls "the western libertarian sensibility – a fusion of social liberalism and western individualism with a special appreciation for technological know-how focused on living with the challenging environments of the region."[15] In doing so, they tapped into both national and hyper-local trends. Hoedads rejected a timber capitalism that exploited the land but embraced making money through rehabilitating that land and creating an alternative and

[11] Sanders, *Seattle and the Roots of Urban Sustainability*; Kleiner, "Nature's Lovers."

[12] Doug Rossinow, "'The Revolution Is about Our Lives': The New Left's Counterculture," in Braunstein and Doyle, *Imagine Nation*, 117–19.

[13] Mackie, "Success and Failure in an American Workers' Cooperative Movement," 226.

[14] Hartzell, *Birth of a Cooperative*, 107–12.

[15] Kirk, *Counterculture Green*, 18.

vibrant forest economy. Many Hoedads followed the ideas of Stewart Brand, promoting appropriate technologies and small-scale, do-it-yourself solutions to the problems society faced. Brand's *Whole Earth Catalog* had a quarterly magazine that featured the Hoedads on two occasions, one being an article by Hoedad member Gary Rurkun.[16] But they also spoke in the language of collectivism as well, not only through their own cooperative, but also through building social institutions that would help transform the Northwest into a more sustainable and socially just society. Hoedad leader Greg Nagle hoped the group could show "people how a cooperative can employ people without ripping off the land, and thereby point out some obvious deficeincies [sic] in the capitalist system."[17] They built upon larger national and regional trends, but also defined themselves through the interaction between themselves and the Northwest forests, building experience in a unique terrain, crafting relationships with regional forest supervisors, and helping to create a form of the counterculture that specifically placed alternative forest work within a Northwestern context, helping to transform the region while doing so.

Despite an aversion to bureaucracy, a growing organization required centralization. To ensure maximum democracy while keeping crews autonomous, each crew elected a representative to a weekly council in charge of administrative matters, financial issues, and parceling out work contracts. An annual meeting was open to all who wanted to attend. To join a Hoedad crew, each worker had to pay a $1,000 fee to the central cooperative, built up through an 8 percent withdrawal from earnings until the total was reached, returnable within a year of withdrawal from the Hoedads. The fee built up the cooperatives' ability to bond projects and meet payroll.[18] The Natural Wonders crew, comprised of friends that met at a spiritual consciousness gathering, worked as a collective unit in the group's early days to promote its philosophy of "unity rather than individualism."[19] However, the lack of incentive for some planters as well as differences in experience, dedication, and skill led most crews to pay individuals by the number of trees planted, incentivizing hard individual work to maximize personal reward.

[16] Kirk, *Counterculture Green*, 16; J.D. Smith, "The Hoedads," *Co-Evolution Quarterly*, Summer 1976, 61–65; Gary Rurkun, "The Foredads," *Co-Evolution Quarterly*, Fall 1976, 76–77.

[17] Greg Nagle, "The Timber Industry in Oregon," *Together*, Spring 1976, 20–22.

[18] Mackie, "Success and Failure in an American Workers' Cooperative Movement," 224–25.

[19] Hartzell, *Birth of a Cooperative*, 159–60.

Hoedads rejected materialism, American militarism, sexual repression, and exploitative capitalism. Like much of the counterculture, Hoedads were a post-New Left personalization of politics; realizing that their work would not lead to revolution overnight, they sought to change the work culture of the forest, contributing to a slow transformation of the region while living their lives on their own terms. The group embraced feminism, consciously creating crews that blended men and women, and later forming all-women crews. Despite the often patriarchal and sexist nature of the counterculture, women's labor played a central role in hippies' economic survival, whether through collecting food stamps for their children, cooking, or selling bead work. By the 1970s, a growing feminist consciousness and political women's movement had empowered many countercultural women to demand equality with men in household labor, the bedroom, and in paid labor.[20] Women had worked periodically in the forests since the early twentieth century, sometimes in family operations, sometimes substituting for men during wartime, occasionally making a longer career in a man's world. However, for most of the century, their presence was notable for its unusualness and much of our information comes from news stories expressing wonderment. Women began working for the U.S. Forest Service in the early 1970s; Wendy Milner Herrett started working for the USFS in 1970, rising to become the first female district ranger in the USFS and first female forest supervisor in Region 6.[21]

Hoedads opened itself to female labor by accident. Most of the early women were wives and girlfriends of male Hoedads who wanted to accompany them to the woods. The first was Molly Scott, who had originally signed on as the camp cook before realizing she could make more money planting trees. In 1973, the Hoedads were 11 percent women; by 1974, that had risen to 25 percent.[22] Women sometimes faced hostility from local residents who assumed the all-female crews were radical lesbians, many of whom had settled in rural Oregon during the 1970s. One crew working near Roseburg, Oregon, faced obscenities from men, with one waving his gun in front of a woman. Once locals were assured this was not a lesbian commune, they stopped but as one tree planter said, "the

[20] Lemke-Santangelo, *Daughters of Aquarius*, 86–112; Debra Michals, "From 'Consciousness Expansion' to 'Consciousness Raising': Feminism and the Countercultural Politics of the Self," in Braunstein and Doyle, eds., *Imagine Nation*, 41–68.

[21] Gerald W. Williams, *The U.S. Forest Service in the Pacific Northwest: A History* (Corvallis: Oregon State University Press, 2009), 212–16.

[22] Hartzell, *Birth of a Cooperative*, 53, 78–83, 260.

implication was clear, that if we had been Lesbians, it would have been okay to harass us."[23]

These women also fought against sexism within Hoedads. They complained about the macho culture of the group's founders who maintained their dominant position within the organization during its early years. They claimed the men showed a lack of credit for women's work and accused them of using female members as a charm weapon against surly forestry officials inspecting their operations. In response, an all-female crew called Full Moon Rising formed in 1977 to force both male reforestation workers and the government officials they dealt with "to relate to us as workers, not mascots."[24] Women hoped to "learn skills from one another in an atmosphere free from intimidation that some wimmin feel from men," said a collective letter from four Hoedads.[25] Other crews remained gender-mixed while women pressured men to embrace feminism. In January 1978, the Potluck crew resolved to "actively look for wimmin planters" in order to keep a gender balance and to consciously promote women to become the crew's representatives in dealing with the Forest Service.[26] By 1982, Hoedads called opening the reforestation industry to women its "proudest achievement in social change."[27]

For women and for men, working in the forest while rehabilitating nature was a liberating experience. Sidney Rust rejected the Vietnam War and instead embraced voluntary poverty and do-it-yourself living in nature. She talked about how "it felt good to live without money for the first time in my life" while in the Hoedads, values she wanted to impart to her baby.[28] As *Together*, the Hoedad newspaper, stated in 1974, cooperative labor gave one an "overwhelming feeling of love and hope." Through "leaning on each other, helping each other to live out of fantasies about day to day living … our fantasies *can* become realities."[29] The publication of Ernest Callenbach's 1975 novel *Ecotopia* was on the minds of Hoedads as they attempted to reshape the forest workforce for a better future.[30]

23 "Winter Tree Planters Praised," *Roseburg News-Review*, March 6, 1980. Hoedads Box 29, Folder 12. On lesbian communes in Oregon during these years, see Kleiner, "Nature's Lovers."
24 "Women in Hoedads," *Together*, Winter 1975, 24.
25 "Wimmin's Crew," *Together*, Spring 1978, 4.
26 "Crew Feed Back on the Sexism Issue," *Together*, Spring 1978, 9.
27 "Unity" *Together*, Fall 1982, 17.
28 Hartzell, *Birth of a Cooperative*, 42.
29 *Together*, July 1974. Emphasis in original document.
30 Ernest Callenbach, *Ecotopia: The Notebooks and Reports of William Weston* (Banyan Tree Books, 1975).

Hoedad writers frequently referenced the novel as central to their mission. Richard Small Bear wrote in 1977 about the "struggle to bring about Ecotopia: a lifestyle in harmony with nature and emphasizing the cooperative side of human nature," for it allowed him and his fellow reforestation workers to explore "alternatives to the wider culture's dead end road of ecological and social alienation."[31] Experiencing ecotopia certainly helped attract workers to the Hoedads. Peter Roscoe remembered a Hoedad camp near Alsea Falls, where salmon congregated to jump. When Rick Herson saw his first salmon, Roscoe described it as "watching a kid see his first whale."[32]

Fantasies became reality through hard work in the forest. The task of carrying heavy bags of trees up hills challenged most members, who largely came from suburban middle-class backgrounds. Betsey Wemple remembered her first time planting trees, on a unit near Mapleton, Oregon, in 1974. She "strapped on this bag that felt like a ton of bricks on my waist and practically buckled me to the ground. I staggered down the road with my waist aching." She then got stuck between logs climbing into the site. By the time she reached the planting site, she attempted to bend over with what she estimated was a 100-pound bag hanging from her waist. She remembered, "slowly, slowly I got the trees out of my bag and into the ground."[33] Understanding the land and ecology was another challenge and could lead to costly mistakes. One crew won a bid for a parcel near Waldport, Oregon, but underestimated the thickness of coastal vegetation, leading to a warning to "be careful of growing plants in estimating production."[34]

Crews often lived in tents or campers near the planting site. They ate what they brought with them, collected wild berries, and fished. As they worked in the rainy season, which in the mountains often meant snow, they faced constant exposure to the elements. Working on a steep mountainside during a Northwestern winter rain storm, with cold winds blowing rain sideways into your body for eight hours, tested the meddle of any worker and led many to quit after a few days or weeks. Eddie Landon's first night working near the Oregon Coast consisted of a storm blowing over his tent and soaking his sleeping bag with rain, forcing him to drive to Portland and borrow his father's trailer to sleep in. When the sun finally

[31] Richard Small Bear, "A Speculation in Hoedad Futures," *Together*, Summer 1977.

[32] Untitled document, Hoedads Box 23, Folder 16.

[33] Hartzell, *Birth of a Cooperative*, 135–37.

[34] Paul Ferguson, "Waldport," *Together*, Summer 1980, 9.

shined again in February, "the people were yelling out across the unit, so full of energy and life."[35] To get to the worksite from the camp, the crews climbed into a large van, known as the "crummy," where, John Sundquist remembered, twelve or thirteen people would cram in the back and "everybody had their knees touching and were facing each other. I was half-nauseated with everything that was going on. The ceiling was dripping. We got out of the crummy … and immediately started going into hypothermia, even though we didn't know the name for it."[36]

Although planting was less dangerous than falling trees, falls, cuts, sprains, and broken bones were still common from working on the difficult terrain. Working down steep slopes meant the constant unloosing of debris. Usually that was dirt and small stones, but it could mean large rocks and boulders on a hillside stripped of the vegetation that would hold down soil. Jerry Rust was hit with a baseball-sized rock on his head. Marcia Brett remembered how on her first day of work, a coworker knocked a stump loose and both he and the stump went rolling down the mountain. He "could still actually walk" but Brett was terrified and nearly quit that day.[37]

Yet it was the physicality and outdoor nature of this work that serviced both personal accomplishment and a political agenda of reforestation that appealed to Hoedads. Betsy Wemple struggled to carry that 100-pound bag up a mountain, but when she did it, she felt liberated, remembering, "I had done it. It wasn't impossible! I could plant trees and it was a big myth all along that I couldn't."[38] Hoedad poet Howie Horowitz's writings gave voice to both the freedom and drudgery of the work. In "Lunchtime," Horowitz expressed the sentiments of many Hoedads about the complexity of living and working outdoors, "The tent blew down/last night,/Hot oatmeal sure tastes good./Six weeks of rain/and you don't feel wet anymore."[39] The reality of the hard work and terrible weather might have driven many prospective Hoedads back to the cities, but for those who stuck it out, driving their bodies for the regeneration of the forest became a point of pride, a dream made true through hard labor for oneself.

For both men and women, the realities of laboring in the forest and fulfilling contractual requirements for planting trees could create friction

35 Hartzell, *Birth of a Cooperative*, 49–50.
36 Ibid., 40–41.
37 Ibid., 162.
38 Ibid., 137.
39 *Together*, September 1974, 14.

with the countercultural freedom they cherished. Cheap Thrills took a contract agreeing to plant 4.5 acres per day. It fell behind almost immediately. At the end of the first week, the crew threw a "wild drunken party," after which a number of workers left, "leaving about 10 people in low spirits unsuccessfully trying to prevent the contract from getting further and further behind." Finally, other crews came to the rescue and helped Cheap Thrills finish the contract on time. Yet it was not an auspicious debut for the crew.[40]

Cheap Thrills may have nearly blown the contract, but the fact that it got done separated Hoedads from other reforestation workers. It gained a reputation with forestry officials as a serious group of workers who did quality work honestly. Hoedads disallowed the traditional contractor practice of burning or dumping unplanted trees, which made extra money because contracts paid by the tree. Given the low wages, some Hoedads wanted to replicate this practice, but instead the group returned extra trees. A befuddled Bureau of Land Management agent compensated the group since he had never seen this before. Joe Earp felt strongly on the matter, saying dumping "was dishonest and colored the whole relationship the person had with their livelihood," while Peter Roscoe described how "our no burying policy helped cement a friendly relationship" with government planting inspectors.[41] Such relationships, however, would face strict challenges over forest practices that made Hoedads ill.

Hoedads defined itself as the future of forest work. Accessing the same information about declining employment and old-growth timber stands that frightened loggers and their unions and fueled environmentalists' push for legislation to restrict timber, Hoedads believed future forest labor would rehabilitate rather than harvest it. The cooperative lambasted corporate logging for ecologically unsound logging practices and fooling the region's workforce into believing the future of timber was secure. Greg Nagle coordinated Hoedad research on forest issues. Citing a 1976 Oregon State University report projecting a 22 percent drop in timber production by 2000, Nagle called logging "as it exists now a dead-end and unless people find ways to diversify the wood products industry ... this area is going to go belly-up economically in a short time."[42] Noting the industry's rapid employment decline, Edd Wemple told the Oregon State

40 "I Got Involved With the Women's Conglomerate Crew," *Together*, Spring 1978, 5.

41 Hartzell, *Birth of a Cooperative*, 75–76; Untitled document, Hoedads Box 23, Folder 16.

42 Greg Nagle, "The Timber Industry in Oregon," *Together*, Spring 1976, 20–22. See also, Greg Nagle, "Whose Land, Whose Timber," *NWFWA News*, Fall 1981, 20–22.

Public Interest Research Group that Hoedads promoted "a labor-intensive management of public and private lands," which "would do a lot to eliminate the coming timber gap." Cooperatives would eliminate exploitative contractors and end "people doing poor quality work." Wemple called for state and federal legislation to stabilize communities through labor-heavy forestry projects such as selective logging and reforestation, while forcing companies to announce plant closings at least six months before closure.[43]

TOXIC EXPOSURE

Hoedads' critique of forestry resulted from its members' experiences fighting chemical exposure. They created their vision of independent collective work in the forests. That vision was shattered by the experience of herbicide poisoning. The timber industry used phenoxy herbicides primarily to control red alder growth. Red alder replaces Douglas fir after clearcutting, creating a cycle of succession that chokes out fir and benefits hemlock, another tree with little commercial value. As foresters claimed manual removal of the trees was labor intensive and expensive, the USFS turned to aerial spraying to control the alder. Within months of a spraying, workers would be on the slopes replanting.[44]

Chemical solutions to forestry problems were the order of the day for much of the twentieth century. Aerial pesticides were first applied to agriculture in 1921 in Ohio and soon expanded throughout the nation.[45] Soon after DDT's invention in 1939, forestry officials began applying the chemical in large doses. The Federal Pest Control Act of 1947 charged the government to protect forests from undesirable insects and diseases. In the 1950s, the USFS turned to DDT mixed with fuel oil to treat spruce budworm, a disease affecting fir trees, primarily in eastern Oregon. Between 1949 and 1955, USFS planes sprayed DDT over 3.84 million acres of forest with the Bureau of Land Management and state forests spraying millions of additional acres. Tussock moth outbreaks in the dry forests of eastern Oregon and Washington also led to DDT spraying, even in 1974, after the Environmental Protection Agency had declared it illegal in the wake of Rachel Carson's *Silent Spring*. As DDT was the only known

[43] Edd Wemple, "Osprig Forestry Conference," *Together*, Spring 1978, 16.

[44] Richard White, *Land Use, Environment, and Social Change: The Shaping of Island County, Washington* (Seattle: University of Washington Press, 1980), 109.

[45] Daniel, *Toxic Drift*, 49.

insecticide to eradicate the moths, the federal government approved the last legal use of it. DDT was only one of many chemicals used to eliminate competition for Douglas fir and other marketable evergreens, developed and applied with little to no research as to their effects upon forest workers.[46]

The experiences Hoedads would face on these chemically treated forest plots would challenge their visions of working to restore nature and themselves. Like countercultural members throughout the nation and especially in the American West, laboring in nature would prove much more difficult than originally conceived, creating significant disillusionment among many members. Poverty, gendered divisions of labor, and the sheer brute labor it took to live off or restore the land would drive many countercultural members off communes and alternative work sites within weeks or months. For those who did stick it out, the realities of work would be very different than they originally conceptualized.[47]

In February 1978, the Potluck crew won a contract to replant BLM lands in the Smith Umpqua Resource Area of southwestern Oregon. One unit was sprayed with defoliants in 1975. In March 1977, it received another spraying of Silvex, followed by a spraying of Krenite that August. Both were dioxin-based chemicals; Silvex was used as a defoliant during the Vietnam War. The Hoedads had a pamphlet from DuPont, the company that manufactured Krenite, which recommended not mixing the chemical with other pesticides. This made workers concerned about a forest so recently doused with heavy herbicide doses. Two Hoedads met with BLM official Bill Wessel in Coos Bay to inquire about whether that unit could be deleted from their contract to protect their health. The Hoedads described the meeting as "not productive." They then called DuPont and asked about risks to their health. The corporate representative said he did not know since the company had never tested the effects of Krenite in conjunction with other chemicals.[48]

Rather than give up the contract, Hoedads decided to send in extra crews to finish the job quickly and minimize exposure. Gail Slentz and

[46] Williams, *The U.S. Forest Service in the Pacific Northwest*, 179–80, 233–35; William G. Robbins, *Landscapes of Conflict: The Oregon Story, 1940–2000* (Seattle University of Washington Press, 2004), 120–43, 190–97.

[47] Ryan H. Edgington, "'Be Receptive to the Good Earth': Health, Labor, and Nature in Countercultural Back-to-the-Land Settlements," *Agricultural History* 82, no. 3 (Summer 2008): 279–308. For a first-hand account, see Roberta Price, *Huerfano: A Memoir of Life in the Counterculture* (Amherst: University of Massachusetts Press, 2004).

[48] Coos Bay, 22 Acre Hoedad Unit, Hoedads Box 14, Folder 24.

many of her coworkers would soon regret this decision, as this was the contract that made them ill.[49] One problem for Slentz and others was the expense of a chemical test for a poorly paid reforestation worker. The test cost $90, a significant expense for an organization making little money. The test ideally took place within forty-eight hours of exposure. By the time Slentz realized she probably had suffered chemical poisoning time was running out and her crew was deep in the forest. Without access to a doctor, Slentz went to the emergency room at a Eugene hospital where she received a test that eventually came back positive for Silvex. A second test confirmed the herbicide still in her body fifty days after exposure. A survey of seventeen workers found that nine reported tasting chemicals, six had headaches, four had nausea, and three had early bleeding in their menstrual cycles. After this incident, Fred Miller and Norma Grier again met with the BLM in Coos Bay, discussing herbicide use for an hour. Coming out of this unsatisfactory meeting, Hoedads began articulating a series of demands for reforestation worker safety from pesticides. They wanted more research into the effect of herbicides on workers, which was poorly studied, re-entry guidelines for exposed workers, and adequate monitoring of exposure. Effectively, they demanded the government take responsibility for the health of reforestation workers.[50]

From almost their first contract, Hoedads had experienced exposure to the chemical regime of industrial forestry. In January 1973, Hoedads started replanting on the first big federal contract they won, a unit near the North Umpqua River west of Roseburg. Jerry Rust remembered, "there was this junk called Thiram on the trees. Bruce vomited one night just from a bottle of beer. We think it had to do with the Thiram. It was a bad trip." Tetramethylthiuram disulfide, or thiram, stopped rodents, deer, and elk from eating newly planted seedlings. It shared chemical properties with Antabuse, a drug given to alcoholics that makes them sick upon a single taste of alcohol. Joe Earp, who had six years in reforestation work and thus was the most experienced early Hoedad, had worked on the Roseburg job for three weeks when he attended a wedding. Upon his first sip of wine, he suffered an excruciating headache, which helped him make connections between the chemical and the illnesses so many Hoedads were

[49] Gail Slentz testimony on House Bill 300, April 26, 1979, Hoedads Box 29, Folder 4; Untitled Document from March 21, 1978, Hoedads Box 4, Folder 6; Coos Bay, 22 Acre Hoedad Unit, Hoedads Box 14, Folder 24.

[50] Coos Bay, 22 Acre Hoedad Unit, Hoedads Box 14, Folder 24.

suffering. Earp became a leader in the Hoedads' first political action, fighting the use of thiram.[51]

Hoedads supported a successful 1975 Oregon bill to ban thiram from the woods. Its leaders testified to legislative committees on their experiences. When the bill passed, it ended the use of the chemical by June 1977 unless the state Workers Compensation Board (WCB) concluded it posed no serious health hazard. When the state Department of Agriculture refused to immediately stop its use, Hoedads fought for a reversal of the decision. The WCB did file a report to fulfill the new requirements, but state Attorney General James Redden suspended the chemical's use after calling it insufficient, although it received a ninety-day reprieve in November after the report was expanded. Between the 1975 law, pressure from citizens about the effect of poorly researched chemicals upon human health, and scientific research finding thiram to be a mutagen, which causes mutations in cells that has a high correlation with carcinogens, the timber industry faced increased pressure to halt its use. The state of Oregon reduced the number of trees treated with thiram from "6 or 7 million trees" to "2 or 3 million," according to Carl Smith, Oregon's assistant state forester, who added, "Thiram is applied only when the purchasers request it."[52]

The timber industry bemoaned thiram's decline. Smith warned that rodent damage to seedlings would rise without thiram. But for Hoedads, rodents brought the forest one step closer to ecological health. Although thiram was not permanently banned, Hoedads took credit for the chemical's decline. One wrote of his surprise when he realized that some new workers in the co-op had never planted a tree treated with thiram, "largely due to the efforts of Joe Earp and David Straton, supported by Hoedads."[53] Many planters turned to biodegradable tubing to protect seedlings. For the cooperatives, the tubing demonstrated how the use of appropriate technology through worker activism could transform industrial forestry into something more ecologically sustainable.[54]

Hoedads saw the thiram victory as a model to apply to the herbicide battle. Workers were exposed, went to the library to learn about the

[51] Hartzell, *Birth of a Cooperative*, 72, 76–78; "How Perilous the Planting," *Eugene Register-Guard*, February 19, 1978.

[52] "The Thiram Bill," *Together*, June 1975, 3; "How Perilous the Planting," *Eugene Register-Guard*, February 19, 1978; "Hoedads Asking State to Ban Pesticide Use," *Eugene Register-Guard*, undated; "Hoedads Appeal Ban Refusal," *Eugene Register-Guard*, undated; Hoedads Box 30, Folder 2.

[53] "Thumb, Cont," *Together*, Fall 1977, 20.

[54] "Thiram," *Together*, Winter 1977, 41–42.

powder, took it to government forestry agencies, and started a process where after years of testing and political fighting, the industry began to abandon thiram as a management tool. Having to restart this process against 2,4,5-T and other herbicides, Gerry Mackie was "quite skeptical" about industry-based scientists who claimed workers were safe, and urged workers to develop their own scientific knowledge.[55] Indeed, workers needed to "make a conscious practice of observing changes to their health," according to Marla Gilham, a leader in the Hoedads' Herbicide Committee, in order to empower themselves to understand the effects of working on their own bodies. Gilham urged crews to interrogate forestry agency supervisors and find out the spraying history of a given unit, study description sheets of the various pesticides, and make choices on whether to drink water or collect edible wild plants depending on that history. If workers became sick, she suggested walking off the job, documenting the symptoms, attempting to discover probable cause for the exposure, and drawing blood immediately for scientific testing.[56]

Hoedads positioned itself in this fight as representing not only its members, but also both the majority of reforestation workers without access to the political system and the forest ecosystem that could not speak for itself. Hoedad members admitted their own privilege as middle-class whites with access to the needed knowledge to fight against chemicals. Thus they had the obligation to represent the silenced transient and undocumented laborers who could not speak out. Hoedads realized that nearby the unit where Slentz became ill, "a contractor whose crews were arrested a couple of times this winter because they were illegal aliens" won a large contract. "A worker with illegal status is unlikely to mention unusual health effects," noted the Hoedads.[57] The fight was also to keep the forest ecosystem healthy, of which reforestation workers were just a small and transient part. Marla Gilham wrote, "I look around at the death produced by herbicides … cancer rates in humans and other animals, the pollution of the air and water and land and space, that we're getting pretty damn close to the point of no reversing."[58]

Such sentiments about the relationship between poisoning the land and people were far from uncommon in the Northwest or around the nation

[55] Gerry Mackie, "Portions of Remarks Submitted to USDA/EPA Symposium on the Use of Herbicides in Forestry," Together, Spring 1978.
[56] Maria Gilham, "Herbicides," *Together*, Spring 1978, 13.
[57] Coos Bay, 22 Acre Hoedad Unit, Hoedads Box 14, Folder 24.
[58] Marla Gilham, "Herbicides," *Together*, Spring 1978.

during the 1970s. In the Northwest, people started intentional communities. Individuals or families bought remote land to farm goats and organic food, or to live self-sufficient lives. Marijuana farms helped supply the nation's growing market for the illicit drug. People arrived in the rural Northwest from across the country with a hope of transforming themselves and the land through an ecologically sustainable life of working in nature. But like for the Hoedads, government use of herbicides shattered this idealized relationship between labor and nature. Carol and Steven Van Strum were anti-war activists and bookstore owners in Berkeley before moving to Oregon's Coast Range in 1974, where Carol planned to write while both farmed. After the USFS sprayed their land with 2,4,5-T and 2,4-D in 1975, their ecotopia fell apart. Birds, trout, and crayfish lay dead all around them. Their children experienced headaches, nausea, and bloody noses. Like Hoedads, the Van Strums understood the nature where they lived through their daily work in it, and when forestry officials used chemicals to elide the need to understand the forests, they were the first people to feel its effects.

When the government ignored their complaints, the Van Strums organized their friends into an organization called Citizens Against Toxic Sprays (CATS), one of dozens of anti-pesticide organizations developing around the United States during these years. CATS quickly made alliances with other Oregon environmental organizations, including Hoedads. On May 12, 1976, CATS, the Oregon Environmental Council, and the Hoedads filed a suit in a federal district court for an injunction against the spraying of 2,4-D, 2,4,5-T, and 2,4,5-TP in the Siuslaw National Forest, charging the USFS Environmental Impact Statement on herbicide use was inadequate. Hoedad Gerry Mackie played a key role in this case, noting that the USFS had quoted the cost of herbicide use at a price far lower than one of its own foresters and had inflated the cost of manual control. This led to a 1977 court order banning spraying until the USFS issued a new environmental impact statement, which it did in 1978, lifting the injunction. However, in 1979, the EPA banned the use of 2,4,5-T and 2,4,5-TP in the forests after studies suggested connections between the herbicides and miscarriages from women who lived in the forest[59] Herbicide use continued in the forest, however. Hoedads and its offshoot

[59] Carol Van Strum, *A Bitter Fog: Herbicides and Human Rights* (San Francisco: Sierra Club Books, 1983); Carol Van Strum, "Ask the Women," *Co-Evolution Quarterly* (Summer 1979): 44–47; Williams, *The U.S Forest Service in the Pacific Northwest*, 277–81; "Oregon Woman Wages War against Bitter Fog," *Eugene Register-Guard*, July 7, 1991.

cooperative, Second Growth, filed a 1979 lawsuit to halt the use of 2,4-D on the Siuslaw National Forest. The cooperatives hoped to build from the health concerns that led to the banning of the other herbicides, charging that the Forest Service had replaced them with poorly researched 2,4-D. The USFS agreed to "apply very strict criteria" in response to the suit, even if it did not agree to stop using it. These were major victories for Hoedads and its allies.[60]

The United States' most famous usage of these chemicals framed how Hoedads, CATS, and others fought against them. During the Vietnam War, the U.S. military had relied heavily on Agent Orange, a 50:50 mix of 2,4-D and 2,4,5-T. The massive damage inflicted upon Vietnamese forests and people led many scientists to begin a campaign against the "ecocide" committed by the United States and galvanized international opposition to U.S. efforts.[61] Exposure to the same chemicals outraged reforestation workers who had come to the forest in part to escape from a society that would commit such acts. A Hoedad named Wolfgang wrote in *Together* how the herbicide industry "put their mark on the soil of the earth, not only in the forests," but "in southeast Asia in the form of Agent Orange. The dirty dogs." Implicitly comparing the Hoedads to Vietnamese freedom fighters, Wolfgang went on: "the forests and jungles [have] notoriously been the home of dissidents, revolutionists, and outcasts of society. Herbicide poisoning may be an effective means of keeping these segments of society unhealthy."[62] Many in the anti-herbicide coalition made these connections between Oregon and Vietnam explicit. CATS founder Carol Van Strum's 1983 book *A Bitter Fog*, detailing her struggle against herbicides, devoted two chapters to building connections between the two places, with Dow Chemical as the antagonist to the people, flora, and fauna in both forests.[63]

Although CATS and then the Northwest Coalition for Alternatives to Pesticides (NCAP) played the leading role in the spraying fights, Hoedads not only provided important testimony from forest workers, but also sought to empower its own members to educate themselves on the

[60] "Suit Asks Siuslaw Spray Ban," *The Oregonian*, May 23, 1979; "Forest Service Restricts Use of 2,4-D," *Eugene Register-Guard*, October 20, 1979; Robbins, *Landscapes of Conflict*, 197–205.

[61] David Zierler, *The Invention of Ecocide: Agent Orange, Vietnam, and the Scientists Who Changed the Way We Think about the Environment* (Athens: University of Georgia Press, 2011).

[62] "Please Mr. Spaceman," *Together*, Spring 1979.

[63] Van Strum, *A Bitter Fog*, 107–47.

herbicides and forestry. Hoedads brought a worker perspective into the anti-spraying movement, providing powerful first-hand testimony against the timber industry on the effectiveness of the chemicals in the forest, something that traditional reforestation labor could not provide. Greg Nagle began collecting documents and books on the history and science of forestry, including on soil and water quality, herbicides, and wilderness issues, making them available to Hoedads in the office library in Eugene and encouraging members to contribute to the larger political effort.[64] This research helped Gerry Mackie testify in a CATS lawsuit against the Department of Agriculture, placing the lack of safety Hoedads felt from the spraying regime in a larger context of questioning the effectiveness of herbicide spraying.[65]

Hoedads' Herbicide Study Committee took the lead within the group on researching herbicides. In doing so, it built upon the "citizen science" movement of the era, as everyday people increasingly challenged scientific-corporate expertise on toxicity.[66] It worked up an economic assessment of 2,4,5-T, designed an experiment to test the timing of brushing on growth and resprouting, and measured the effect of spraying on replanting sites.[67] In the summer of 1978, it undertook the Groundwork Lowell Project, a research effort on the efficacy of spraying, gathering information on spraying in the Lowell Ranger District of the Willamette National Forest. It compared sprayed to unsprayed acres on a parcel that had previously gone a decade without herbicide treatment, demonstrating that the brush herbicides targeted did not interfere with proper growth as "most of the crop trees are quite healthy . . . and the presence of brush doesn't constitute a problem necessarily." Actual spraying was haphazard, with evidence suggesting areas near helicopter launching points receiving the vast bulk of herbicides. Finally, it found that areas receiving herbicide treatment had significantly less Douglas fir growth in the following year. Noting the disparities between its report and the Forest Service's judgment of its own brush problem, the Herbicide Committee concluded, "it calls into question

64 Greg Nagle, "Forestry Library (and Other Thoughts)" *Together*, Winter 1977, 18.

65 Gerald Mackie testimony in *Citizens Against Toxic Sprays, Inc.* v. *Earl Butz, Secretary, United States Department of Agriculture* et al., Hoedads Box 29, Folder 1.

66 Samuel Hays, *Beauty, Health, and Permanence: Environmental Politics in the United States, 1955–1985* (New York: Cambridge University Press, 1987), 171–206, 329–62; Michael Egan, *Barry Commoner and the Science of Survival: The Remaking of American Environmentalism* (Cambridge: MIT Press, 2007).

67 "The Present (and the Future)," *Together*, Spring 1979.

the whole array of confident statistics which are the very underpinnings of justification for aerial herbicide use."[68]

If sprayed herbicides were dangerous, inefficient, and ineffective, Hoedads had an answer to the problem of brush clearing: manual reduction of brush, mostly through letting the alder grow until the time of planting and then cutting it with chainsaws. With declining employment in the timber industry, Hoedads argued the experienced workforce existed for widespread manual clearing, even if it lacked any meaningful connections with other timber workers, calling it "a source of jobs and dollars in areas of chronic unemployment."[69] Hoedads placed hope in a proposed congressional bill in 1977 to create 300,000 new government jobs and gave concrete support to an Oregon bill that would have created a Forest Conservation Corps.[70] However, the manual labor argument was more a projection than a reality it could implement. In 1977, the Alsea District of the BLM modified some reforestation contracts to include manual labor for brush clearing but they went unbid. Howie Horowitz urged Hoedads to bid on these contracts because "no bidders on herbicide-alternative contracts may very well be fatal to our cause. We can't shuck the responsibility off to someone else, because as of yet there is no one else who can take it." Unfortunately for Horowitz, the Hoedads' bidding committee said the group lacked the labor to bid the contract, "saying the exact same thing as the herbicide apologist." Horowitz urged Hoedads to "put our bodies where our mouths are."[71]

To advance its forestry agenda after the success of the Groundwork Lowell Project, the research committee urged members to approve a 1 percent dues increase to fund forestry research and press its herbicide agenda against a well-funded opposition.[72] In fact, devoting resources to the herbicide fight was a real problem for the Hoedads. In 1979, it estimated costs for the year at $40–50,000 to fight for the suspension of 2,4,5-T. Officers urged that each replanting group take on one piece of the shortfall, with each member offering $75–100 of their pay. At 300 members, this could raise up to $30,000.[73]

Hoedads may have lacked the membership to put all their plans in practice, but by critiquing herbicides, its members became a small but

[68] "Willamette Herbicide Study," *Together*, Fall 1978.

[69] Hoedads, Untitled document on manual brush clearing, Hoedads Box 23, Folder 13.

[70] "Subject H.B. 320," April 25, 1977. Hoedads Box 3, Folder 19.

[71] Howie Horowitz, "Brush with Destiny," *Together*, Fall 1977, 3.

[72] "1% for Forestry Research and Development Proposal," *Together*, Winter 1978.

[73] "Spring Herbicide Work Day or Cruise for the Co-op," *Together*, Spring 1979.

important voice in the growing green challenge to national forest policy. They saw all the problems they faced as a result of poor forestry practices that affected all timber workers. Only "when timber harvesting is approached in a very sane manner, harmonious with the forests we take from," would the problems forest workers and the forests themselves face be relieved.[74] In 1976, Hoedads and the smaller cooperatives created the Northwest Forest Workers Alliance (NWFWA) as a region-wide organization to promote their legislative needs, with members in Washington, Oregon, and California. The NWFWA effectively worked as an informal labor union, even to the point of collecting $6 yearly dues from reforestation workers. As by far the largest coop, Hoedad leaders ran the NWFWA's entire political operation, much to the frustration of its leaders. Concentrating those most interested in politics in one group, the NWFWA also started a process that divided the Hoedads between an increasingly politicized minority and a majority primarily interested in working for themselves without engaging larger social issues.[75]

Hoedad's political success added to its emerging voice on forestry. Jerry Rust won election to the Lane County Commission in 1976, where he became a leading regional voice on environmental issues for two decades, including pushing at the county level against herbicide use, while the well-connected and politically astute Hoedad leaders crafted a close relationship with Congressman Jim Weaver, who represented the Eugene area in Washington. The timber industry began feeling pressure on herbicide use from Hoedads and its allies. When four Hoedads attended the 1977 Western Forestry Association Conference in Olympia, they were surprised at the extent to which they had changed the conversation about herbicide use. Reporting back to the organization, the delegation noted, "almost every big-shot speaker pushed the need for more and better PR to convince the public that herbicides are safe and necessary."[76]

Hoedads forced a government response to its spraying critique. In 1980, the Bureau of Land Management gave a tour of sprayed lands for cooperative workers. These interactions with government officials gave a new appreciation for the challenges of forestry. A write-up of the tour for members noted that there "are no simple solutions. You can go around

[74] Herbicide Committee Minutes, September 30, 1980, Hoedads Box 29, Folder 4.

[75] "1% for Forestry and Research Development Proposal," *Together*, Winter 1978; "Western Forestry Association Conference, *Together*, Winter 1977, 25; Minutes: NWFWA Regional Conference, July 28–31, 1978, Hoedads Box 31, Folder 7.

[76] "Western Forestry Association Conference," *Together*, Winter 1977, 24.

screaming 'DON'T SPRAY!!' but that isn't an answer. The problems people like Norm [Gantley, silviculturist for the Eugene office of the BLM] face are legitimate, so together we must all come up with safe, workable solutions."[77] However, while this dialogue helped build understanding between different stakeholders, in the absence of those solutions, the radicalizing experience of sickness and the challenges from traditional reforestation contractors placed some Hoedads on a path toward securing their rights as workers.

HOEDADS: A LABOR UNION?

Because Hoedads was a cooperative of owners, they were exempt from much labor law. The co-op originally did not have to pay minimum wage, withhold income taxes, or contribute to workers' compensation plans. This was the key to its competitive bidding and it raised the ire of reforestation companies threatened by this challenge. In 1976, several reforestation companies formed an industry group called the Associated Reforestation Contractors (ARC). Originally, Hoedads was a member of this organization, but was kicked out in January 1977 as ARC lobbied to reclassify the cooperatives as employers to take away Hoedads' bidding advantages.[78] Hoedads responded harshly to ARC attacks, pointing out the companies' rampant exploitation of its largely undocumented reforestation labor force, including low wages and indifference to worker safety, that the Hoedads rejected, while they had "given our workers job security and satisfaction, self-respect, time to do quality work . . . and are not subject to certain costs because of the democratic benefits inherent in their operation."[79]

Workers' compensation was the core of Hoedads' battle with ARC. As a whole, Hoedads emphasized safety on the job, passing out homemade flyers about safe work practices to members, but in reality the onus was largely on individual members to remain in good health. Hoedads admitted to themselves they did not deal well with injury. Janet Essley wrote, "Hoedads who have been injured have faded into bourgeois society to try to earn a living in less strenuous occupation."[80] In December 1976,

77 Herbicide Committee Minutes, September 30, 1980, Hoedads Box 29, Folder 4.

78 Associated Reforestation Contracts, Inc. to John Klump, January 5, 1977, Hoedads Box 3, Folder 18.

79 Hoedads to Jim Weaver, n.d., Box 3, Folder 18.

80 List of medical supplies and untitled accident prevention document, Hoedads Box 17, Folder 19; Janet Essley, "Workmen's Compensation: A Philosophical Argument," *Together*, Autumn 1976, 51.

a contractor named John Foster protested a Hoedad operation on the Umpqua National Forest over the lack of workers compensation. Foster was a member of ARC, which argued that Hoedads must have an insurance plan for its members. This forced Hoedads to spend precious resources at first fighting it and then implementing a solution. It claimed that paying into workers' compensation would undermine its ability to compete for contracts, precisely what ARC hoped.[81] ARC then joined an AFL-CIO initiative to push for an expanded workers' compensation law in Oregon. ARC placed language in the bill ensuring it would cover reforestation contractors, creating new costs the Hoedads could not pay. This infuriated Hoedads, who helped defeat the bill by lobbying Ted Kulongoski, the ambitious Democratic state representative and future governor who supported the bill but "also didn't want the Hoedads upset with him for the next election." Hoedads convinced Kulongoski to not allow the bill out of committee unless the AFL-CIO could demonstrate it had the votes to pass it. It did not, and the bill died. This success led Edd Wemple to justify his political lobbying to the membership, writing, "we made some friends in Salem ... Had we not gone there we would now be covered by Workers' Compensation."[82]

For Hoedad veterans such as Janet Essley, although dealing with a corrupt insurance system and government was counter to their impulses in taking alternative work, it opened an opportunity to start thinking about how the group could collectively insure each other. While she preferred "socialized medicine a la China," until that came, a group insurance plan made the most sense to Essley, especially since in a cooperative no employer would try to fight legitimate compensation claims.[83] This is the path Hodeads took, setting up a mandatory insurance plan in order to avoid workers' compensation. Yet administering this took significant time and resources and explaining confusing regulations to members, all of which took away from the Hoedads' central mission.[84]

Hoedads faced federal pressure in addition to that from their competitors. In 1978, the Department of Labor issued an order applying the 1965 Federal Service Contract Act to cooperative workers, deciding that cooperatives were service employees of the federal government when they

81 Hoedads to Jim Weaver, n.d., Hoedads, Box 3, Folder 18.

82 "Salem Report," *Together*, Summer 1977.

83 Janet Essley, "Workmen's Compensation: A Philosophical Argument," *Together*, Autumn 1976, 51.

84 Edd Wemple, "Salem Report," *Together*, Summer 1977, 3; "Ask Your Insurance Person," *Together*, Winter 1977, 6–7.

worked on federal forestry contracts. This regulation meant workers must receive a minimum wage determined in the planting contract, a significant departure from the collective pool of money Hoedads received before without regard to the number of workers who would labor on the plot, which often meant they did not receive the minimum wage. The decision also forced Hoedads to pay an additional benefits package, paid holidays, and one week of paid vacation. Essentially, the Labor Department legally voided the cooperative work arrangement of the Hoedads and reclassified them as regular wage workers subject to federal labor law. Refusal to comply meant the potential loss of all government contracts and a federal lawsuit to reimburse below minimum wage workers for the past two years. Hoedads saw no choice but to comply. It considered challenging the ruling and engaging in a mass mailing campaign to alert voters as to the absurdity of the Labor Department enforcing rules to "pay money we don't even feel we owe ourselves," as Gail Slentz put it. However, because the workers' compensation issue was not settled when the decision was announced, it forced the group to choose which employment battle to fight. Slentz argued that fighting the Labor Department designation before the lawsuit's conclusion would overextend the group and "could have many bad effects on us," potentially including the extinction of the group.[85] Slowly, Hoedads began complying with federal labor law, even as it saw itself as outside the traditional labor system.

These decisions had two major consequences for the Hoedads. First, they significantly changed the emphasis of the organization's leadership away from the joys of working in the forest to fighting rearguard actions to protect members' cherished autonomy from traditional work life. For people who wanted to labor in the forests, many began spending a lot of time in an office or lobbying politicians in Salem. Second, the pressure to provide insurance and minimum wages, as well as its inability to pass legislation that would protect themselves from herbicides, fostered among some Hoedads a deeper analysis into the history of worker organizations. If the government would force the cooperatives into a system designed for traditional work arrangements, perhaps it made sense for co-ops to use the beneficial parts of American labor law to their advantage. Slowly, some members of the organization began to think of themselves in the tradition of labor unions. In exploring the history of cooperative economics in the United States, Smitty from the Cougar Mountain crew went as far back as the National Labor Union in the 1860s to provide examples of

85 "Minimum Wage Report," *Together*, Spring 1979.

how the working class sought to band together to remain independent from capitalist control over their lives.[86] Calling worker-owned cooperatives "in conflict with the whole basis of capitalist controlled corporations," Richard Small Bear urged his fellow Hoedads that "keeping this in mind can help us come to a unified stand on the numerous issues that have polarized the membership in the last year," such as workers' compensation and the minimum wage.[87]

Historical parallels between reforestation workers and past labor unions only went so far in an organization with constantly churning membership of people attracted to the forests as self-employed individuals who worked and lived together, but remained autonomous agents untied to long-term collective structures. Such divides tended to fall generationally, as new members with full voting rights often eschewed political organizing. Although Hoedads had a vision for the future of forest labor, its members rarely articulated thoughts about workers laboring in the forest other than themselves. When they did, the sentiment tended to treat them as just part of an exploitative industry. As a Hoedad named Wolfgang put it when writing about the timber industry, "it's a loggers world and it makes some of them feel good that they can rape the forests and leave their slash and trash and who gives a shit about a bunch of hippie trippie commie treeplanters and how much herbicides they have to eat."[88]

Yet by 1977, some Hoedads involved in the NWFWA began to talk seriously about unionization. This came out of their frustration with fighting the Forest Service and private owners without a support structure and their inability to bargain collectively, not only around herbicide exposure, but pay and contract specifications.[89] In Edd Wemple's 1978 speech to the Oregon State Public Research Interest Group meeting, he said, "unionization of labor is a consideration for the IWA, UFW, and Northwest Forestry Workers Association." Here he thought of NWFWA as a labor organization akin to the other two rather than promoting its affiliation with an established union, but the comparison suggests the movement taking place within the Hoedad leadership.[90] Gerry Mackie noted that collusion laws interfered with cooperatives organizing collectively to improve all workers' conditions. Because of this, unionization

[86] Smitty, "A Short History of American Co-ops," *Together*, Winter 1977, 14–15.
[87] Richard Small Bear, "A Speculation in Hoedad Futures," *Together*, Summer 1977.
[88] "Dear Mr. Spaceman," *Together*, Spring 1979.
[89] "Union," *Together*, Fall 1978.
[90] Edd Wemple, "Forestry Conference," *Together*, Spring 1978, 16.

was the best option for cooperative workers because they "need not compete with each other," and rather could bargain with the government. Mackie placed the tree planters in context of radical unionism in the Northwest, compared them to the International Longshoremen and Warehouse Union (ILWU). Similar to the Hoedads' fight, Mackie believed the ILWU during the era of the left-leaning Harry Bridges struggled against work that was "tough, injurious, sporadic, arbitrary." Yet after a half-century of organizing, "today, the ILWU all but controls the docks." Impressed by the ILWU's democratic traditions, Mackie asked for $1,000 from Hoedads to explore the initial steps toward unionization.[91]

In 1978, a spin-off group of the NWFWA formed. Called the Forest Workers Organizing Committee, the FWOC sought to build alliances with labor unions with the hope of eventual affiliation.[92] Probably the most emotionally appealing union for most Hoedads was the United Farm Workers (UFW). Hoedads wanted to ally with the Latinos who made up many reforestation crews. In 1974, while working on a fire during the summer offseason, a group of Hoedads became friends with some immigrant planters on their crew. This grew into the short-lived Hoedad Latino crew, Los Broncos. To Hoedads, Los Broncos seemed an entry point into transforming the core labor planting labor force. However, Los Broncos faded quickly. Communication problems provided one barrier. Gary Sanchez thought working with Los Broncos was great because "they were singing Mexican rancho songs at the top of their voices." But Walter Pudwill remembered the Broncos' poverty and their lack of English, noting, "it was hard to communicate." They would not take time for lunch so they could maximize their earnings, a surprising moment for Pudwill.[93] Los Broncos never came to a single organizational meeting and "had not realized the responsibilities of a cooperative Hoedad crew," according to Hal Hartzell.[94] Los Broncos' leader, Aurelio, wrote to the cooperative office in December 1974 to thank Hoedads for working with them, but noted that they lacked enough work to sustain themselves. He wrote, "the day that we do not work, we do not eat, and things have been going bad lately."[95] Not long after, Los Broncos faded into Hoedad

[91] Jerry Mackie, "One Big Union," *Together*, Summer 1977.

[92] "Union," *Together*, Fall 1978.

[93] Hartzell, *Birth of a Cooperative*, 303–304.

[94] Ibid., 321.

[95] "His and Her Story," *Together*, Fall 1977. Original letter, as transcribed in newspaper: "Nosotros vivimos del trabajo. El dia que no trabijamos no comemos y oy a sido al Rever."

memory as a missed opportunity, although the organization would occasionally work with Latinos over the years.[96]

The cooperatives put out feelers to UFW, but were told that the union was focusing on California farmworkers.[97] Therefore FWOC leaders soon settled on the International Woodworkers of America as the likely union home. By 1978, the NWFWA looked to the IWA because of its history "extending to the Wobblies" and reputation for "progressive politics" that made it different to most AFL-CIO unions.[98] That Hoedads would consider membership in the IWA made sense as both fought against the effects of herbicide spraying on workers' health. A 1977 meeting with the U.S. Department of Agriculture saw IWA representatives question the agency's commitment to replacing dioxin-based herbicides with alternative spraying. Like the Hoedads, the IWA supported manual vegetation control instead of aerial spraying, both because of its environmental impact and because it would lead to greater employment.[99]

Like the IWA, Hoedads also strongly critiqued the timber industry's false choice between environmental protection and jobs. Hoedads criticized Willamette National Forest's Draft Environmental Statement and Management Plan in 1975, saying the USFS and timber industry "have literally propagandized the public, workers in particular, into believing the alternative short of increasing the forests allowable cut would cost thousands of jobs."[100] Both the IWA and Hoedads demanded working voices be taken seriously in forestry debates, rejecting industry control over bodily exposure and calling for a right of the public to know about chemicals. Hoedads complained that industry's position was such that "workers and the public have no right to challenge their expertise on the usefulness of chemicals even though these same workers may be poisoned by them," words that could have been spoken by IWA members.[101]

However, there were serious challenges to this potential alliance. Hoedads were independent people who worked together in the forest to escape the corrupt institutions of mainstream America. Organized labor's

[96] "Unity," *Together*, Fall 1982, 18.

[97] "Union," *Together*, Fall 1978.

[98] Minutes: NWFWA Regional Conference, July 28–31, 1978, 10, Hoedads Box 31, Folder 7.

[99] "Topics for Discussion," July 19, 1977, IWA Box 108, Folder 14; Bud Rahberger to John Evans, July 16, 1982, IWA Box 310, Folder 17.

[100] Jonathan Walker and David Straton untitled report, Hoedads Box 23, Folder 11.

[101] "Thiram," *Together*, Winter 1977.

terrible reputation among the counterculture did not help. The staid leadership of George Meany, the AFL-CIO's support of the Vietnam War, union corruption, and construction workers beating antiwar protestors in New York City led many members of the counterculture to see organized labor as part of the immoral and dishonest nation they wanted to transform. Perhaps nothing sums up countercultural views of unions more than the union member of the jury in the 1971 dystopian film *Punishment Park*. In the film, arrested protestors are provided the choice of long prison sentences or to survive in Punishment Park, where they will be hunted and murdered by members of the police. Among the most vocal members of the jury is a union representative who repeatedly lectures those on trial about their lack of patriotism and finds them guilty of subversion. With Meany's AFL-CIO so strongly supporting the Vietnam War, in the aftermath of Kent State, such distrust of organized labor summed up popular leftist feeling about unions in the early 1970s.[102]

So many Hoedads needed a lot of convincing to consider joining a labor union. During the workers' compensation fight, one anonymous Hoedad responded to organized labor's position by stating, "I get a perverse pleasure thinking that George Meany might be crapping his dead drawers every time we reject Comp."[103] Nevertheless, Hoedad leaders tried to convince the rank and file. Issa Simpson assured members that like a cooperative, a union is what its members make of it. Moreover, they made the case that the IWA was the right union for them. Simpson stated the IWA not only offered a union of woodworkers, but they had "one of the best working democratic systems of any union" that included salaries for union officers no higher than the highest paid worker. He believed a politically progressive membership would allow them to maintain their cooperative structure and resist the bureaucracy that so turned off the counterculture from organized labor.[104]

Hoedads reached out to the IWA in 1977, originally without success.[105] However, they then contacted sociologist and labor activist

[102] On organized labor and the counterculture, see Jefferson Cowie, *Stayin' Alive: The 1970s and the Last Days of the Working Class* (New York: The New Press, 2010); Joshua Freeman, "Hardhats: Construction Workers, Manliness, and the 1970 Pro-War Demonstrations," *Journal of Social History* 26, no. 4 (Summer 1993): 725–44; Penny Lewis, *Hardhats, Hippies, and Hawks: The Vietnam Antiwar Movement as Myth and Memory* (Ithaca: Cornell University Press, 2013).

[103] "Thoughts on the 'Necessary Evil,'" *Together*, Summer 1980, 21.

[104] "Union," *Together*, Fall 1978.

[105] Roy Ockert to Fernie Viala, December 29, 1977, IWA Box 300, Folder 10.

Jerry Lembcke, who was writing his history of communism in the IWA and serving as the vice-president of the Oregon Federation of Teachers.[106] Lembcke alerted IWA leaders, who were interested because of the possibility of opening this sector to unionization and stemming the union's membership decline. This culminated in a 1979 meeting between the NWFWA, Denny Scott, and Lembcke. Scott declared the union's openness to a variety of possible relationships with the co-ops, assuring them that their views about forestry would be respected and heard within the larger union structure. He made connections between the Hoedads' environmental risk and that of the original IWA members by painting a history of loggers resisting the early twentieth-century's unsanitary camps to form unions. Lembcke built upon this by talking about the IWA as the direct successor to the Industrial Workers of the World in the woods, an appealing historical reference who, to quote historian Doug Rossinow, "became icons of decentralist radicalism" for many members of the counterculture.[107] The co-ops found the IWA's flexibility and success in improving members working conditions appealing. After the meeting, Hoedads called for a resolution to support the formation of a local within the IWA at the next general meeting the following month.[108]

For many workers, however, not only was a union bureaucracy undesirable, but Hoedads themselves had become too bureaucratic. An anonymous member urged Hoedads to shrink, complaining of the large office in Eugene and of the "bigness that breeds alienation and anomie." This member rejected the entire lobbying and political program, calling it "pouring good money after bad" to a state legislature with no interest in reforestation workers' concerns and saying the smaller co-ops around the Northwest should have to take the lead on dealing with the Forest Service and state agencies after five years of Hoedad leadership. Shrinkage would lead to a more personal co-op and allow Hoedads to avoid helping other groups "with their ridiculous requests for assistance."[109]

Supporters reassured skeptical members that the IWA "were not your typical AFL-CIO bureaucrats." Instead, they told the members to drop "critical and negative" feelings about unions "based on myths and fallacies about union organization," and instead join a union that "had a

[106] Jerry Lembcke and William M. Tattam, *One Union in Wood: A Political History of the International Woodworkers of America* (New York: International Publishers, 1984).

[107] Doug Rossinow, "'The Revolution Is about Our Lives': The New Left's Counterculture," in Braunstein and Doyle, *Imagine Nation*, 118.

[108] NWFWA Regional Conference, January 5–8, 1979, Hoedads Box 31, Folder 9.

[109] "Off the Wall," *Together*, Spring 1979.

strong and militant history of fighting for the rights of woodworkers."[110] One Hoedad urged the group's members to consider themselves no different from other workers and join the union, arguing, "we should be concerned with the rights and protection of all working people, not just cooperative woods workers. I don't feel that I'm in a privileged class of co-op workers. I don't think we have any more rights than anyone else."[111]

However, a core group of members deeply engaged in herbicide prevention drove the group's political agenda. Continued frequent turnover, reaching 50 percent per year, combined with full voting rights for new members, meant a constant need to educate new members on why it made sense to ally with an organization that represented the corrupt bureaucracy they rejected by entering the counterculture.[112] After four years, Greg Nagle was one of the most experienced members of his crew. He expressed frustration that these newcomers were so unaware of the importance of herbicide policy.[113] The NWFWA admitted that most "want to work with their friends, be their own boss, live and work at their own pace in their own style."[114] This divide between politics and culture had long plagued Hoedads. Fred Miller urged member involvement to avoid a situation where "decisions about the company will be made by a very small number of people, which is not healthy." But many workers preferred "just hanging out in camp when not planting."[115]

Although the minutes to the meeting where the union proposal was presented do not survive, the reforestation workers' efforts to affiliate with the IWA collapsed immediately in the face of opposition from the rank and file. A reference to the matter in February 1980 noted, "the issue of a reforestation union has angered and upset more cooperative members than any issue," while a 1982 article blamed Hoedads' anarchist and individualistic philosophy for the inability of the organization to ally with more established organizations.[116] Denny

110 "Towards an Industry Wide Forest Workers Organization," *Together*, Summer 1979.
111 "Associated Oregon Industries Letter," May 5, 1980, Hoedads Box 5, Folder 12.
112 Gerry Mackie, "Success and Failure in an American Workers' Cooperative Movement," 226.
113 General Meeting Minutes, Winter 1981, Hoedads Box 7, Folder 18; Greg Nagle, "Hodeads," Box 21, Folder 12.
114 "Duty Now for NWFWA," Oregon NWFWA newsletter, February 1980, Hoedads Box 31, Folder 1.
115 "Our Herbicide Experience," *Together*, Summer 1978.
116 "Re-Unions," Oregon NWFWA Newsletter, February 1980, Hoedads Box 31, Folder 1; "Turning Under Turnover," *Together*, Spring 1982.

Scott remembered the Hoedads favorably, but also confirmed that they never came close to joining the IWA.[117] The possibility of traditional and alternative labor uniting in a union collapsed before it could get underway.

The use of toxic chemicals declined after the EPA ordered the suspension of 2,4,5-T and Silvex use in the forest in 1979 and the use of them ended entirely in 1981. However, so did the tree-planting cooperative movement. Hoedad membership began to slip in 1981 and collapsed to seventy members by 1983. President Carter's decision to not report on known employers of undocumented labor for the 1980 census and the Mexican economic crisis following the oil price collapse in 1981 and 1982 led to the widespread growth of undocumented labor in the forests. These workers were paid as little as 10 percent what the Hoedads made, making it impossible for it to win contracts. In 1983, reforestation costs had fallen so far that the Forest Service returned $80 million to the U.S. Treasury. The percentage of U.S. residents working in reforestation fell from 90 percent in 1979 to 20 percent in 1984. A contractor who had served time in prison for exploiting undocumented labor won half the contracts in western Oregon in 1985. Hoedads and other cooperatives could not compete. The NWFWA disbanded and the cooperatives' ability to influence forest policy ended.[118]

Certainly the changing labor culture of reforestation was important to the decline of the cooperatives. However, larger cultural changes were also in the air. By the 1980s, recruiting new members became difficult, even in Eugene, where the counterculture remained relatively strong. As Hal Hartzell said in an undated year-end report from the mid-1980s, "we are a shrinking group of aging members. If we do not take on new blood, new life at every juncture than [sic] we will wither and die."[119] By 1984, the Hoedads had only thirty members and continued at around that number until it chose to dissolve in 1994.[120]

Toxic exposure created an atmosphere for alliance building across class and culture, but the divide between organized labor and countercultural ideals of labor was too great a barrier to overcome. The IWA never could break into reforestation workers, nor would Hoedads realize their broader vision

117 Oral interview with Denny Scott. In author's possession.

118 Mackie, "Success and Failure in an American Workers' Cooperative Movement," 218.

119 "Board Review," Hoedads Box 23, Folder 7.

120 Mackie, "Success and Failure in an American Workers' Cooperative Movement," 229–32.

of cooperative labor transforming the forests. Reforestation workers remained some of the most exploited in the industry, and still are today.[121] Yet the Hoedad story is important for the history of workplace organizations and environmental change in the history of Northwest forests. In the most degraded and exploited labor force in the forests, workers demanded their voices be heard in forestry debates. Aware of their own privilege as well-educated, middle-class whites, Hoedads sought to fight for those who did not have access to political power to speak for themselves. The experience of illness and frustration over the forestry policy that wantonly poisoned workers created a more class-conscious tone to Hoedad political activism. But in an industry so prone to turnover, a transient industry not unlike that which the IWW organized six decades earlier, and in the face of democratic decision making that privileged new members' voices, Hoedad leaders did not have the power within their own organization to craft alliances with unions for the benefit of all workers. Debates over the future of the forests would be impoverished without these voices.

The cooperatives' experience in forestry also demonstrates the fraught relationship countercultural workers had with the larger forces shaping industrial forests. Hoedads' interactions with industrial agencies and the state-corporate alliance behind them meant that work in the forests might regenerate nature as its members as envisioned, but not without serious impact on workers' bodies and long-term engagement with federal bureaucracies and the corporate forces supporting them. Like countercultural workers around the West, the reality of laboring in nature was sharply different to romanticized visions of that work by people looking to escape mainstream employment. That reality check did not mean the work was not worth doing or that these organizations could not persist; the story of Hoedads shows just how effectively countercultural elements could influence natural resource policy over a long period of time. However, their story also shows how escaping mainstream society into alternative forms of work was much harder than many originally thought.

Yet Hoedads also brought a new kind of voice to the Northwest's forests, one with great relevance today. As the timber industry declined in importance in the regional economy, new ways of working in the forest developed that privilege sustainability, ecology, and independence from

[121] Sarathy, *Pineros*.

industrial capitalism. Hoedads and reforestation cooperatives might not have survived in the 1980s, but their ideas about a forest that had a greater economic value standing than harvested, and the power of the forest to regenerate people and a region, were alluring and remain influential in the twenty-first century.

6

Organized Labor and the Ancient Forest Campaigns

Convoys of log trucks festooned with yellow ribbons rolling down the road to cheering crowds of angry workers and their families. Environmentalists sitting in trees to prevent logging companies from cutting them down. Bearded greens talking of the need to save the forest ecosystem. Mill workers in mesh caps and denim jackets talking of feeding their families. These are the images of my teenage years in Oregon timber towns, displayed across the country on the evening news. Between 1970 and 2000, battles over the fate of the Northwest's last old-growth forests roiled the region. Once-obscure places such as Opal Creek and Warner Creek became nationally famous as the site of conflicts between environmentalists and the timber industry. Timber workers saw environmentalists prioritizing trees and spotted owls over jobs and families. Environmentalists protesting and spiking trees only raised tensions, as did workers harassing treesitters with chainsaws and locals killing owls in anger. Greens successfully mobilized national public opinion and legal cases, using the courts to decrease timber harvests from public lands by the 1990s. Through this period, media narratives simplistically portrayed the conflict as jobs versus owls.

This book's final chapter complicates that narrative by examining the relationships between organized labor and environmentalists in the ancient forest campaigns. Both contemporary and historical accounts of these conflicts have largely marginalized or ignored timber unions. Yet as they had for decades, timber unions asserted themselves into the region's environmental debates, sometimes taking the position of their employers and sometimes not, but always hewing their own path to influence policy to ensure jobs in the forest they hoped would last for generations. How the United Brotherhood of Carpenters and International Woodworkers of America responded to the environmentalist challenges depended in part on individual union cultures developed over decades. Focusing on their responses and relationships to environmentalists suggests a nuanced history of working-class environmental goals that adds to a debate that too often papers over the diversity of working-class perspectives. This chapter is not a complete history of the ancient forest campaign, a topic that has already received significant attention from journalists and scholars.[1] Instead, it centers the experiences of workers and their labor organizations in this history. It begins by exploring how transformations in the timber industry laid the groundwork for the tensions between labor and environmentalists

[1] Contemporary accounts include David Seideman, *Showdown at Opal Creek: The Battle for America's Last Wilderness* (New York: Carroll and Graf, 1993); William Dietrich, *The Final Forest: The Battle for the Last Great Trees of the Pacific Northwest* (New York: Simon & Schuster, 1992); Timothy Egan, *The Good Rain: Across Time and Terrain in the Pacific Northwest* (New York; Vintage, 1991); Kathie Durbin, *Tree Huggers: Victory, Defeat, & Renewal in the Northwest Ancient Forest Campaign* (Seattle: Mountaineers Books, 1998); Chris Maser, *Forest Primeval: The Natural History of an Ancient Forest* (San Francisco: Sierra Club Books, 1989). Among the still small but rapidly growing scholarly literature on these events, see Beverly A. Brown, *In Timber Country: Working People's Stories of Environmental Conflict and Urban Flight* (Philadelphia: Temple University Press, 1995); Susan R. Schrepfer, *The Fight to Save the Redwoods: A History of Environmental Reform, 1917–1978* (Madison: University of Wisconsin Press, 1983); James Morton Turner, *The Promise of Wilderness* (Seattle: University of Washington Press, 2012); Gerald W. Williams, *The U.S. Forest Service in the Pacific Northwest: A History* (Corvallis: Oregon State University Press, 2009); David A. Clary, *Timber and the Forest Service* (Lawrence: University Press of Kansas, 1986); Paul Hirt, *A Conspiracy of Optimism: Management of the National Forests since World War II* (Lincoln: University of Nebraska Press, 1994); Harold K. Steen, *The U.S. Forest Service: A History Centennial ed.* (Seattle: University of Washington Press, 2004); Darren Speece, "From Corporatism to Citizen Oversight: The Legal Fight over California Redwoods, 1970–1996," *Environmental History* 14, no. 4 (October 2009): 705–36; Speece, "Defending Giants: The Battle over Headwaters Forest and the Transformation of American Environmental Politics, 1850–1999," Ph.D. Dissertation, University of Maryland, 2010; Douglas Bevington, *The Rebirth of Environmentalism: Grassroots Activism from the Spotted Owl to the Polar Bear* (Washington, D.C.: Island Press, 2009); William Robbins, *Nature's Northwest: The North Pacific Slope in the Twentieth Century* (Tucson: University of Arizona Press, 2011); Nancy Langston, *Forest Dreams, Forest Nightmares: The Paradox of Old Growth in the Inland West* (Seattle: University of Washington Press, 1995); Christopher McGrory Klyza and David J. Sousa, *American Environmental Policy, 1990–2006: Beyond Gridlock* (Cambridge: The MIT Press, 2007); Christopher Klyza, *Who Controls Public Lands?: Mining, Forestry, and Grazing Policies, 1870–1990* (Chapel Hill: University of North Carolina Press, 1996); Thomas R. Wellock, "The Dickey Bird Scientists Take Charge: Science, Policy, and the Spotted Owl," *Environmental History* 15, no. 3 (2010): 381–414; Hans Brendan Swedlow, "Scientists, Judges, and Spotted Owls: Policymakers in the Pacific Northwest," Ph.D. Dissertation, University of California, 2002. More popular recent works include Kate Coleman, *The Secret Wars of Judi Bari: A Car Bomb, the Fight for the Redwoods, and the End of Earth First!* (San Francisco: Encounter Books, 2005).

and then highlights the complexity of working-class responses to ancient forest protection and declining jobs. Workers articulated a view of themselves as stewards of the forest that validated their use of the forest for economic subsistence and recreation, and sought to protect it from corporate rapaciousness. But they also saw preservationism as a threat that would undermine their livelihoods, which environmentalists too often simplified into reflexive support for employers.

While reforestation cooperatives demonstrated how work in the forest was changing in the 1970s, most timber industry workers still labored for logging companies and their world became more unstable by the year. In the 1940s, IWA Research Director Ellery Foster claimed the Northwest's timber industry would die if corporations retained control over timber policy. By the 1980s, his predictions seemed to be coming true in the face of technological and corporate transformations that drastically reduced employment numbers and decimated old-growth stands. Workers' economic insecurity conditioned responses to wilderness protection. As it had from its founding in 1937, the IWA sought to protect forests for its members' enjoyment and timber for jobs. But it found this position increasingly difficult to take, particularly after the expansion of Redwood National Park in 1978, the first pitched battle between workers and environmentalists in the Northwest. The United Brotherhood of Carpenters led labor's response here due to its higher membership density in the region. The UBC's historical opposition to environmental protection led to an aggressive anti-park stance while the IWA struggled to maintain a middle ground with greens. But new leadership in 1987 shifted the IWA away from working-class environmentalism and the last years of the ancient forest campaigns were marked by significant hostility and frustration on both sides, partly because of the decline of long-standing relationships between the two movements. By 1994, the northern spotted owl received federal protection and the IWA was no more, its remnants having merged with the International Association of Machinists (IAM) that year. The Northwest forests remained sites of labor, but mushroom pickers, trail builders, and rafting guides became more common than loggers and mill workers in many parts of the region. Environmentalists won the ancient forest campaigns, but at the cost of alienating much of the labor movement, the repercussions of which it still faces today.

Focusing on the relationships between labor unions and large environmental organizations necessarily simplifies the ancient forest campaigns. This chapter pays little to no attention to scientists, federal agency heads, judges, or politicians, all of which have received attention from historians previously. Nor can it tell the entire story of workers and environmentalists. Not all loggers were union members. If labor was fractured, greens were even more so, with grassroots organizations often accusing large national groups like Sierra Club of compromising with rapacious timber interests. Emotions on the ground were high on both sides. This chapter highlights moments where local people had conversations about the region's future, but most of those talks took place between union officials and leaders of national environmental organizations. Both movements did hope to work with the other to find solutions to the forest problems of the Pacific Northwest, but ultimately the challenges of a transforming industry and economy proved too great.

THE TIMBER INDUSTRY IN TRANSITION

After World War II, timber harvesting on federal lands grew rapidly. Political pressure from the timber industry and politicians to build homes at low cost and support employment numbers led to a "conspiracy of optimism" that long-term management would maintain the forests. Massive congressional appropriations for national forest roads, rising from $13.3 million in 1950 to $24.3 million in 1953, opened the vast forests to harvest. In 1950, 3.5 billion board feet of timber was harvested from national forest land. By 1969, that was 11.9 billion board feet. Ninety percent of this harvest came from west coast old-growth forests.[2]

At the same time, the timber industry looked to increase profits through automation and opening new markets. More advanced saws run by automated controls, machines for moving and sorting logs, and the consolidation of sawmills and chipping mills that turned pulp into paper all drastically reduced the need for employment. Smaller mills began going out of business en masse in the 1970s. In 1978, the timber industry employed 136,000 people in Oregon and Washington. Four years later, that number had declined to 95,000.[3] Surviving mills made heavy capital investments to increase efficiency. Weyerhaeuser invested $400 million to modernize its mills in Everett and reduced its work force from 900 to

[2] U.S. Forest Service, "Managing Multiple Uses on the National Forests, 1905–1995," www.foresthistory.org/ASPNET/Publications/multiple_use/chap3.htm; Hirt, *A Conspiracy of Optimism*, xxiv, 93.

[3] Eban Goodstein, *The Trade-Off Myth: Fact and Fiction about Jobs and the Environment* (Washington, D.C.: Island Press, 1999).

500.[4] The number of workers needed to produce one million board feet of lumber fell by approximately 20 percent, from 9.1 between 1976 and 1982 to 7.4 between 1982 and 1991.[5] Meanwhile, the emergence of Japan, Taiwan, and South Korea as economic powerhouses opened new markets for Northwest timber. Rather than process that wood in American mills, companies found it more profitable to ship it unprocessed to Asia. If they cut too much on their own lands, companies could still buy inexpensive federal timber for their own mills.[6] By 1970, more than 2.5 billion board feet of timber was exported from west coast ports, a number up 16.6 percent from the previous year. Of that timber, 96.2 percent went to Japan.[7]

Automation and exports had profound effects upon timber union membership. Between October 1978 and February 1981, IWA membership in the Northwest fell from 36,000 to 22,000.[8] Not only did this mean lost jobs, but also lost union dues for the IWA to fight for workplace safety, sustainable forestry, and progressive social policy. The IWA's situation mirrored much of the nation's organized labor during these years, with automation and capital mobility leading to millions of lost industrial jobs.[9] The IWA had a fatalistic attitude toward mechanization. However, it took a much harder line on log exports. Ironically, an environmental disaster created the modern log export market. The 1962 Columbus Day storm in Oregon and Washington toppled more than 11 billion board feet of timber, far more than the American market could use. The federal government encouraged the sale of that timber to its Asian allies and a profitable market emerged. By the 1970s, 16 percent of Northwestern log production went to the export market.[10] In 1964, IWA mills in Port Angeles demanded the

[4] Patricia Marchak, *Green Gold: The Forest Industry in British Columbia* (Vancouver: University of British Columbia Press, 1983), 169–71 has a good short description of the changes in automation. See also Edward C. Weeks, "Mill Closures in the Pacific Northwest: The Consequences of Economic Decline in Rural Industrial Communities," in Robert G. Lee, et al., *Community and Forestry: Continuities in the Sociology of Natural Resources* (Boulder: Westview Press, 1990), 127.

[5] Goodstein, *The Trade-Off Myth*, 87, 94.

[6] "New Controversy in Log Exports," *Union Register*, February 15, 1974.

[7] "1970 Log Exports from West Coast at All-Time Record High," *International Woodworker*, February 24, 1971; "Northwest's Timber Harvest Declined Sharply in 1970," *International Woodworker*, August 25, 1971.

[8] Delegate Handbook, Region 3, 1981–82, IWA Box 54, Folder 12.

[9] Jefferson Cowie, *Stayin' Alive: The 1970s and the Last Days of the Working Class* (New York: New Press, 2010).

[10] Christine L. Lane, "Log Export and Import Restrictions of the U.S. Pacific Northwest and British Columbia: Past and Present," (Portland: USDA, USFS, Pacific Northwest Research Station, 1998), 6; A. Clark Wiseman and Roger A. Sedjo, "Effects of an

union fight exports after a mill laid off union members for a lack of logs while ships departed the port laden with trees headed for Japan. By the next year, the Carpenters estimated that 1,000 timber workers were unemployed due to raw log exports. Both unions officially registered their opposition with politicians.[11] Pressure from the Washington and Oregon congressional delegations convinced the Johnson administration to negotiate a quota on exports from public lands in 1967. The Morse Amendment to the Foreign Assistance Act of 1968 went further, limiting log exports from federal land to 350 million board feet per year, and in 1974 the government prohibited the export of softwood logs from federal lands in the West.[12]

While unions and congressmen could pressure the federal government for change, the states proved trickier and private owners intractable. A 1968 attempt to ban the export of timber from Washington state lands lost at the polls and the state had no meaningful restrictions until 1990. Oregon did restrict exports from the early 1960s but effectively stopped enforcing the laws in the 1980s, leading to a rapid increase in the state's timber sold to Asia.[13] Private timber owners had no restrictions. Sending 800 empty lunch buckets to Washington, in 1974 the Carpenters demanded that President Ford cease all exports of raw logs, claiming this alone would allow the timber industry "to return to full employment within a few weeks."[14] In 1977, the IWA estimated that processing timber in the United States for the Asian market would create 11,000 jobs.[15]

The IWA connected log exports to sustainable forestry practices. When the Carter administration proposed increasing exports, Keith Johnson

Export Embargo on Related Goods: Logs and Lumber," *American Journal of Agricultural Economics* 63, no. 3 (August 1981): 423–29.

[11] Resolution No. 32, 1953 IWA Convention, IWA, Box 40, Folder 9; Al Jernigan to Al Hartung, May 5, 1964; Hartung to Jernigan, May 8, 1964, IWA Box 80, Folder 11. On the history of the IWA and trade, see Denny Scott, "The IWA and International Trade," *International Woodworker*, September 17, 1975; On the 1,000 unemployed loggers estimate, "Unregulated Log Exports Cause Job Loss for Mill, Ply Workers," *Union Register*, January 1, 1965.

[12] A. Clark Wiseman and Roger A. Sedjo, "Effects of an Export Embargo on Related Goods: Logs and Lumber," *American Journal of Agricultural Economics* 63, no. 3 (August 1981): 423–29; Lane, "Log Export and Import Restrictions of the U.S. Pacific Northwest and British Columbia: Past and Present," 8–10.

[13] Lane, "Log Export and Import Restrictions of the U.S. Pacific Northwest and British Columbia: Past and Present," 28–32.

[14] "Solons Act to Ease Log Export Problem," *Union Register*, April 9, 1965; "Curb on Log Exports Sought by Magnuson," *Union Register*, July 28, 1967; "Forest Service Acting on Log Export Rules!" *Union Register*, December 29, 1967; "Willamette Valley Sends 800 Lunch Buckets to D.C." *Union Register*, November 1, 1974.

[15] 1977 IWA Convention Minutes, IWA Box 26, Folder 2.

wrote to the president that the union worried about undermining the long-term forest sustainability, noting U.S. Forest Service studies projected a 24 percent decline in timber harvests from the national forests by 2000. Instead, keeping wood for the American market by restricting the exports of raw logs would both reduce the price of wood and maintain a healthy, productive forest. For an IWA suffering 2,000 job losses from seven mill closures in 1980, exporting logs while increasing harvests made neither ecological nor economic sense.[16] Exports exploded during the Reagan years, peaking in 1989 at 1.944 billion board feet of timber, twice that of peak levels during the Carter administration. Between 1979 and 1989, lumber production in the Northwest increased by 11 percent while employment dropped by 24,500 jobs. Liberal congressman from the Northwest such as Oregon's Jim Weaver and Washington's Don Bonker introduced bills to limit exports, but powerful timber-friendly senators such as Oregon's Mark Hatfield, alongside strident corporate resistance, ensured they went nowhere.[17]

Thanks to mechanization and log exports, the number of people laboring in the timber industry plummeted, even as the Pacific Northwest enjoyed robust economic growth through the 1980s. Whereas timber worker employment in Washington and Oregon fell by nearly 25,000 workers in the 1980s, total employment in the two states grew by 625,000 jobs and these new residents had a different stake in the forests than loggers. The timber industry's political power decreased as the Northwest became more urban and those citizens wanted to consume the forest as recreation. The economic value of the forests was increasingly thought of in trees standing rather than trees logged. When residents organized to fight the timber industry for the last ancient forests in the 1970s and 1980s, timber workers feared for their jobs and timber worker unions would be a rapidly declining shell of their previous incarnations.

[16] Keith Johnson to Jimmy Carter, April 29, 1978, IWA Box 289, Folder 11; "White House Aides Get IWA Log Export Views," *International Woodworker*, January 23, 1980.

[17] "Ancient Forests and the Economy: Evolution and the Law of Static Perceptions," Wilderness Society-Northwest Region, Box 4, Folder Speeches and Writings; "Bonker Trying to Brake Log Flow," *Olympian*, May 7, 1978; "Duncan Opposes Weaver's Tough Log Export Legislation," *Eugene Register-Guard*, May 27, 1975; "Weaver Bill Would Curtail Log Exports," *Eugene Register-Guard*, May 2, 1980; Jean M. Daniels, *The Rise and Fall of the Pacific Northwest Log Export Market* (Portland: USDA, USFS, Pacific Northwest Research Station, 2005), 12–14. See also C. Brant Short, *Ronald Reagan and the Public Lands: America's Conservation Debate, 1979–1984* (College Station: Texas A&M Press, 1989) for the Reagan administration's public land policies.

THE IWA AND ENVIRONMENTALISM

Although the IWA failed to implement its forestry program in the 1940s, its vision of a forest sustainably managed for working-class people's needs – economic, recreational, and ecological – never disappeared. Much of organized labor, including the United Auto Workers, United Steelworkers of America, and International Association of Machinists, began supporting environmental protection during the 1960s and early 1970s to improve workplace environments and to secure public lands for members' recreational use. For the Oil, Chemical, and Atomic Workers, connecting workplace health with environmentalism led to meaningful alliances with environmentalists based around the idea that a healthy environment was a working-class issue. However, the labor tide began turning against environmentalism with the post-1973 economic crises and oil embargo. Early labor support for environmentalism was predicated on believing in an ever-expanding economy. Actual job losses combined with job blackmail, or employers' threatening to close factories if forced to clean up pollution and protect workers, quickly put environmentalists on the defensive. For unionists committed to environmentalism, convincing members of its importance in hard economic times proved challenging.[18]

Despite plummeting membership numbers due to the industry's structural changes, IWA leadership robustly defended the interest of their members in a forest managed for steady work and recreation. As the previous two chapters show, the IWA worked with environmental groups to protect the Occupational Safety and Health Administration and the Clean Air Act while positioning itself as a union countercultural reforestation workers could respect. During Keith Johnson's presidency, the IWA connected its long-standing position on resource management in

[18] Scott Dewey, "Working for the Environment: Organized Labor and the Origins of Environmentalism in the United States, 1948–1970," *Environmental History* 3, no. 1 (January 1998): 45–63; Robert Gordon, "'Shell No!': OCAW and the Labor-Environmental Alliance," *Environmental History* 3, no. 4 (October 1998): 460–87; Les Leopold, *The Man Who Hated Work and Loved Labor; The Life and Times of Tony Mazziocchi* (White River Junction, VT: Chelsea Green, 2007); Brian Mayer, *Blue-Green Coalitions: Fighting for Safe Workplaces and Healthy Communities* (Ithaca: ILR Press, 2009); Fred Rose, *Coalitions across the Class Divide: Lessons from the Labor, Peace, and Environmental Movements* (Ithaca: Cornell University Press, 2000); Lisa Fine, "Workers and the Land in U.S. History: Pointe Mouillée and the Downriver Detroit Working Class in the Twentieth Century," *Labor History* 53, no. 3 (August 2012): 409–34; Robert Gottlieb, *Forcing the Spring: The Transformation of the American Environmental Movement*, Rev. and updated edn. (Washington: Island Press, 2005), 347–88.

defense of long-term working class interests to the growth of environmentalism, even when this meant bucking the AFL-CIO.

Many workers saw wilderness protection as a real threat. Mrs. Gordon Meyers, whose husband worked as a logger near a proposed addition to the Mt. Jefferson Wilderness Area, wrote to Senator Wayne Morse in 1967, "we love the outdoors and like to see nature conserved for future generations as much as anyone." But this was a secondary priority to supporting Oregon's timber economy for Meyers, who claimed it would reduce the available timber for his company by twenty years and asked, "Which is more important? More area for recreation when there is enough already, or leaving jobs entact [sic], by leaving the area as it is."[19]

The IWA tried to articulate an answer to that question, arguing both work and wilderness were possible through ecologically conscious management that treated the forest as a renewable resource while defending a broad range of environmental values. IWA officers saw themselves as defending the forest from a rapacious timber industry, asserting workers' interest in the forest as both play and work, and promoting a moderate and respectable environmentalism to its members through the union newspaper, communication with locals, and union resolutions. The IWA simply did not trust companies to manage the forest. When Georgia-Pacific (G-P) began investing in the Pacific Northwest in the 1970s, the IWA expressed serious concern over the company's poor environmental record in the South. Vice-President Landon Ladd warned of G-P's indifference to sustainable forestry and told of the union's need "to balance our job needs for lumber and wood products against our life need for clean streams, clean air, forested mountains, fish and game, and other wildlife."[20]

As Ladd stressed, working-class recreation was central to that balance. Beginning in 1956, the IWA hired Oregon freelance nature writer Fred Goetz to write a newspaper column titled "About Open Spaces." Running for more than three decades, it was a statement to the importance of forest recreation in workers' lives. The column's title itself, selected by a union member from Klamath Falls, speaks to the value loggers placed upon a forest maintained for their use. Through Goetz, Stanley Platt of Local 3–246 could tell fellow union members about the 170-pound mule deer he shot near LaPine, Oregon. Jack Larson of Lebanon, Oregon, could

[19] Mrs. Gordon Meyers to Wayne Morse, January 19, 1967, Morse Papers, Series B, Box 117.

[20] Ladd to Locals, August 4, 1972, IWA Box 102, Folder 39.

promote his adaption of a logging pack to hunting to his fellow members, hoping to make a little money through his ingenuity. Workers could also quiz an expert about their own observations of the natural world. Ralph Heegle of Local 3–427 asked Goetz about fluctuations in deer populations over time. Workers wrote for advice about which tent to buy, fishing equipment, and the merits of hunting various fur-bearing animals. Goetz provided information on how new Forest Service regulations would expand opportunities for recreation or talked to biologists about the mysterious ways of mountain lions.[21]

As the 1970s dawned, Goetz's column took on an ecological edge. He began educating members on how pollution affected the open spaces they loved. He recommended IWA members in Portland vote for anti-pollution measures that would stop raw sewage from floating into the Willamette River. Even if members lived elsewhere, Goetz believed it relevant "to IWA members who may have a similar problem in their home town." In other columns, he noted the effects of water pollution on fishing, urging workers to report polluters to government agencies and call them to the attention of "fellow environmentalists," clearly claiming the name for loggers. Reporting polluters included their own employers; Goetz himself talked about reporting Weyerhaeuser to state officials for logging practices that degraded a salmon-spawning habitat on Oregon's Molalla River.[22]

Goetz's changing column reflected broader IWA philosophies concerning educating its membership about nature, recreation, and environmentalism through the union newspaper. The IWA used the paper to teach its members about new wilderness permit policies. It ran stories announcing Earth Day events and encouraging members to participate. It publicly supported the Conservation Foundation's attack on Richard Nixon's tiny anti-pollution budget. It showed workers evidence that industry frequently exaggerated job losses because of pollution regulations and told them to listen to EPA estimates instead. This all validated workers'

[21] Fred Goetz, "About Open Spaces," *International Woodworker*, December 26, 1956; Goetz, "About Open Spaces," *International Woodworker*, May 22, 1957; Goetz, "About Open Spaces," *International Woodworker*, February 11, 1959; Goetz, "About Open Spaces," *International Woodworker*, January 24, 1968; Goetz, "About Open Spaces," *International Woodworker*, August 26, 1970.

[22] Fred Goetz, "About Open Spaces," *International Woodworker*, October 25, 1972; "About Open Spaces," *International Woodworker*, May 13, 1970; Goetz, "About Open Spaces," *International Woodworker*, March 10, 1971; Goetz, "About Open Spaces," *International Woodworker*, February 11, 1970.

own view of themselves as consumers of nature and helped connect their enjoyment of the forest with broader environmental policies the union supported to maintain this working-class paradise.[23]

Protecting the forest for working-class recreation also shaped IWA relations with politicians. Union officials congratulated Washington Senator Henry Jackson on shepherding the National Environmental Policy Act through Congress and lobbied him to press for a greater budget for USFS research projects in order to "increase production of all the products of the forest – wood, water, wildlife, and recreation." IWA Vice-President D.C. Gunvaldson emphasized to Jackson that loggers had "our share of skis and tents and woods-loving children," leading them to "an abiding respect for environmental integrity."[24] These positions could surprise those who expected a timber union to oppose environmentalism. In 1973, James Searce, EPA Administrator William Ruckelshaus's labor consultant, wrote to the IWA to ask for labor's perspective on the agency. Ruckelshaus worried about "the problems that actions by the EPA might create for a labor leader." Roy Ockert responded not with the anti-EPA sentiment the Nixon appointee expected, but instead noted, "the members of the IWA are deeply concerned that our environment be protected ... Since many workers in our industry are hunters, fishers and campers, the interests go beyond the pure economics of logs and jobs."[25]

The IWA used environmental language to make connections between poor forest policy and other regional environmental problems. A 1977 union resolution criticized President Gerald Ford for cutting reforestation funding, noting that it would depress timber industry employment and "result in floods and erosion because lands are bare but should be forested."[26] Instead, it urged Ford to crack down on pollution that "kills trees and animals and is injurious to the health of all living beings including humans," and argued that "a cleaner, more healthy

[23] "USFS Sets Wilderness Permit Plan," *International Woodworker*, March 13, 1974; "Earth Week '73 Set April 9–15," *International Woodworker*, March 14, 1973; "Conservation Group Raps Nixon's Meager Budget to Combat Pollution," *International Woodworker*, March 25, 1970; "Washington Window: The True Costs of Pollution Controls," *International Woodworker*, July 30, 1980.

[24] D.C. Gunvaldson to Henry Jackson, April 29, 1971, IWA Box 102, Folder 36; Gunvaldson to Jackson, March 3, 1972, IWA Box 102, Folder 38.

[25] James Scearce to Roy Ockert, April 10, 1973; Ockert to Scearce, April 24, 1973, IWA Box 301, Folder 10.

[26] "R-62, Revival of the Lumber and Wood Products Industry," IWA Box 54, Folder 10 Delegate Handbook, Region 3, 1977.

environment" would create jobs.[27] This was not only expressed at the union offices in Portland, but among at least some local officials. For instance, Tim Skaggs, business agent for a local at Arcata, California, excoriated Georgia-Pacific in testimony in 1982 over its water pollution, urging stricter controls over pesticide usage. Skaggs talked about how environmentalism had come about as a result of "outrageous forest practices" that "led to the adoption of regulations to protect water, wildlife, and the multiple uses of public and private lands." But more was needed because G-P and other companies relied on "massive clear-cutting" that "caused substantial erosion and stream siltation, resulting in a loss of water quality."[28]

These positions, like the union's work on chemical spraying and workplace environments discussed in previous chapters, created relationships with environmental and consumer organizations. The IWA leadership's criticisms of American energy policy helped solidify these connections. Most of organized labor, both nationally and regionally, supported nuclear energy expansion because of the union jobs it would create. In Oregon, the AFL-CIO and Carpenters fought against a 1976 ballot measure to institute new safeguards on the construction of nuclear plants; that same year, the AFL-CIO stated, "rapid development of nuclear power is a 'must' without which the nation's economy would falter."[29] But the IWA rejected the federation's stance and in 1977 decided to oppose nuclear power due to risk of radioactive contamination in the transportation and disposal of waste, and the lack of safety systems to prevent a core meltdown. It submitted testimony to the congressional Water and Power Resources Subcommittee that December, joining environmental groups in support of non-nuclear energy production that provided jobs in an environmentally responsible manner that protected public health.[30] The IWA urged its members to avoid the trap of supporting any project for a few jobs, running articles in its union newspaper explaining nuclear power's unreasonable expense and promoting alternative energy resources such as hydroelectric,

[27] "R-61, Revival of the American Economy," Box 54, Folder 10 Delegate Handbook, Region 3, 1977.

[28] "IWA Demands Safe Jobs and Clean Water," *Hard Times*, February 1983, 7.

[29] "Northwest Industry, Labor Oppose Anti-Nuclear Measures," *Union Register*, October 15, 1976. Alan Miller, "Towards an Environmental/Labor Coalition," *Environment* 22, no. 5 (June 1980): 32–39. Quote from Brian Obach, *Labor and the Environmental Movement: The Quest for Common Ground* (Cambridge: MIT Press, 2004), 51.

[30] "Statement of the International Woodworkers of America before the Water and Power Resources Subcomittee on the House Committee on Interior and Insular Affairs," December 8, 1977, IWA Box 300, Folder 7.

wind, and solar as cost-efficient, job creating, and environmentally sustainable.[31]

The IWA also participated in the Citizen/Labor Energy Coalition (CLEC), a group of labor unions and progressive organizations that attempted to revive Great Society-era liberalism by focusing on energy policy. CLEC believed that the petroleum industry lowered oil supplies to generate profit and called for greater public participation in energy policy. The IWA embraced a 1979 CLEC campaign to flood Congress with "Big Oil Discredit Cards," signed cards protesting price gouging by oil companies. Denny Scott instructed each local to get members to sign the cards, calling its CELC work "one step in developing a political voice, and a political agenda for the IWA for the 1980s."[32]

The union even challenged timber companies directly on their environmental footprint. In 1978, Weyerhaeuser decided to build a new export facility at Dupont, Washington, that would allow it to centralize its export of raw logs at one large facility. The proposed facility occupied 250 acres with a quarter-mile-long dock servicing ships up to 1,000 feet in length. Weyerhaeuser hoped to ship two million tons of forest products a year from it, largely raw log exports to Japan. Environmentalists opposed it because it bordered Nisqually National Wildlife Refuge, one of the last wild spots on the heavily industrialized south Puget Sound. The Washington Environmental Council sued to block the facility. The IWA briefly joined in the opposition. Opposing a facility to export logs certainly contributed to this, but the facility's environmental impact made some union leaders uncomfortable. Denny Scott noted that while the export facility itself was relatively small, Weyerhaeuser owned 3,000 acres around the site and he did not believe the company would leave it "in a natural, undeveloped state." Weyerhaeuser put pressure on the union to reverse its stance, giving local union officials a tour of the facility to demonstrate the environmental soundness of the project. This succeeded in getting the region's locals to withdraw the union's official opposition based upon the relatively low impact.

This was not the only time the IWA considered job losses an acceptable cost for environmental protection. The Oregon Wilderness Coalition

[31] Bob Baugh, "The Energy Equation, Part III," *International Woodworker*, August 1979; Baugh, "The Energy Equation, Part IV," *International Woodworker*, September 1979.

[32] On CELC, Andrew Battista, "Labor and Liberalism: The Citizen Labor Energy Coalition," *Labor History* 40, no. 3 (1999): 301–21. Quote from Keith Johnson to Brothers and Sisters, August 13, 1979, IWA Box 290, Folder 24.

(OWC) sent Denny Scott a Wilderness Economic Impact study it conducted in 1977, finding that significantly increased wilderness protection would have only minor impact on employment. The study noted that increased wilderness would reduce forest employment by 1.1 percent. Scott corrected the OWC's numbers to 2.9 percent, but he also called it "a minimal reduction" in jobs and offered his support.[33]

On the other hand, sacrificing any jobs to expand wilderness was already a difficult position for a timber union in the late 1970s. There were limits to union environmentalism and the IWA would oppose environmentalists when it was in its interest to do so. While the eruption of Mt. St. Helens in 1980 proved a moment when the union flexed its muscles on worker safety, environmentalists' calls to protect the fallout zone and create federal protection for the land concerned the union because "it would jeopardize the jobs of our members."[34] Still, the IWA maintained lines of communication with environmental organizations. As jobs disappeared, companies shifted the blame from their own responsibilities over cutting the resource and exporting logs to Asia to environmental restrictions. Keith Johnson urged workers to ignore their employers blaming environmental protection for job losses and instead listen to the Sierra Club: "We cannot permit industry their motion alone to determine when the natural resources of your country can be depleted and you, in turn, will be out on the bricks looking for a job."[35] For Johnson, employers, not environmentalists, had destroyed jobs through unsustainable forestry.

Ultimately, the IWA saw itself as holding a middle ground on environmental issues between corporate rapacity and greens' overreaching. It framed its support for the Environmental Protection Agency by respecting members' discomfort with environmentalists. It worried about "unrealistic EPA actions" that could cost workers in other industries jobs but also hoped greens would force corporations to clean up their polluted factories instead of relocating to the developing world. IWA leaders saw themselves as mediators between "those who never cut down another tree and those who feel a full stomach is a fair exchange for a few more particles of crud in their lungs." But ultimately, they believed the EPA

33 Denny Scott to Kurt Kutay, May 16, 1977, IWA Box 300, Folder 25.

34 "Western States Regional Council No. 3 Officers' Report to the 22nd Constitutional Convention," p. 11, IWA Box 54, Folder 12.

35 Address of Keith Johnson to IWA Western States Regional Council, March 11, 1974, IWA Box 31, Folder 22.

could provide workers "a paycheck *and* a decent world to live in" if workers' voices played a central role in environmental debates.[36]

The IWA had many limitations on its ability to mobilize members for a vigorous working-class environmentalism. Declining employment numbers meant its members felt threatened by environmental legislation. Union policy did not always reflect the personal interest of union members. Political diversity among union members meant many loggers opposed environmentalism regardless of what union leaders said. The IWA also did not control relations between workers and environmentalists. The ancient forest campaigns began in Carpenters territory and the contentious tone between the two movements set in northern California would become more common in Northwest by the 1980s. It was here that unions and environmentalists would find themselves at odds for the first time, where loggers vulnerable to job loss and long-term economic instability clashed with changing cultures and political values. In the redwoods, internal union cultures went far in determining how timber workers responded to the challenge of environmental protection.

REDWOOD NATIONAL PARK

The redwood forests had served the San Francisco timber market since the 1850s. By the turn of the twentieth century, they had become a central part of the industrial logging empire transforming the Pacific Northwest. Beginning in the Progressive Era, reformers had sought to save some of the great redwood forests of northwestern California from the timber industry. For decades, this activity largely resided in the Save-the-Redwoods League, an elite conservation organization relying on private philanthropy and which worked closely with the timber industry to preserve small, cathedral-like groves. Beginning in the late 1950s, citizens in northern California and environmental organizations across the nation began lobbying for protecting the redwoods in a national park. By this time, companies had logged nearly 90 percent of the original redwood forest. The administration of Lyndon Johnson proved a propitious time for such organizing and Johnson dedicated the 66,000-acre Redwood National Park on October 2, 1968. The timber industry and Carpenters opposed the park but the bill did not lead to a sustained campaign by organized labor to fight it. However, the 1968 bill did not end the controversy, for

[36] Spohn to Ladd, October 23, 1974, IWA Box 300, Folder 9. Emphasis in original document.

the new park excluded a great deal of virgin forest. Almost immediately environmentalists organized for a larger park.[37]

Northern California was changing rapidly in the 1970s. The region attracted hippies and back-to-the-land advocates who brought an environmental consciousness and a new illicit marijuana economy to the region. They combined with long-time residents and tourists from San Francisco and farther abroad to save the redwoods. Local grassroots organizations like the Environmental Protection Information Center (EPIC) would help lead the fight for a larger park. Philip Burton, a liberal Democrat who represented a San Francisco district in Congress, sponsored a bill to expand the park by 74,000 acres. Environmentalist rhetoric against the timber industry was far harsher than before 1968. The Emerald Creek Committee, an environmental group based in Arcata, released a pamphlet in 1976 entitled "Redwood National Park: The Final Assault," which came with images suggesting an industry war against the forest, with gashes in the forest as stark as the napalmed forests of southeast Asia. This sort of imagery could prove effective in raising consciousness about the land, but also could alienate those who relied on that logging for survival.[38]

The move to park expansion coincided with the same widespread layoffs in northern California as the rest of the timber industry. Between 1976 and 1978, Carpenters representation in the north coast timber industry fell from 2,500 to 1,800, while the IWA agreed to a 15 percent wage cut in order to keep one mill open. One Carpenters local estimated a loss of 516 jobs in the mills it represented by April 1978. The IWA represented workers in eight regional mills in 1978; three closed within a year.[39] Workers' fear of losing their jobs melded with the Carpenters' long-standing vitriol for environmentalism to solidify labor's response against the park. The UBC bemoaned the snail darter decision that temporarily stopped construction of Tennessee's Tellico Dam in 1977, with UBC legislative director Charles Nichols sardonically noting of the

[37] For the story of Redwood National Parks' creation, see Schrepfer, *The Fight to Save the Redwoods*. On opposition to the Redwood National Park in 1968, see Dave James, "Land Management Concepts Affecting the Redwood Empire," September 24, 1964, United Brotherhood of Carpenters Papers, Humboldt State University, RG 1, Box 7, Folder 42; Don Cave, "Management and Labor Meeting," UBC RG 1, Box 7, Folder 41; Eureka Chamber of Commerce, "List of Assessed Value by Districts and Counties under Redwood Park Plan #1: Humboldt County Assessed Valuations," UBC RG 1, Box 7, Folder 41.

[38] Emerald Creek Committee, "Redwood National Park: The Final Assault," IWA Box 289, Folder 24.

[39] Noel Harris, "District No. 1 Redwood District Council Area," January 1978 UBC RG 1 Box 7, Folder 41.

environmentalists' celebration, "if this is a great victory, the maiden voyage of the Titanic was a tremendous exercise in superb seamanship and the Edsel was the Ford Company's greatest financial success."[40] Nichols' anti-environmentalist rhetoric was on full display during the park expansion fight. Writing a letter angrily denouncing the Washington Post for editorializing in support of expansion, Nichols envisioned a future where environmentalists would not allow enough trees to be cut to "print the necessary paper to print the Washington Post. Now wouldn't that be a tragedy!"[41]

The Carpenters worked closely with Don Clausen, a firm timber industry supporter who represented the north coast in Congress. Clausen courted the Carpenters to unite with him in opposition to the park, writing local union leader Noel Harris that only by standing up together to the "antidevelopment movement" could they resist "attacks on your industry" that "have only begun – and they promise to become more intense, more inaccurate, and more misleading."[42] The California state AFL-CIO also joined the fight, saying there was "no ecological basis for the expansion."[43] This was a sharp turn away from the state federation's 1972 statement calling for alliances with environmentalists for broader progressive change and stating, "we believe it unnecessary to choose between environmental preservation and economic security."[44] But much had changed since 1972. Like many early union statements about environmentalism, California labor pulled back with the economic shocks of the 1970s. With park expansion, California unions indeed believed they had to choose between preservation and economic security.

The UBC turned its antipathy for park expansion into direct action. It organized a 5,000-person rally in Eureka on April 13, 1977. Local UBC leaders were proud to unite with industry in the rally, with Louisiana-Pacific President Harry Merlo joining AFL-CIO leaders on the platform, hailing the effort as "a FIRST."[45] It followed with a May 24 rally in Washington, D.C., that notably protested President Carter's support for

[40] Charles E. Nichols statement, May 18, 1977, UBC RG 6, Box 8, Folder 19.

[41] Charles Nichols, "Letter to the Editor," *Washington Post*, n.d., UBC RG 6, Box 8, Folder 19.

[42] Don Clausen to Noel Harris, July 27, 1972, UBC RG 6, Box 8, Folder 15.

[43] John Henning to All Affiliates, August 22, 1977, UBC RG 6, Box 12, Folder 6.

[44] "Statement of Policy and Environment," UBC RG 2, Box 14, Folder 9.

[45] "Local 2592 Business Rep Lauded in Fight to Save Redwood Jobs," *Union Register*, May 13, 1977.

environmentalism with a sixteen-foot long, seven-foot high, 18,000-pound redwood log shaped as a peanut.[46] Union executive Ray Nelson was proud of his role in organizing an event that brought workers and bosses together: "the guys were with us, industry was with us and everything." Yet Nelson also wondered whether it was worth it, with one local spending $10,000 bringing members to Washington in an ineffectual protest when Carter had already announced his support for the park.[47]

These protests began the harsh and sharp rhetoric from organized labor toward environmentalists in the Northwest. It was one thing for John Henning of the California AFL-CIO to say at an Oakland protest, "the trees come next; our people come first." It was quite another for him to talk about the Sierra Club as having "no social instinct, no social compassion ... These people don't give a damn about the people who are displaced by their social frustrations." At the same protest, Al Lasley, the business agent of Local 2592 in Eureka, said that environmentalists have called timber companies "rapists of the land," but he also said "environmentalists are every bit as much rapists. They care about their greed and not our need."[48]

The IWA leadership avoided these rallies and this harsh language. It had favored greater protection for the redwoods since at least 1951.[49] Spurred by the IWA, the CIO told conservationists in 1953, "the Coast Redwood Belt in California is being destroyed by present cutting methods and that only the establishment of a National Forest there can save the situation," something the American Forestry Association strongly opposed.[50] Union leadership wanted to support park expansion. It did not encourage members to participate in anti-park rallies, nor did it send members to the Washington protest. But its northern California locals opposed the expansion as much as the Carpenters and they provided a rank-and-file challenge to IWA environmentalism. At the 1977 IWA Convention, leadership proposed a resolution in support of wilderness, as it had in the past. It talked of the need to protect special places, balance

[46] "Preservationists Barking Up Wrong Tree; Thousands of West Coast Members Rally in San Francisco and D.C." *The Carpenter*, June 1977, 8; "Loggers Protest Redwood Park Plan in Rally at White House Steps," *Union Register*, June 3, 1977.

[47] Ray Nelson Oral History, UBC Box RDC manuscript XXV, Folder Oral History Transcripts.

[48] "Redwood Loggers Roll into S.F. in Fight to Save Jobs," *Union Register*, May 6, 1977.

[49] Resolution 33, 1951 IWA Convention, IWA Box 39, Folder 3.

[50] Anthony Smith to Friends, June 23, 1953, IWA Box 319, Folder 7.

biological and ecological needs with jobs for woodworkers, and criticized the companies for attempting to split workers and environmentalists by putting out "false or misleading statements with respect to wilderness or park proposals to enhance their own selfish interests" and for using "'job blackmail' to enlist labor's assistance in opposing wilderness additions." It continued to support a combination of increased wilderness protection and more intensive forest management on acres designated for logging.

Unlike past conventions, in 1977 delegates took to the floor to oppose the resolution. Local 3–98 from Arcata spearheaded this protest. Gerald Barnes said, "as far as California is concerned, we're opposed to anything else being put into wildlife or park areas." Other delegates applauded. Barnes took union leadership to task for not consulting with the locals over wilderness resolutions, explaining, "when you people are looking into these environmental impacts and looking into the situations around us, be sure and come and talk to us who live in the area to see if somebody is not planning to snow us." Other delegates followed who questioned the entire idea of wilderness and criticized politicians like Idaho Senator Frank Church for pandering to "environmentalists from Seattle and Moscow, Idaho" and for supporting roadless Idaho areas. Finally, Vice-President Fernie Viala suspended the debate and the resolution passed when taken up later in the day without further discussion on the record.[51]

The final bill, expanding the park by 48,000 acres, passed 63–26 in the Senate and 317–60 in the House. Carter signed it on March 27, 1978. But despite the insulting language used by the AFL-CIO and UBC at anti-park rallies, the Sierra Club allied with labor to include a clause in the final bill that provided displaced workers a generous compensation package. Administered by the Department of Labor, the Redwood Employee Protection Program (REPP) guaranteed full salary and health benefits until 1984 for any timber worker laid off between May 31, 1977 and September 30, 1980.[52] REPP allowed environmentalists to fight back against labor's claims they did not care about workers. For unions, REPP was an important precedent for employee compensation when the nation preserved public lands from development. In the words of Carpenters' local representative Al Lasley, who had recently used rape metaphors to describe park supporters, "environmentalists were helpful

[51] 1977 IWA Convention Minutes, IWA Box 26, Folder 2.

[52] Redwood Park Employee Protections, U.S. Department of Labor Highlights, March 1978, UBC RG 1, Box 8, Folder 42; Draft Proposal for United Labor Coalition, UBC RG 2, Box 4, Folder 29.

in getting it through. This shows that there are ways for labor to work with environmentalists. In the end, it is easier for labor to work with environmentalists than it is to work with the companies."[53]

REPP became a lifeline in a region devastated by layoffs and recession. By December 1981, Del Norte County had a 25.1 percent unemployment rate and Humboldt County 18.7 percent.[54] Local IWA leader Tim Skaggs said, "the workers and community have relied on REPP benefits to ease the serious economic problems caused locally by the park expansion."[55] The Carter administration named Al Lasley as a liaison to the Department of Labor for administering REPP, providing additional assurance that the program would serve workers.[56] Lasley helped Lloyd Shumard, a 38-year-old timber faller in Eureka, receive benefits that paid him nearly $36,000 a year, enough to support his family.[57]

REPP had potential as a model for reducing tensions between labor and greens. It was the closest approximation to the later proposal by Oil, Chemical and Atomic Workers official Tony Mazzocchi to create a "Superfund for Workers" to provide direct payments to workers unemployed through environmental protections.[58] But the generous benefits loggers like Shumard received made many in Washington uncomfortable. REPP always had shaky political support. Its liberal income guarantee worried the Carter administration about expanding the welfare state at a time of rising inflation and growing conservatism. When Carter signed the bill, he stated, "I must express my serious concerns with the extraordinary worker protection provision," claiming that all workers who lose their jobs "should be treated equally by the Federal Government."[59]

As of January 1980, exactly 1,783 residents of northern California had received more than $14 million in benefits since the program began in

[53] Quoted from Richard Kazis and Richard Grossman, *Fear at Work: Job Blackmail, Labor, and the Environment* (New York: Pilgrim Press, 1982), 261.

[54] Unemployment Statistics from Northcoast Center for Displaced Workers, UBC RG 8, Box 2, Folder 11.

[55] Albert Lasley to To Whom It May Concern, April 3, 1978, UBC RG 1, Box 8, Folder 42; Declaration of Tim Skaggs in *Local 3–98 IWA, AFL-CIO v. Donovan and California Employment Development Program*, UBC RG 1, Box 12, Folder 6.

[56] Proceedings, California Labor Federation, AFL-CIO, 1978, 150. UBC RG 6, Box 12, Folder 7.

[57] "Timber Faller Makes It Big," *Sacramento Bee*, February 18, 1979.

[58] See Leopold, *The Man Who Hated Work and Loved Labor*, 417–18.

[59] Jimmy Carter: "Redwood National Park Expansion Bill Statement on Signing H.R. 3813 Into Law," March 27, 1978. Online by Gerhard Peters and John T. Woolley, *The American Presidency Project*. www.presidency.ucsb.edu/ws/?pid=30562.

September 1978. But a federal grand jury investigated whether people had enrolled for REPP benefits fraudulently. Allowing workers to enroll for REPP without defined proof of park expansion as the reason became an easy way for unions and companies to limit friction caused by layoffs or firings.[60] An unnamed worker claimed he was laid off as normal for two weeks around Christmas. But since everyone assumed all regional layoffs were because of the park expansion, he signed up for REPP benefits.[61] Ronald Reagan's ascendance to the presidency led to new restrictions on REPP benefits. Secretary of Labor Raymond Donovan issued new rules in 1981 that forced workers to reestablish REPP eligibility after each layoff and disallowed benefits to anyone who lost their job after the end of 1978. The decision affected about 1,300 workers. Further cuts in 1982 trimmed funding for REPP from $10 million to $5 million for the 1983 fiscal year.[62]

While the Carpenters led the fight against park expansion, the IWA took the lead in the fight to save REPP. Both unions protested the cuts, claiming congressional approval was needed for such a drastic change to the law, organized workers to write letters in favor of the program, and held rallies in Eureka and Redding.[63] IWA Local 3–98 worked with community leaders to create the Displaced Worker Center, housed at a local church to help the unemployed seek out resources. More than 600 unemployed loggers had reentered the workforce thanks to DWC assistance by 1984.[64] Tim Skaggs became president of the Union Defense Committee to fight for REPP. The IWA successfully sued for an injunction against the federal government and state of California over the changes. California appealed the decision and refused to pay benefits until the settlement of that appeal, resisting a court order to do so for several months. The IWA filed several additional lawsuits over benefit payments and eligibility requirements. Several were still pending when the program ended in 1984. Overall, REPP brought about $40 million in benefits into Humboldt County, although by the time of its final demise,

[60] "Timber Faller Makes It Big," *Sacramento Bee*, February 18, 1979.

[61] "Fraud Riddles Redwood Park Program," *Del Norte Triplicate*, January 30, 1980.

[62] "Redwood Employee Protection Program Rules Changes," UBC RG 1, Box 12, Folder 5; Declaration of Tim Skaggs in *Local 3–98 IWA, AFL-CIO v. Donovan and California Employment Development Program*, UBC RG 1, Box 12, Folder 6; "Reagan Cuts Heavily into REPP," *San Francisco Chronicle*, February 9, 1982.

[63] Workshop on Job Protection, May 24, 1982, UBC RG 1, Box 12, Folder 6. Labor-Community Roundtable, UBC RG 1, Box 12, Folder 6.

[64] IWA Local 3–98, Northwest Dislocated Workers Project, UBC RG 8, Box 2, Folder 37.

most commentators considered it a failure because of the controversy surrounding it.[65]

The Carpenters hoped that allying with industry to oppose park expansion would convince companies to keep jobs in northern California. Simpson Lumber President G.W. Oswald assured the California Federation of Labor he would "continue in business in northern California."[66] Many workers already felt that corporations blamed environmentalists for plants they intended to close. Arcata logger Bruce Miller accused Simpson of using environmentalists as a "whipping boy to get us workers in a fret," and distract them from how corporate greed had led to unemployment.[67] When Louisiana-Pacific closed its Samoa, California, mill in 1977, it blamed the likely expansion of the park and the California Department of Forestry's refusal to grant the company its harvest requests. The Carpenters had agreed to a new contract with L-P on October 4. Two days later, the company announced its closure. The union filed an unfair labor practice complaint with the National Labor Relations Board claiming the plant manager admitted the closure was actually because of labor costs and not environmental restrictions, but the plant did not reopen.[68] Closures continued. Simpson closed its Fairhaven plywood operation in July 1981, citing reduced housing demand. Two hundred and thirty-seven workers lost their jobs.[69] Then in 1983, Louisiana-Pacific decided to eliminate its unions in the Northwest to reduce wage rates to that of the South.[70] Pulling out of industry-wide contract talks, the company offered a one-year contract with drastically reduced benefits, compulsory overtime and arbitrary days off. Workers at seventeen mills, both UBC and IWA-represented, struck throughout the Northwest. They stayed on strike until giving up the fight in 1986. State Senator Barry Keene, who represented Humboldt

[65] Charles Nichols to Raymond Donovan, April 16, 1981, UBC RG 1, Box 12, Folder 5; IWA Local 3–98 v. Raymond J. Donovan court decision, December 14, 1981 UBC RG 1, Box 12, Folder 5; John Cumming to Jay Arcellana, February 16, 1982, UBC RG 1, Box 12, Folder 5; Cumming to Stanley Weigel, March 26, 1982, UBC RG 1, Box 12, Folder 5; "REPP Winds Down; Battles in Court Continue," *Eureka Times-Standard* June 14, 1984; Chronicle of REPP Program and Union Defense Lawsuits, UBC RG 8, Box 1, Folder 43.

[66] G.L. Oswald to Ray Nelson, April 10, 1978, UBC RG 8, Box 1, Folder 38.

[67] Bruce Miller to unknown newspaper, UBC RG 2, Box 17, Folder 21.

[68] P.E. Neil to Employee, October 6, 1977; Neil to Les Johnson, December 12, 1977; From Leslie Johnson's Affadavit to the National Labor Relations Board, December 2, 1977; UBC RG 7, Box 4, Folder 27.

[69] Tom Croft to Doug Patino, July 21, 1981, UBC RG 8, Box 2, Folder 19.

[70] "Lumber's Man in Washington," *People's World*, January 5, 1985.

County in Sacramento, summed up the disappointment of the community in Louisiana-Pacific's actions. Writing to company executives, Keene bemoaned the loss of the labor-industry cooperation, reminding them that "community-wide opposition to the expansion of Redwood National Park was one important example of that working relationship."[71]

Park expansion was just a blip in the larger shifts in corporate strategy in the Northwest's timber industry, but environmentalists proved a useful scapegoat. The growing division between labor and greens over Redwood National Park in 1978 became commonplace throughout the region in the 1980s as the continued corporate drive to export timber and reduce manufacturing costs combined with an increasingly robust and powerful environmental movement using the courts and halls of political power to enact widespread forest protections. Both phenomena would make loggers' place in Northwestern society increasingly unstable, but only the timber industry effectively placed its changes in rhetoric that claimed to represent working-class interests. Environmentalists' failure to communicate with labor would turn workers against them as spotted owl protection became the Northwest's hot-button political issue in the 1980s.

LABOR AND THE SPOTTED OWL

The ancient forest campaigns only became more contentious after the Redwood National Park expansion. Environmentalists organized to save the last old-growth forests and scientific evidence of declining wildlife populations gave them the tools to win. Although relatively few timber mills relied exclusively on old-growth timber by the late 1980s, while mills continued closing in the face of corporate decisions about log exports and automation, workers directed their ire toward environmentalists. Timber unions continued advancing workers' interests in the forest debates, but as the IWA continued to bleed membership, new union leadership brought it in line with the Carpenters and labor presented a united front against environmentalists after 1987. Labor's fierce resistance to spotted owl protections caught the major environmental organizations off guard, as they had come to expect at least fruitful dialogue with labor. Yet even during the most contentious debates, people on both sides of the divide

[71] John Ross, "L-P Strike: A Bitter Harvest," *Econews*, August-September 1983, UBC RG 8, Box 3, Folder 11; Marilyn Chase, "Lengthy Strike at Louisiana-Pacific Tests Chairman's Resolve to Cut Starting Wages," *The Wall Street Journal*, October 17, 1983; Barry Keene to Harry Merlo, November 14, 1983 UBC RG 8, Box 3, Folder 12.

tried to initiate conversations with the other side, demonstrating belief that they had one thing in common: a mistrust of the timber industry forged over a century of forestry and labor practices.

Americans' increased environmental awareness after World War II had enormous legislative and legal implications for forest policy. Expanding recreational use of the national forests helped build a citizen-based environmental movement that resulted in the growth of environmental organizations and spurred demands for legislated wilderness protection. The Wilderness Act of 1964 created official wilderness withdrawn from Forest Service land for the first time. In response, the USFS undertook the Roadless Area Review (RARE) in 1971, identifying and classifying all roadless areas on national forests that could potentially become federally protected wilderness. When the USFS recommended only sixteen of 255 roadless areas in Oregon and Washington for protection, the Sierra Club Legal Defense Fund sued the agency and the out-of-court settlement mandated new reviews of all its roadless areas. In 1977, the USFS undertook that second review. RARE II intended to find permanent solutions to the issue, ending the lawsuits bogging down logging and providing the timber industry with clarity on its future. However, in 1979 the Carter administration announced its decision to protect only 15.4 million of the 62 million acres of roadless lands in the national forests. Environmentalists again filed suit and a 1982 Ninth Circuit Court decision ruled the RARE II environmental impact statement inadequate. The future of roadless areas remained in limbo.[72]

A second legal change that transformed the timber industry occurred in 1974, when the Izaak Walton League won a lawsuit challenging USFS clearcutting practices in West Virginia's Monongahela National Forest. *Izaak Walton v. Butz* ruled that the USFS violated the Organic Act of 1897 by allowing clearcutting, as the law gave federal authority to log only "dead, matured or large growths of trees" that had been "marked or designated." This threw forest policy into chaos since it challenged the main silvicultural practice in use for decades. Congress responded by superseding the Organic Act with the National Forest Management Act (NFMA) of 1976, which codified USFS control over forest management

[72] Turner, *The Promise of Wilderness*, 190–96; Williams, *The U.S. Forest Service in the Pacific Northwest*, 241–42, 290–94; Clary, *Timber and the Forest Service*, 175–77. On the issue of RARE II and clarity of future logging for the industry, see for example, "Wilderness Decision Removes Uncertainty on Timber Supply," *Union Register*, April 27, 1979.

and explicitly legalized clearcutting, but also required each national forest unit to develop environmental impact statements with public comment periods, a significant victory for environmentalists. RARE II and public comment periods gave environmentalists tools to challenge the industry–government cooperation that had left the Northwest's last old-growth forests in peril.[73]

Commenting on the Monongahela decision, the IWA called clearcutting "an accepted practice" and urged it in Douglas fir forests because it "facilitates rapid replanting and rapid regeneration of new seedlings." But the union criticized the practice on steep southern slopes where reforestation was difficult, as well as the dry pine forests of eastern Oregon and eastern Washington, saying "there have been abuses of clearcutting and these abuses should be corrected through sound forest practice regulations."[74] Unlike timber companies and the Carpenters, the IWA supported the NFMA, hoping that environmentalists' input would lead to a more sustainable industry. The union also supported the principle behind RARE II, reiterated its support of wilderness with "unique geographic, biological, or wildlife habitats" and if the withdrawal of timber did not have a "substantial negative impact" on jobs, but also called for a final decision so that it could evaluate future timber supplies.[75]

By the 1980s, falling spotted owl populations outpaced wilderness protection as the key environmental issue in the forests. The NFMA required the Forest Service to maintain "viable populations" of native species, mandating the agency to manage for endangered species populations for the first time. In the 1970s, USFS biologists noticed declining populations of the northern spotted owl, a species that requires old-growth forests as its habitat. When the Fish and Wildlife Service and Forest Service were reticent in providing enough habitat for healthy spotted owl populations, environmentalists used NFMA requirements to sustain owl populations as a tool not only to protect the owl but also to save the last old-growth forests. In 1985, environmental organizations appealed to the Department of Agriculture to fulfill its duties under the NFMA but in 1987, the U.S. Fish and Wildlife Service refused to list the

[73] Hirt, *A Conspiracy of Optimism*, 260–65; Williams, *The U.S. Forest Service in the Pacific Northwest*, 272–76; Steen, *The U.S. Forest Service: A History*, Clary, *Timber and the Forest Service*, 190–94.

[74] Keith Johnson statement to Senate Committee on Agriculture and Forestry, March 22, 1976, IWA Box 289, Folder 11.

[75] "R-62, U.S. Wilderness Legislation," Western States Regional Council No. 3 Delegate Handbook, 1984 IWA Box 54, Folder 13.

owl under the Endangered Species Act. The Sierra Club Legal Defense Fund then filed the first lawsuit to force federal land agencies to protect the northern spotted owl. The FWS listed the northern spotted owl as threatened under the ESA on June 26, 1990, but in 1991, Judge William Dwyer ruled that the USFS had violated the NFMA by not properly managing the spotted owl and ordered all logging on potential owl habitats closed until the USFS instituted a plan that would protect the bird. This immediately halted nearly all logging in old-growth forests.[76]

The spotted owl crisis coincided with the IWA's decline. As late as 1986, the union still gave newspaper columns to environmentalists, publishing a letter from a Washington woman advocating old growth and spotted owl preservation.[77] But in 1987, the IWA split when its semi-autonomous Canadian locals withdrew over a dispute over U.S. timber imports from Canada.[78] Keith Johnson was unceremoniously dumped from the union presidency and replaced with Wilson Hubbell, a logger from Coos Bay who started in the woods in 1951, rose through the union ranks, and had served as union vice-president since 1978.

Hubbell did not share the left-leaning social movement tendencies of Johnson and when the union split, the fifty-year tradition of IWA environmentalism died with it. Hubbell joined with the Carpenters and organized labor around the Northwest to create the Timber Labor Coalition, which opposed further wilderness areas and urged the rejection of spotted owl protection.[79] The IWA moved toward the "Wise Use" stance so many stakeholders in western public lands had taken in the wake of the Sagebrush Rebellion in the late 1970s.[80] The union newspaper began publishing bitter anti-environmentalist screeds and encouraged members to buy "Save a Logger, Eat an Owl" bumper stickers. Local 3–2 placed a wood statue of an owl pierced by an arrow on its roof, which the newspaper proudly reproduced in a picture.[81]

[76] See Brendan Swedlow, "Scientists, Judges, and Spotted Owls: Policymakers in the Pacific Northwest," *Duke Environmental Law and Policy Forum*, 13, no. 2 (Spring 2003): 187–278 for an in depth discussion of the legal process behind spotted owl protection.

[77] Angela Olson, "Spotted Owls Have Been around the Northwest Longer than People," *International Woodworker*, October 16, 1986.

[78] "34th Convention Approves Creation of Two National Unions: Members to Vote," *International Woodworker*, February 13, 1987.

[79] "Forest Products Unions Form Coalition on Timber Supply," *The Woodworker*, August 18, 1989.

[80] John D. Echeverria and Raymond Booth Eby, eds., *Let the People Judge: Wise Use and the Private Property Rights Movement* (Washington, D.C.: Island Press, 1995).

[81] Photos published in *The Woodworker*, October 20, 1989.

This new stance did not go unchallenged from the rank and file. Retired logger Crawdad Nelson wrote to the newspaper befuddled at the new anti-environmental stance. Nelson lambasted the IWA's participation in "anti-preservation rallies" and asked union leadership whether "it is in the interest of workers to continue working as if old-growth were an infinite resource?" He called supporting bosses, "the practical equivalent of suicide." The official union response to this disgruntled member stated the Timber Labor Coalition "was not formed to further the position of our unscrupulous employers, it was formed to bring some reason to the question of timber supply." But the new IWA position could not answer the longer-term questions Nelson asked about the effects of disappearing old growth on jobs.

A more common response from loggers was to defend themselves as stewards of nature, perfecting the forest through work. They took pride in harvesting the earth's bounty for people and then watching it grow back. They knew nature through their labor of transforming the forest for the expanding benefit of the American middle class.[82] IWA member Jim Menefee stated in opposition to wilderness, "I think we're all ecologists, but we're ecologists in that we like to preserve things and want things to grow. Trees, to me, are like a farm. They are meant to be harvested." Menefee drew on ecological debates of the day to make his point, referring to tussock moth epidemics that killed millions of trees in eastern Oregon during the 1970s as a reason environmentalists were wrong about preserving old-growth trees.[83]

Loggers' claims to stewardship extended far beyond union meetings. Workers routinely defended their work, saying that clearcutting was good for the forest because Douglas fir needed sunshine to grow back and create another crop. They asserted the open spaces of clearcuts improved habitat for deer and elk, leading to better hunting and a cycle of logging and replanting that improved the ecosystem by eliminating dead and dying trees. As Judy Peltier of Orick, California, said, "most of my family and many of my friends are loggers and I know of no one personally who does not believe in conservation ... No tree lives forever, not even old growth redwood. No one wants our streams or wildlife hurt. Every one of us wants our children to enjoy the things we enjoy now, including our jobs."[84] Logger Jim Apukka defined

[82] Rose, *Coalitions across the Class Divide*, 62–63, explores this issue a bit.

[83] 1977 IWA Convention Minutes, IWA Box 26, Folder 2.

[84] "Letter to the Editor," unknown newspaper, February 24, 1975, UBC RG 8, Box 1, Folder 24.

himself as a member of the environmental movement but believed that other greens just did not understand the timber industry. He was "very concerned about global pollution and the destruction of the Rain Forest," but completely rejected the environmentalist critique of Pacific Northwest logging, urging anyone who doubted it to come to Washington "and look at our magnificent trees. Look at how green and lush it is around here."[85]

Working-class claims to environmentalism did not easily mesh with the ecology-based arguments of the environmental movement. Greens correctly diagnosed the impact of corporate logging practices upon the forest, but they erred in not taking loggers' claims seriously. Loggers defined themselves as the real environmentalists in the ancient forest campaigns, "caught up between the extreme environmentalists and the greed of companies who want to cut every tree in the world to satisfy their greed, then shutting down, leaving thousands unemployed," as an IWA story about a rally for jobs in 1990 proclaimed.[86] Workers uniting with industry in opposition to spotted owl protections and articulating their own environmentalism was a real public relations challenge for the large environmental organizations organizing and funding the court challenges to federal timber policy and owl protection.

Countering this alliance, environmentalists argued that the nature of forest work had changed. The Wilderness Society and Audubon Society commissioned professional studies of timber industry economics to demonstrate that automation and log exportation created the crisis in timber employment, not environmental protection. As Wilderness Society President George Frampton told the Portland City Club in a 1988 talk, Northwesterners had a choice: "Forty years from now you can have a leaner, more competitive timber industry in the region that employs 50 percent fewer workers, and no more old-growth forests. Or, you can have a leaner, more competitive industry employing 50 percent fewer workers and still have two million acres of old growth to enjoy."[87] Environmental organizations argued for a recasting of work in the forest that would preserve logging jobs on second-growth land as well as create new jobs in forest rehabilitation and tourism that would continue a

[85] Jim Apukka, "Letter to the Editor," *The Woodworker*, September 21, 1990.

[86] "Yellow Ribbon Rally for Jobs and Owls," *The Woodworker*, April 20, 1990.

[87] George T. Frampton to the Portland City Club, September 23, 1988, Wilderness Society-Northwest Region, University of Washington Special Collections Box 5, Ancient Forest Campaign, Folder Old Growth Forest – Statements, 1988–92.

century-long tradition of the forest as the region's economic engine. They embraced alternative forestry practices, limited salvage logging of fallen trees, reforestation, trail building, restoring road beds to forest, and forest thinning as a future economy good for workers and the forest ecosystem. Audubon Society Vice-President Brock Evans, who played a leading role in shaping environmentalists' strategy, argued that the Northwest could protect its old-growth forests and maintain a strong timber economy based around these new forestry practices, if combined with limiting log exports and diversifying the timber economy away from old-growth Douglas fir and toward using a diversity of species on second-growth land.[88] Tourism generated by old-growth forests would also create jobs. Both environmentalists and politicians in rural counties clung to tourism as a partial solution to the employment problem. Linn County, Oregon, began work with the USFS in 1990 to plan for more intensive development of tourist opportunities in a county where the Willamette National Forest made up 32 percent of the land. Outdoor recreation might not replace the well-paid industrial jobs but it did represent both tax dollars and more sustainable work than timbering.[89]

Environmental organizations also supported economic assistance to affected communities. Evans argued "it is not our aim to damage local economies or put people out of work if we can help it," and urged environmentalists to press for legislation for financial assistance to communities affected by logging restrictions.[90] They also hoped, in the words of Mike Standifer, a Wilderness Society consultant, "to neutralize support for the timber industry by devising a plan that would appeal to both labor unions and community leaders." The plan called for extended unemployment benefits for workers and a fee on log exports to pay for community assistance programs that allowed towns to decide how they wanted to spend the money. There was never any chance of this becoming law, especially the export fee opposed by the timber industry, but it did serve a useful rhetorical purpose.[91]

88 Brock Evans, "We Can Protect Our Remaining Ancient Forests and Maintain a Strong Timber Economy in the Pacific Northwest." Wilderness Society-Northwest Region, Box 5, Ancient Forest Campaign, Folder Old Growth Forest – Speech, 1989.

89 Rural Northwest: Exploring Common Ground, Conference Report May 1992, Wilderness Society-Northwest Region, Box 4, Folder Rural Northwest II: Community Transitions, 1992.

90 Memorandum from Brock Evans to Old Growth Activists, August 1, 1988, Wilderness Society-Northwest Region, Box 4, Folder Ancient Forest Conference-Agenda/Strategy, 1988.

91 Mike Standifer to Rindy O'Brien, July 17, 1991, Wilderness Society-Northwest Region, Box 5, Ancient Forest Campaign, Folder Old Growth Forest – Strategy, 1991.

Even in these days of bitter struggle, timber unions and environmentalists could agree on the damage caused by log exports. Exports increased forty percent during the 1980s, from 2.6 billion board feet in 1980 to 3.7 billion board feet in 1989. For environmentalists, attacking exports was central to their strategy of showing their concern for the Northwest's economic future. The Wilderness Society repeatedly stressed that ancient forest protection could protect both ancient forests and jobs.[92] Oregon congressman Peter DeFazio finally shepherded a 1990 law prohibiting exporting raw logs from federal lands, a rare victory for timber unions during these years. IWA President Wilson Hubbell said the law "will increase the job security of every woodworker in the U.S."[93] But regulating logs from state or private lands seemed impossible. When the Wilderness Society reached out to the Carpenters to form a more united front on exports, the UBC rejected it because "Congress, in our view, is not ready to restrict the use of private property."[94] When DeFazio pressed for a bill that would tax private timber exports in 1991, the IWA and UBC supported it, but the International Longshoremen's and Warehousemen's Union, whose workers loaded raw logs onto the ships, angrily opposed it. ILWU Local 24 president Glen Ramiskey lambasted DeFazio "for pitting worker against worker." Congress rejected the bill as it turned toward promoting free-trade policies. Banning log exports would not be a solution to the job problems of the Northwest woods.[95]

There was also genuine sadness and frustration among environmentalists that the dialogue they used to have with labor in the 1970s and early 1980s had completely disappeared. "Shel" wrote to Brock Evans in 1991 that he "shared [Evans'] anguish" over relations with organized labor and lamented that environmentalists had let the OSHA/Environmental Network "dissolve," eliminating a natural place for dialogue.[96] Norm Winn of The Mountaineers, a Seattle-based environmental organization, urged his fellow ancient forest campaigners "to encourage

[92] The Wilderness Society, "Ancient Forest Protection: A Plan of Action for Washington, Oregon, and Northern California," 1990, Wilderness Society-Northwest Region, Box 4, Folder Speeches and Writings.

[93] "Sometimes a Victory," *The Woodworker*, November 16, 1990.

[94] Sigurd Lucassen to Larry Tuttle and Randi O'Brien, June 12, 1991, Brock Evans Papers, University of Washington Special Collections Box 12, Folder Ancient Forests: Labor, 1991.

[95] "Environmentalists Want Laborers to Join Cause," *Tacoma Morning News Tribune*, September 1, 1991; William Robbins, *Hard Times in Paradise: Coos Bay, Oregon*, Rev. edn. (Seattle: University of Washington Press, 2006), 184.

[96] Shel to Brock Evans, June 11, 1991, Brock Evans Papers, Box 12, Folder Ancient Forests: Labor, 1991.

dialogue between environmental organizations, timber workers, and other segments of the public" to place environmentalists in a stronger public position.[97] Environmentalists tried to open channels of communication. In a 1991 open letter to more than fifty labor unions, the Wilderness Society said that "timber workers are getting one of the great con jobs in recent memory" from the timber industry by shifting the blame for unemployment onto greens. To the national AFL-CIO, Brock Evans wrote, "we're puzzled and disappointed over organized labor's reluctance to help the environmental community save both jobs and trees." But this effort suggested that organized labor was poorly servicing its own members. Insulted, Denny Scott, by this time working for the United Brotherhood of Carpenters, replied, "it's a misnomer to say we don't represent our workers' interests." After later meetings with Scott, environmentalists noted his anger over these allegations.[98] Environmentalists also had no interest in compromising on saving the ancient forests. Grassroots groups already viewed the Wilderness Society and Sierra Club with suspicion; moreover, the big green organizations did not have the power to dictate to other environmentalists any terms of compromise. The Oregon Natural Resources Council dismissed compromises with labor, noting, "environmentalists must not be afraid to win." Such attitudes were common.[99]

In 1992, staffers of Washington Governor Booth Gardner mediated a series of meetings to expand dialogue between the two groups. The two sides could agree on the most general principles of forestry as a legitimate function of public and private land if conducted on ecological principles, but the fault lines were deep and conversation challenging. Denny Scott led labor's response and called for old-growth management with protection for owls as required under the Endangered Species Act, but also eliminating most appeals on timber sales and exempting all remaining old-growth from wilderness designation.[100]

97 Norm Winn to Tim Zenk, April 30, 1992, Wilderness Society-Northwest Region, Box 4, Folder General Correspondence 1987–92.

98 "Environmentalists Want Laborers to Join Cause," *Tacoma Morning News Tribune*, September 1, 1991; Tim Cullinan to Jim Pissot, November 19, 1991, Brock Evans Papers, Box 12, Folder Ancient Forests: Labor, 1992–93.

99 Andy Kerr to Julie Norman, March 10, 1993, Brock Evans Papers, Box 12, Folder Ancient Forests "Thinning Heresy," 1993.

100 R. Denny Scott to Rich Nafziger, April 10, 1992, Wilderness Society-Northwest Region, Box 4, Ancient Forest Campaign, Folder Gardner, Booth, 1990–1992; Ad Hoc Labor/Environmentalists Group, April 15, 1992, Wilderness Society-Northwest Region, Box 4, Ancient Forest Campaign, Folder Gardner, Booth, 1990–1992; Ground Rules and Principles, January 15, 1992, Wilderness Society-Northwest Region, Box 4, Ancient Forest Campaign, Folder Gardner, Booth, 1990–1992.

The talks went nowhere. Environmentalists developed a deep mistrust toward Scott, an ironic turn given his work with greens when he was with the IWA. Scott's long experience in timber policy, his negotiating skills, and determination to represent his union's viewpoint made his name shorthand for environmentalists describing their frustration with labor. Recapping the first meeting mediated by Gardner's representatives, environmentalists described Scott as "another hardliner," a sentiment repeated frequently. Bonnie Phillips-Howard of the Western Ancient Forest Campaign went so far as to worry that Scott was funneling information about environmentalists back to his timber industry allies. Others dismissed this notion, but still defined Scott as the problem, saying he "has been sticking a knife in deep."[101] Ultimately, Phillips-Howard rebuked the entire notion of talking with labor, writing, "it has become painfully obvious to me how fruitless and indeed dangerous this path really is." Rather, Phillips-Howard suggested, "getting excellent legislation passed in Washington, D.C., is where we need to focus our attention." While she noted that environmentalists might like to have meaningful alliances with labor, she summarized the real commitment as "wouldn't it be nice if we lived in a world where that would work."[102] Phillips-Howard was correct. By 1992, there was no good political reason for environmentalists to compromise with labor, not with their major recent victories in federal court.

However, at least in northern California, conversations between greens and labor on the grassroots level continued. This seemed an unlikely place for dialogue to develop. The labor movement was still galvanized from the Redwood National Park expansion in 1978. The north coast had developed a robust environmental movement that included Earth First! Founded in 1980, Earth First! took a "by any means necessary" strategy to saving the forests and defined itself against the compromises made by mainstream environmental organizations like the Wilderness Society and Sierra Club. By 1985, Earth First! had become involved in the ancient forest campaigns, introducing direct action tactics like tree-sitting to halt

101 Tim Cullinan to Jim Pissot, November 19, 1991, Brock Evans Papers, Box 12, Folder Ancient Forests: Labor, 1992–93; Bonnie Phillips-Howard to Janet Honteith, et al., April 17, 1992, Brock Evans Papers, Box 12, Folder Ancient Forests: Labor, 1990–91; Mitch Friedman to Steering Committee, April 23, 1992, Brock Evans Papers, Box 12, Folder Ancient Forests: Labor, 1990–91.

102 Bonnie Phillips-Howard to Jean Durning, et al., April 17, 1992, Wilderness Society-Northwest Region, Box 4, Folder, Gardner, Booth, 1990–1992.

logging operations, infuriating loggers and frustrating the mainstream organizations lobbying for legislative solutions to the ancient forest crisis. Moreover, Earth First!'s members also embraced tree spiking, a tactic that involved driving a metal spike into a tree in order to scare timber companies into not cutting it. In 1987, mill worker George Alexander was nearly decapitated when the saw he worked at a California mill struck a spiked log. Alexander survived, but suffered a broken jaw, the loss of a dozen teeth, and a nearly severed jugular vein. Earth First! leader Dave Foreman expressed little remorse: "I think it's unfortunate that somebody got hurt, but you know I quite honestly am more concerned about old-growth forests, spotted owls and wolverines and salmon – and nobody is forcing people to cut those trees."[103] Loggers loathed Foreman. Carey Kinyon, president of the IWA local in Anderson, California, summed up local opinion, calling Foreman "a terrorist who advocates destruction and lawlessness."[104]

But by the late 1980s, the tree spiking and monkey wrenching advocated by its founders was challenged by a new generation. The first decade of Earth First! was marked by a hypermasculine culture promoted by Foreman, co-founder Howie Wolke, and other members whose ideology of defending mother nature lacked sensitivity toward women or workers and avoided larger left-wing politics. New members with anarchist politics and more pro-feminist sensibilities transformed the movement in the late 1980s. Judi Bari and Darryl Cherney worked with Earth First! cofounder Mike Roselle in changing the tenor of the organization, eventually leading to the departure of Foreman and other founding members. Many younger Earth First! members felt solidarity with workers, if in the abstract, and considered themselves anti-corporation, not anti-working class.[105] Some EarthFirst! members began pushing back against industry efforts to tar them with tree spiking, noting accurately in 1987 that they were "heavy-handed tactics designed to bring woodworker wrath upon environmentalists," and declaring that they disavowed any violent tactics or destruction of private property.[106] That might have been true for the

[103] Judi Bari, *Timber Wars* (Monroe, ME: Common Courage Press, 1994), 268.

[104] Carey G. Kinyon, Sr., "Letter to the Editor," *The Woodworker*, April 20, 1990. On the battles between environmentalists and the timber industry in northern California, see Richard Widick, *Trouble in the Forest: California's Redwood Timber Wars* (Minneapolis: University of Minnesota Press, 2009), although his discussion of labor completely ignores everything between 1935 and 1985.

[105] Jeffrey Shantz, "Judi Bari and 'The Feminization of Earth First!': The Convergence of Class, Gender, and Radical Environmentalism," *Feminist Review* 70 (2002): 105–22.

[106] "Earth First," *Country Activist*, July 1987.

people who wrote it, but George Alexander's destroyed face told a different story.

Despite these tensions, the tradition of IWA environmentalism survived locally. In 1982, Local 3–98 business agent Tim Skaggs told the North Coast Regional Water Quality Board, while speaking out for greater pesticide restrictions in northern California forests, that Redwood National Park was necessary because it did "what the timber corporations refused to do: treat the land and the water responsibly." For Skaggs, Redwood Park expansion had proven a hardship for timber workers, "but in a good cause."[107] This sort of rhetoric built trust with environmentalists. In 1985, the IWA's Fort Bragg local filed a protest with the California Department of Forestry over a proposal to clearcut 2,500 acres in the headwaters of the Big River because of its effect "upon water quality and sedimentation of spawning gravel that will adversely affect fish life in the river." Moreover, it excoriated Louisiana-Pacific, the corporation seeking to log this land for "not managing their property on a sustained yield basis" that "will also have an economic impact upon us when L-P has finished cutting over their timberland and we can no longer look to them for jobs." Local environmental activist Ron Guenther called the IWA's stance "not-so-surprising" and praised the union for standing up against the new corporate agenda to liquidate old-growth redwood. He concluded by proclaiming "three cheers for the Woodworkers!"[108]

As IWA executives renounced its environmentalism after 1987, it would be harder for environmentalists to offer three cheers to the union. But locally, the IWA remained an important labor voice on environmental issues. Don Nelson, business agent for the Arcata local, became an important labor voice for responsible timber cutting at a time of great polarization. In 1987, Nelson urged the California State Water Board to tighten regulations on logging, not only to create a more sustainable industry and forest, but because "we do not want to be viewed as rule breakers or rapers of the forest and despoilers of the waters of our state. We do not want our jobs to be continually in jeopardy because of public demands to curtail or eliminate our industry."[109] For Nelson, environmental regulations were necessary for sustainability in an environmental age. Nelson's work opened doors for conversations with environmentalists. At least once, Nelson even debated EarthFirst! leader Judi Bari on public access

[107] "IWA Demands Safe Jobs and Clean Water," *Hard Times*, February 1983, 7.
[108] Ron Guenther, "Loggers Defend Environment," *Country Activist*, January 1985.
[109] "Labor Speaks for Forests," *Country Activist*, July 1987.

television; although the tape no longer exists, the single report of it remembers her excoriating him.[110]

Around the same time, Bob Martel, editor of the *Country Activist* in Humboldt County, opened his newspaper to a variety of voices. He wanted to overcome the differences between loggers and environmentalists to work toward "a dialogue, a discussion about those questions begging answers" concerning the region's future. He had hope, noting that "some individuals in the timber industry are beginning to show signs of understanding environmental concerns," while environmentalists were developing economic models that found space in the forest for reforestation work, environmentally sound timber harvesting, as well as pushing for state support for worker retraining.[111] Martel also opened space for Nelson to express frustration with the environmental community for its lack of compromise. In May 1990, Nelson and environmentalists created a tentative alliance to press timber companies to preserve more jobs. He claimed that "a sustainable lumber industry is possible ... Most knowledgeable foresters agree." But at the same time, when he pointed out the serious consequences of drastic cuts in production, he was "jeered and laughed at by the public and other committee members." He told his erstwhile allies, "it is just as wrong for environmentalists to ignore the needs of workers as it is for the multinational corporations." Instead, "they have driven us to join with some strange bedfellows in opposing them every step of the way!" Martel's response to the increasing difficulty of these conversations simply noted that Nelson was "a decent man," but that "more pain and anger" would follow and "the path of common vision will grow even dimmer."[112]

At a June 1990 Humboldt County Board of Supervisors meeting discussing forestry, supervisors Liz Henry and Norm DeVall, well-known local environmentalists, lambasted Nelson after he supported the delay in a report on county forestry policy to give workers more time to understand the situation. DeVall told Nelson that even though environmentalists wanted to end logging entirely, workers should organize against their employers and if Nelson could not handle it, the workers should find a different union. Nelson assumed this meant the IWW and, exasperated, noted, "he criticized me because I wasn't a Harry Bridges." He reminded

[110] Coleman, *The Secret Wars of Judi Bari*, 93.

[111] Bob Martel, "Editorial: Towards a Common Ground," *Country Activist*, June 1990.

[112] Don Nelson, "Treat Us with Respect," *Country Activist*, June 1990; Bob Martel, "Let's Bridge the Gap," *Country Activist*, June 1990.

environmentalists, "my job is to protect workers' jobs and wages, not to cut wages and jobs," and that environmentalists like the two supervisors "show their complete lack of support in this county."[113] After 1990, Nelson's work with environmentalists effectively ended in the face of these intractable problems.

Redwood Summer made these challenges greater, when Earth First! supporters from around the country descended upon northern California in 1990 to fight against logging. These young people lacked knowledge of local conditions or history. Logger "Woody W. Pecker" wrote to *Country Activist* urging environmentalists to understand loggers' perspectives and announced his offense over Earth First! tactics such as tree spiking and anti-logger graffiti sprayed around Humboldt County. Accusing environmentalists as "No compromise. No deals. Their way or no way," it was difficult to see how even in a forum trying to promote understanding, any could be reached.[114] On the other hand, *Country Activist* published Earth First!'s disavowal of tree spiking in the same June 1990 issue. Although they could not guarantee that other members would accede to their platform, they placed the new stance in the context of solidarity with workers who died from management's indifference to safety and credited conversations with logger Gene Lawhorn of Oregon's Roseburg Lumber Company for opening their minds to the reality of workers' lives. While this was a positive step, EarthFirst!'s ideas of coalitions with workers did not include existing unions. Rather than the IWA or UBC, it talked of "the Georgia-Pacific, Louisiana Pacific and Pacific Lumber employees who are members of IWW Local #1 in northern California." Bari assisted five workers in Fort Bragg file an OSHA violation after they faced chemical exposure on the job, but no hard evidence exists of further concrete actions between Bari and loggers and statements by Bari suggest dismissal of timber workers' existing unions. In any case, Earth First! lacked the ability to create meaningful coalitions with loggers, especially after Bari's injuries when her car exploded in May 1990.[115]

Charles Hurwitz's arrival into northern California provided a common enemy labor and greens could unite around. Hurwitz, a corporate raider and chairman of Maxxam, Inc., who amassed a $4 billion fortune in real

113 Don Nelson, "More from IWA," *Country Activist*, July 1990.

114 Woody W. Pecker, "Tough Words from a Timber Man," *Country Activist*, June 1990.

115 Judi Bari, et al., "An End to Tree Spiking," *Country Activist*, June 1990; Shantz, "The Feminization of Earth First!"

estate and oil before branching out into corporate raiding, bought Pacific Lumber in 1985. Pacific Lumber was one of the oldest companies on the North Coast, founded in 1863, and had a long reputation for relatively sustainable logging. Thus, it had more old-growth redwood than most private landholders by the 1980s. This stable corporate presence ended when Hurwitz sought to immediately pay off the debt he incurred in his purchase by liquidating the timber. That promised more jobs in the short term but long-term economic and environmental disaster. Hurwitz became the enemy of both environmentalists and labor, who saw the writing on the wall of their jobs ending as soon as they felled the last trees. Here, the environmentalists could place their concerns about the ecological future of the region plainly in context of the region's economic future. Tim McKay of the Northcoast Environmental Center said of Pacific Lumber, "they are the most stable lumber company in our region and are about to go into liquidation-of-assets mode. It may be the last boom in the boom-and-bust history of Humboldt County."[116]

Environmentalists challenged Maxxam for over a decade, fighting to save the Headwaters Forest from destruction. Earth First! finally crafted meaningful connections with organized labor, but notably, it was not with local timber workers. Pacific Lumber was a nonunion operation and so the timber unions remained largely silent on the issue. Rather, it was the United Steelworkers of America, many of whose members worked in plants also acquired by Hurwitz, who sought to make alliances with environmentalists to attack him. In 1998, the USWA called a strike at a Kaiser Steel plant in Spokane then owned by Hurwitz. Maxxam recruited Pacific Lumber workers as scabs to replace them. This led the USWA into northern California to attempt to convince the loggers to stop this. They had little success with a workforce desperate for jobs, but the USWA did mold meaningful alliances with the region's active environmental community. Earth First! members Mikal Jakubal and Darryl Cherney took jobs as scabs to spy on conditions in the Spokane mill while USWA members helped northern California environmentalists protest the unsustainable logging practices of Hurwitz. In 1999, the USWA joined environmental groups ranging from the Sierra Club to Earth First! in creating the Alliance for Sustainable Jobs and the Environment to coordinate efforts against Maxxam. Federal intervention led to the purchase of the Headwaters from Maxxam in 2000. But this was a story without much intervention from organized labor. With a fraction of their

[116] Ruthanne Cecil, "Company Town Threatened," *Country Activist*, November 1985, 1–3.

numbers from the 1970s, demoralized and desperate to hold to their jobs, by their end the ancient forest campaigns had relegated labor to the sidelines.[117]

Outside of the Headwaters, the timber wars were coming to a close in the early 1990s. Legal and political victories suggested a final political victory for environmentalists was in sight. The 1991 Spotted Owl Recovery Team's decision to cut harvesting levels to less than half of 1980s levels led IWA President Wilson Hubbell to bemoan the "owl-science cartel that wants Pacific Northwest forests to be locked up for the sole benefit of the spotted owl."[118] Labor hoped a Bill Clinton presidency would reorient the forest debate toward labor's needs. In April 1993, Clinton fulfilled a campaign promise by holding the Northwest Forest Summit in Portland. All the stakeholders presented their positions to Clinton, Vice-President Al Gore, and a panel of government scientists, officials, and experts. Clinton hoped to create a compromise plan all sides could accept. Both sides held large rallies in days leading up to the summit. Clinton directed three working groups under the leadership of Forest Service Chief Jack Ward Thomas to develop different plans to protect the owl while maintaining jobs.

When Clinton selected Option 9 from his choices, unions felt betrayed, even as some environmental organizations felt it allowed too much logging.[119] Option 9 included a 70 percent reduction in forest harvesting, continued to allow log exports, and did not include a short-term boost in harvests. It did mandate salvage logging, which greens felt was a loophole that companies would exploit to destroy much of the remaining old-growth. The IWA claimed a Democratic president's betrayal "may have accomplished what neither President Reagan or Bush could, that is, turn woodworkers into Republicans."[120] The IWA continued defining environmentalism as an intensive, yet sustainable use of natural resources. It claimed Clinton took an environmentally destructive position that "has virtually assured that nonrenewable resources which contribute far greater greenhouse gases will be substituted for relatively ecologically benign wood products." But organizing around this principle was

[117] On the Headwaters campaign, Speece, "From Corporatism to Citizen Oversight"; Bevington, *The Rebirth of Environmentalism*.

[118] "Hubbell Speaks Out on Spotted Owl," *The Woodworker*, December 20, 1991.

[119] An example of the angry environmentalist response is Brian Tokar, "The Clinton Forest Plan," *Z Magazine*, April 1994.

[120] "Option #9 Endangers All Woodworkers!" *The Woodworker*, July 16, 1993.

impossible because "acid rain and cancer are not as visible as tree stumps." Instead, as William Street pointed out, the United States is "exporting our problems to Russian, Costa Rican, New Zealand, Cambodian, or Chilean forests."[121] The IWA's environmental ideology had a point; American consumption of wood products did not decline after protecting old-growth forests.

The automation, log exports, and capital disinvestment that had sent organized labor into a twenty-year decline continued through the ancient forest campaigns. By 1993, the IWA could not maintain itself as a functioning organization. For all the work it had done with industry to promote timber supplies since 1987, it was repaid with letters of appreciation while those same companies, in Hubbell's words, "spent millions of dollars on union busting attorneys to stop organizing activities while making sure they only have to deal with organized labor when it will benefit their corporate agenda."[122] In 1994, the IWA merged with the International Association of Machinists. Choosing the Machinists over the Carpenters showed how the IWA still held its industrial unionism and reformist past central to its identity. During the 1970s and 1980s, the IAM and IWA had worked closely together in support of workplace safety and health in industry, and Keith Johnson and Machinists President Wimpy Winpisinger were close allies, including working with environmentalists on workplace health and safety. The Carpenters were furious with the decision and the IWA accused the Carpenters of interfering in its affairs just like when the union was founded in 1937, and that "IAM leaders respect the democratic tradition of the IWA."[123] Those democratic traditions had made the IWA one of the most member-responsive unions in the AFL-CIO, attracted support from environmental organizations over protecting wilderness, and interested countercultural forest cooperative workers. But it could not survive the combination of massive unemployment and the end of old-growth logging on federal lands. With the IWA's demise, a tradition of work in the forest based around its view of sustainable forestry that maintained communities, provided living wages, and demanded healthy and safe working conditions faded with it.

121 "Option #9 Mismanagement Mean Massive Job Dislocation," *The Woodworker*, August 20, 1993; William Street, "Paper or Plastic," *The Woodworker*, October 16, 1993.

122 Wilson Hubbell, "A Time to Reconsider?" *The Woodworker*, September 17, 1993.

123 Why Would a Woodworker Want to Merge with the Machinists," *The Woodworker*, January 21, 1994.

Conclusion

Spotted owl protection led to a drastic decline in logging in the national forests. In 1987, the U.S. Forest Service sold 5.3 billion board feet of timber for harvest. By 1995, that dropped to 0.4 billion board feet.[1] Yet the job losses involved were not nearly as great as dire industry predictions claimed. Between 1983 and 1988, average timber employment in Oregon and Washington was 105,000. By 1994, it was still 91,000.[2] Largely, this is because the timber industry had used the fear of spotted owl protection as cover for its profit-taking corporate strategies that laid off thousands of workers, including automation, moving operations to more profitable forests, and selling unprocessed logs to Japan. For workers, it mattered little why the jobs were lost. They lacked work and had few options in the increasingly tech-based and urban Northwest economy. For those who could find work, logging remained the nation's most dangerous profession, with a fatal injury rate of 129.9 per 100,000 workers in 2012.[3]

The remnant unions became creative in finding work for unemployed members. Although the relationships between unions and environmentalists remained strained, the increasingly conciliatory atmosphere after the finality of the Clinton Forest Plan did lend itself to tentative conversations to figure out new ways to employ unemployed loggers in the woods. The

1 Fred Rose, *Coalitions across the Class Divide: Lessons from the Labor, Peace, and Environmental Movements* (Ithaca: Cornell University Press, 2000), 40.

2 Eban Goodstein, *The Trade-Off Myth: Fact and Fiction about Jobs and the Environment* (Washington, D.C.: Island Press, 1999), 92–93.

3 Bureau of Labor Statistics, "Fatal Occupational Injuries, Total Hours Worked, and Rates of Fatal Occupational Injuries by Selected Worker Characteristics, Occupations, and Industries, Civilian Workers," 2012, www.bls.gov/iif/oshwc/cfoi/cfoi_rates_2012hb.pdf.

Jobs in the Woods program intended to employ loggers for tearing out old logging roads, watershed restoration, fire fuel reduction, and other ecologically sustainable projects. But it remained small and underfunded, with only 600 restoration jobs funded by the Forest Service and Bureau of Land Management.[4] Ultimately, there was little unions could do to find jobs for most unemployed members.

As a whole, the Northwest economy quickly recovered from the loss of timber jobs as it moved beyond its natural resource economy past into a center of urban, hip America. Seattle became the center of 1990s musical culture and one of America's most attractive cities to live in; Portland picked up that mantle in the 2000s and early 2010s. The Portland portrayed in *Portlandia* is far from the working class city of the 1980s. But Seattle and Portland do not speak for the entire Northwest. In towns dependent on a single timber mill, today likely shuttered, the damage is visible. Visit Coquille, Oregon, Cosmopolis, Washington, or Mill City, Oregon. These towns and their residents continue to struggle to recover from the loss of timber jobs twenty or more years ago. There are a few exceptions that won the proverbial lottery. Forks, Washington, famously became the setting of the *Twilight* series, despite the author never having visited the town before writing the books. A (probably short-term) tourist boost combined with the town's proximity to Olympic National Park has given it a lifeline. But that may not be long-lasting and is certainly not replicable around the region.

People have found other ways to know the forest through labor. The mushroom gathering industry exploded in the 1980s and 1990s, providing some of the nation's tastiest mushrooms for fine restaurants. Morels, matutakes, chanterelles, and truffles all provide short-term and sometimes lucrative employment for gatherers. Moreover, the industry has boomed since the reduction of logging as the ecosystem becomes healthier.[5] There are other products one can grow or create under the cover of the West Coast's verdant forests: marijuana and crystal methamphetamine. One 2013 drug bust near Oakridge, Oregon, discovered 3,000 marijuana plants worth $30 million on Willamette National Forest land.[6] These

[4] Goodstein, *The Trade-Off Myth*, 102–4.

[5] David Pilz and Randy Molina, "Commercial Harvests of Edible Mushrooms of the Pacific Northwest United States: Issues, Management, and Monitoring for Sustainability," *Forest Ecology and Management 5593* (2001): 1–14.

[6] "Sheriff: Thousands of Pot Plants Found in Forest," *KVAL.com*, August 25, 2013, www.kval.com/news/local/Sheriff-Around-10000-pot-plants-found-in-Willamette-Natl-Forest-221078501.html.

operations can have enormous environmental effects, particularly from the pesticides used to protect marijuana plants from predators. A recent study of mortality in the rare Pacific fisher showed that 79 percent of carcasses had rat poison in their systems from marijuana grow operations in their habitat.[7] Yet in the absence of well-paid legal work, the temptations of illicit work in the forests remain powerful.

Legal work based on the region's natural beauty has also created a few jobs. Oakridge became a poster child for the struggles of the post-logging economy, with its long-term poverty receiving a feature story from *The New York Times* as recently as 2006.[8] Yet some hope has returned. The town has become a mountain biking mecca, creating new jobs based upon a new kind of work in the forest: supplying those who play in it. It is also the home of the unique Brewers Union Local 180, Oregon's only all-cask microbrewery. It attracts enough visitors that the town government has placed road signs directing visitors to it from Highway 58. Finally, twenty years after the Clinton Forest Plan cut off access to logging old growth on the national forests, the town has begun developing economic alternatives that create jobs and give hope for its future. But who does this work benefit? A single brewery and a few bike shops hardly replace hundreds of mill jobs. Moreover, these are jobs largely held by new residents. It is not the now-aging ex-loggers or their children riding bikes where they used to log or repurposing abandoned buildings into breweries.

Whether through marijuana farms or mountain bike stores, like the loggers of the past, modern forest residents are actors in creating the Northwest forest landscape. From the dawn of the twentieth century and industrial logging to the early twenty-first century of rafting and breweries, those making a living off the forest have used their voices to influence how the timber industry and state powers shape the resource residents need to feed their families. The Industrial Workers of the World did not have the language of environmentalism to shape its challenge to the timber industry. But its struggle for environmental justice transformed the forests and the lives of workers through the largest labor struggles the Pacific Northwest had ever seen. The Loyal Legion of Loggers and

[7] Mourad W. Gabriel, Leslie W. Woods, Robert Poppenga, Rick A. Sweitzer, Craig Thompson, Sean M. Matthews, J. Mark Higley, Stefan M. Keller, Kathryn Purcell, Reginald H. Barrett, Greta M. Wengart, Benjamin N. Sacks, and Deana L. Clifford., "Anticoagulant Rodenticides on Our Public and Community Lands: Spatial Distribution of Exposure and Poisoning of a Rare Forest Carnivore," *PLoS One* 7, no. 7: e40163.

[8] Erik Eckholm, "Rural Oregon Town Feels Pinch of Poverty," *The New York Times*, August 20, 2006.

Lumbermen did not provide workers real representation on the job, but the creation of a sanitary workscape to undermine labor radicalism demonstrates the power workers expressed in forcing first the military and then individual employers to grant their demands. The International Woodworkers of America fought for sustainable forestry to stabilize the industry and provide steady work for the future. In its failure, it became a prophet for the future of an industry that misused the forests. The union also struggled to keep its members healthy and safe on the job, leading it to deploy a variety of creative tools to empower workers to take safety into their own hands. In both campaigns, the IWA formed tentative connections and alliances with environmentalists that provided important outside assistance. Its unionism also proved appealing for some Hoedads when their ideal of regenerating the forest through labor ran up against the reality of the chemical-technological regime that went far to define the late twenty-century forest. Union leaders and rank and file workers had a variety of reactions to the wilderness campaigns and lawsuits that began restricting logging on the national forests. Whether it was IWA leaders urging compromise on wilderness or Carpenters' rank and file protesting against Redwood National Park expansion, timber workers consistently identified what they saw as threatening their work in the forest. Whether log exports or spotted owl protection, workers acted in their own best interests. In doing so, they played a central role in shaping the history of the Northwest forests.

Examining a century of labor struggle and the environmental impact of the timber industry on workers' lives, it becomes clear that articulated concerns about forest protection usually remained reserved for union leadership while the rank and file played a much greater role in demanding and creating safe and healthy workplace environments. There are a number of reasons for this. First, workers simply had a greater personal stake in health and safety. Whereas forest policy might affect workers in the future, the workplace environment threatened them every day. Union contracts and safety committees could not provide a truly safe workplace but the continuum from the IWW to the IWA to the Hoedads demonstrates the centrality of worker activism to healthy timber industry workplaces. Yet even here, the specifics of those struggles usually fell to IWA or Hoedad leadership rather than rank-and-file activism, even if in response to membership demands, due to the complex scientific and political knowledge needed to create reform.

Second, forest policy was complicated, shaped in regulatory agency meetings and the halls of Washington, state capitols, and corporate boardrooms. Workers, laboring at hard jobs in the forests and mills, hardly had time to become forestry experts on their own. These complex policy questions are part of the reasons why unions hire professional staff. Ellery Foster and Denny Scott were not loggers, but their expertise in forestry policy asserted working-class interests into larger forestry debates. It is possible that the IWA could have engaged rank-and-file workers and created a democratic, unionized forest culture that challenged employer prerogatives over logging practices on the job site. But it is hard to imagine how this would have played out successfully, even if the IWA leadership had not ejected the communists from the union and even if Taft-Hartley had not forced it to redirect its political agenda. Forestry issues were also only one of the challenges timber unions faced, which included lobbying at the state and national levels for candidates and issues, organizing new workplaces, negotiating contracts, servicing the needs of members in the grievance process, and many other duties. If forest policy only became central to labor's agenda during times of crisis, that is because unions are complex organizations sifting constantly shifting priorities that are largely determined by the union's latest crisis.

Third, as scholars and activists have long noted, workers have concrete interests in environmental protection but their own economic security largely predicates how much support they can give these measures. The unionization of much of the forest workforce by the 1940s and enormous forest production of the postwar decades opened up space for the IWA to support wilderness legislation, even if rank-and-file workers near a given affected forest might oppose the idea. By the 1970s, the transformation of not only the timber industry but American industry at large to one shedding jobs due to mechanization and capital mobility undermined the willingness of unions to support any legislation that might put workers out of a job. In such an atmosphere, even workplace safety standards can be too risky for unions to support, although this was never an issue with the IWA. So if workers were going to involve themselves in forestry debates, as they did in the 1980s and 1990s, it was almost inevitable that it would revolve around an emotional appeal to save their own jobs. There's little environmentalists could say to alleviate this problem, even if they could have handled the issue with a lot more sensitivity to timber workers' economic plight.

The complexities of working class interactions with environmentalists have in no way diminished in the United States today. As I conclude this book, two major issues roil relations between labor and greens. The first is the fate of the Keystone XL Pipeline, which would pipe oil from the

Alberta tar sands to processing and shipping facilities on the Gulf Coast of Texas. The second is Environmental Protection Agency regulations on emissions from coal-fired power plants. Both of these issues are complex. The Obama administration reducing climate change-causing emissions with new coal regulations while often promoting increased domestic gas and oil production is evidence of a less than consistent environmental policy. For working people reliant upon the fossil fuel industry, both projects are of the utmost importance.

Today, both the labor and environmental movements are at multi-decade low points in political power. The failure of environmentalists to pass a cap-and-trade bill in 2009 demonstrated their increasing weakness in Washington. In 2013, I attended a conference of major environmental leaders on the aftermath of the bill's failure. Despair defined it as much as any labor movement gathering I have ever attended, especially the private dinner after the event when greens talked amongst themselves. Labor's decline is of course well documented. Today, only 11 percent of workers and less than 7 percent of private sector workers belong to a union, numbers on the decline as Republican governors push through so-called "right to work" laws in formerly union-dense states such as Michigan and Wisconsin. So both movements, two of the most important progressive in the country, need to ally with one another to create change that brings greater equity to working people and moves us toward a more sustainable future.

Like in the Northwest forests, unions themselves take a variety of responses to these current environmental issues. The Transport Workers Union, Amalgamated Transit Union, and National Nurses United have come out against the Keystone XL pipeline, while larger and more powerful international bodies like the International Association of Machinists and United Steelworkers have tread carefully but nevertheless made clear attempts to reach out to greens. On the other hand, the Laborers, the union whose members stand to receive jobs from the pipeline's construction, has not only come out in favor of it, but has castigated other unions for questioning it and pressed the AFL-CIO for an endorsement of the project, while lambasting the entire idea of blue–green alliances. Unfortunately, this attitude confirms the stereotypes of environmentalists who see unions as backward, corrupt institutions that are not worth making alliances with.[9]

[9] Andrew Restuccia, "Labor Union Quits Alliance with Greens over Keystone Pipeline," *The Hill*, January 20, 2012, http://thehill.com/policy/energy-environment/205441-labor-union-leaves-bluegreen-alliance-over-keystone-disagreement.

I am frequently in western Pennsylvania, where "Obama's War on Coal" road signs festoon the region's highways. The same can be seen throughout Appalachian coal mining country. Once-solid Democratic union members, the coal mining communities have turned politically conservative in recent years. Yet the number of people employed in the coal industry plummeted long before the Obama administration. Today, coal employs 18,000 people in Kentucky, down from 48,000 thirty years ago.[10] Meanwhile, in Rhode Island, Massachusetts, and Maine, restrictions on depleted fish populations outrage fishermen who claim that the fish are still out there if the government would just let them work. Much like timber workers disputing solid scientific findings about the northern spotted owl twenty-five years ago (and today), fishermen claim the science charting depleted fish populations is politically motivated and flawed. Coal is hardly the economic lifeline to Appalachia the industry claims, nor does fishing provide many jobs in New England at this point. Like the timber industry, automation has played a leading role in the employment decline in these industries. Economic instability has reinforced local loyalty to industries despite their huge environmental costs to the community and the planet. Similarly, all of these scenarios paint environmentalists as outsiders opposing economic progress and the right of citizens to profit off the land. There is at least one significant difference, however. Whereas the Northwest had significant homegrown environmental movements that propelled the spotted owl lawsuits on the grassroots, these groups are much smaller in Appalachia, despite organizations like Kentuckians for the Commonwealth and Save Our Cumberland Mountains leading opposition to mountaintop removal mining. But at the core of resistance to environmentalism among the natural resource workers of Oregon, West Virginia, and Rhode Island is a lack of economic opportunities for working-class people. As this book has shown, timber workers' unions pressed the environmental agenda of their members, which could include wilderness protections when economic abundance made workers prioritize their own recreation in nature as a goal. But when the jobs disappear, environmental protections become an unaffordable luxury.

Yet there remains much common ground between labor unions and environmental activists. When environmentalism remains primarily about improving people's lives, there is a seat at the center of the table for the representatives of working-class Americans. Only when we narrow

[10] Kentuckians for the Commonwealth, "Coal Production and Employment Trends," www.kftc.org/campaigns/appalachian-transition/coal-production-and-employment-trends.

environmentalism down to the protection of spaces from human activity does that go away. That is not to say that environmentalists were wrong to try to protect the last old-growth timber. Quite the opposite in fact, and the ancient forests campaigns in many ways confirm the IWA's pessimistic view of a century of corporate control over Northwestern forests. But greens' indifference over loggers' fate in the 1980s continues to be used against them around the country today. Yet the environmental community has learned a great deal from its mistakes during the ancient forest campaigns and even local radical greens today are familiar enough with the beliefs of Judi Bari to know the need to try and build some kind of dialogue with workers. If greens begin to actively support the struggles of workers to protect themselves on the job from industrial hazards, the chances of building meaningful alliances will only grow. Environmentalists taking workplace environments seriously and allying with unions to keep American workers healthy and safe provides one tool to more broad-based support for the environmental movement. Creating a holistic environmentalism that centers the contributions and experiences of working people is a necessary part of building a sustainable and equitable future for people and the planet. Labor unions must play a central role in that future and, therefore, so must work in nature.

Index

Printed in the United States
by Baker & Taylor Publisher Services

Printed in the United States
by Baker & Taylor Publisher Services